A PEOPLE'S HISTORY
OF THE
VIETNAM WAR

ALSO BY JONATHAN NEALE

Memoirs of a Callous Pickett
The Cutlass and the Lash
The Laughter of Heroes, a novel
Mutineers, a novel
Lost at Sea, a novel for children
Tigers of the Snow
"You Are G8, We Are 6 Billion"

A PEOPLE'S HISTORY
OF THE
VIETNAM WAR

A New Press People's History

JONATHAN NEALE

HOWARD ZINN,
SERIES EDITOR

THE NEW PRESS

NEW YORK
LONDON

First edition published as *The American War: Vietnam 1960–1975* by Bookmarks,
London, 2001. This edition published by The New Press, New York, 2003
Distributed by W. W. Norton & Company, Inc., New York

LIBRARY OF CONGRESS CATALOGING-IN-PUBLICATION DATA
Neale, Jonathan.
[American War]
A people's history of the Vietnam War / Jonathan Neale.
p.   cm.
Originally published: The American War. London: Bookmarks, 2001.
Includes bibliographical references and index.
ISBN 1–56584–807–1 (hc)
1. Vietnamese Conflict, 1961–1975.   I. Title.
DS557.7.N373   2003
959.704'3—dc21   2003043645

The New Press was established in 1990 as a not-for-profit alternative to the large,
commercial publishing houses currently dominating the book publishing industry. The
New Press operates in the public interest rather than for private gain, and is committed
to publishing, in innovative ways, works of educational, cultural, and community value
that are often deemed insufficiently profitable.

The New Press
38 Greene Street, 4th floor
New York, NY 10013
www.thenewpress.com

In the United Kingdom:
6 Salem Road
London W2 4BU

Composition by Westchester Book Group

Printed in the United States of America

2   4   6   8   10   9   7   5   3   1

To Nancy Lindisfarne,
with all my love

CONTENTS

Series Preface

Turning history on its head opens up whole new worlds of possibility. Once, historians looked only at society's upper crust: the leaders and others who made the headlines and whose words and deeds survived as historical truth. In our lifetimes, this has begun to change. Shifting history's lens from the upper rungs to the lower, we are learning more than ever about the masses of people who did the work that made society tick.

Not surprisingly, as the lens shifts the basic narratives change as well. The history of men and women of all classes, colors, and cultures reveals an astonishing degree of struggle and independent political action. Everyday people played complicated historical roles, and they developed highly sophisticated and often very different political ideas from the people who ruled them. Sometimes their accomplishments left tangible traces; other times, the traces are invisible but no less real. They left their mark on our institutions, our folkways and language, on our political habits and vocabulary. We are only now beginning to excavate this multifaceted history.

The New Press People's History Series will roam far and wide through human history, revisiting old stories in new ways, and introducing altogether new accounts of the struggles of common people to make their own history. Taking the lives and viewpoints of common people as its point of departure, the series will re-examine subjects as different as the Renaissance, the Industrial Revolution, the Cold War, the settlement of The New World, World War Two, and the American Civil War.

A people's history does more than add to the catalogue of what we already know. These books will shake up readers' understanding of the past—just as common people throughout history have shaken up their always changeable worlds.

Howard Zinn
Boston, 2000

ACKNOWLEDGMENTS

My first debt is to books by Marilyn Young, Christian Appy, and James Gibson, and for their wonderful eyes for quotes. I have often gone to their sources and found myself using the same quotes they chose.

Secondly, Sharon Smith and John Rees encouraged me to write this book. Joel Geier gave very useful advice. Fil Hearn gave me the chance to go to Vietnam in 1998. Ian Birchall, Martin Smith, Dharma Thapa, Nigel Davey, Charlie Hore, Bruce Self, and Judith Orr read it and told me what to change and cut. Nancy Lindisfarne and Anthony Arnove in particular read with the eagle eyes of really good editors and insisted on many changes, most of which I have made. I am very grateful.

Rob Hoveman at Bookmarks began work on this project and was always kind and encouraging. Emma Bircham did the copy-editing and saw the book through production. She was a joy to work with. Emma and Mike Marqusee were also instrumental in finding an American publisher for this edition. Marc Favreau and Andrew Hsiao at The New Press were careful and helpful editors, and their suggestions for updating and changing the book have substantially improved it.

I owe two personal debts. Liz de Boisgelin stood by me through a difficult time in 1970, and I have not forgotten. Nancy Lindisfarne, by her love and the example of her courage, gave me the strength to write this book.

Finally, I would not have written this book had I not been

involved in the movement against the Kosovo war with my comrades in the Amherst branch of the International Socialist Organization (ISO). My thanks for their inspiration, and particularly to Doug Murray.

CHRONOLOGY

1883	France completes conquest of Vietnam.
1924	First Vietnamese Communist organization founded.
1935	Five friends begin meeting in the village of My Thuy Phong (Beautiful Waters).
1939	French round up nationalists and Communists.
1940	Germany defeats France. French colonialists rule Vietnam under Japanese supervision.
1941	Ho Chi Minh returns to Vietnam.
1945	In April, Japan takes over formally from France in Vietnam. In the spring and summer, famine kills 1 million in northern Vietnam. In August, Japan surrenders and crowds led by Viet Minh (Vietnamese League) take power in Saigon and Hanoi, and across the country. In September, Ho Chi Minh declares independence in Hanoi, and in Saigon British-led troops put down a rising and try to restore French power.
1946–54	War between France and Viet Minh.
1949	Communists, led by Mao Zedong, win power in China.
1954	French defeated at Battle of Dien Bien Phu. Peace negotiations in Geneva divide Vietnam into two countries, North Vietnam under the Communists and South Vietnam allied to the United States. A great majority of Communist troops and political workers are withdrawn from the South to North Vietnam.
1954–59	South Vietnamese government of President Ngo Van Diem arrests and executes remaining Communists in the South. Communist leadership in the North urges nonviolent response.

1959   Communists in the South push northern leadership into back-
            ing an insurrection in the South.

1960–65   Communist-led National Liberation Front (Viet Cong) is win-
            ning guerrilla war in the villages in South Vietnam.

1961   President John F. Kennedy sends the first American troops to
            Vietnam—3,200 by the end of the year.

1963   Urban unrest and demonstrations led by Buddhists in South
            Vietnam. United States backs coup and assassination of Pres-
            ident Diem. President Kennedy assassinated, replaced by Pres-
            ident Lyndon Johnson. 18,000 U.S. troops in Vietnam.

1965   United States begins sustained bombing of North and South
            Vietnam. Large numbers of U.S. troops committed—180,000
            by the end of the year, will eventually rise to over 500,000.

1967   First large demonstrations against war in United States. Public
            opinion shifts against the war.

1968   Tet Offensive by Viet Cong in January shows strength of pop-
            ular support. President Johnson, shaken, says he will not run
            for president again that year. My Lai massacre in Vietnam.
            Peace negotiations begin in Paris and will last five years. Bitter
            demonstrations at Democratic convention in Chicago. Rich-
            ard Nixon elected president, promises to solve Vietnam prob-
            lem.

1969   Nixon does nothing. United States remains in Vietnam. Very
            large demonstrations in United States in October and Novem-
            ber.

1970   United States invades Cambodia. In reaction, wave of student
            demonstrations and strikes in the United States, and four stu-
            dents are shot dead. United States withdraws from Cambodia
            and begins serious troop withdrawals from Vietnam. Wide-
            spread refusal to fight and killing of officers by U.S. military
            in Vietnam.

1972   Spring offensive by North Vietnamese army in South Viet-
            nam. Sustained bombing of North by United States. Nixon
            goes to China. U.S. troops still in revolt, being rapidly with-
            drawn—only 24,200 remain at the end of the year.

1973   United States and North Vietnam sign peace agreement in
            Paris. United States promises to withdraw troops and pay $5

billion compensation. Last troops are withdrawn—money not paid. President Nguyen Van Thieu of South Vietnam cannot live with peace settlement. War continues, but Communists do not try to take power.

1974   Nixon resigns in Watergate scandal.

1975   Khmer Rouge take power in Cambodia. South Vietnamese army collapses. Communists take Saigon, set up new South Vietnamese government.

1975–78   Killing fields of Cambodia under Pol Pot and Khmer Rouge.

1976   South and North merge into one Vietnam. China cuts aid to Vietnam.

1978   Refugees, primarily of Chinese ancestry, begin fleeing Vietnam. In December, Vietnam invades Cambodia.

1978–79   Vietnamese occupation of Cambodia and war with Khmer Rouge, who are backed by U.S., Chinese, and Thai governments.

1979   In January, Vietnam takes Phnom Penh, Cambodia, and sets up new government there. In February, China invades Vietnam, meets unexpected level of resistance, and withdraws.

1985   Communist leadership in Vietnam formally backs change to partial market economy.

1989   Fall of Communist governments in Russia and Eastern Europe. Vietnam begins to withdraw from Cambodia.

1990   Last Vietnamese soldiers leave Cambodia. UN arrives.

A PEOPLE'S HISTORY
OF THE
VIETNAM WAR

INTRODUCTION

The Vietnamese call it the American War. In America it's called the Vietnam War. This is a short history of that war, from the point of view of the peasants and GIs who fought it.

In 1945, when World War Two ended, Vietnam was a French colony. Vietnamese Communists then led a nine-year peasant guerrilla war against the French. In 1954 a peace settlement divided Vietnam in two. North Vietnam became a "Communist" dictatorship allied to Russia and China, and South Vietnam became a private capitalist dictatorship allied to the United States. Some Communists stayed behind in South Vietnam. The southern government persecuted them, and in 1959 they began a peasant guerrilla insurgency, the Viet Cong or National Liberation Front. By 1965 it looked as if the Communists would soon take power in South Vietnam, and the United States began sending in large numbers of troops to prevent this.

But why another book on the war?

There are a lot of books on different aspects of the war, many of them very good. This is an attempt to synthesize them into a short history that both tells the story and makes sense of what happened. It is particularly written for a new generation of activists who were small children, or were not even born, during the war years.

But there are two other audiences that particularly matter to me. One is the Vietnam generation in America—the people who fought in the war, the people who opposed it, and the hundreds of thousands who did both. I have tried to write a book that is true to their experience. The other audience is in Vietnam. Large numbers of young Vietnamese feel a deep sympathy for the guerrilla struggle, but they also feel oppressed by the corrupt government that came to power by winning that war. I hope that this book makes sense to them too.

This is a history from below. It tells what Vietnamese peasants, American soldiers, and American protesters did, and how they felt. It is a history from above as well. I write about what the generals and politicians on both sides did—although I am less concerned with what they felt. But the most fascinating, and important, thing in history is the intersection between below and above—the struggles where the ordinary people and the powerful meet. So the book looks at the conflicts between Vietnamese peasants and landlords, between guerrilla fighters and Communist bureaucrats, and between GIs and generals. It also deals with the conflicts back in the United States between the interests of ordinary working people and the policies of government and corporations. In short, to use an old-fashioned phrase, it looks at "class struggle."

Most historians separate class struggle and international relations. One is domestic policy and the other is foreign policy. They exist, in most accounts, in different worlds. This book looks, all the time, at how internal conflicts affect both international and domestic relations.

So Chapter 1, about why the Vietnamese fought, begins with an account of the class struggle in South Vietnam between a government backed by landlords and businessmen on one side, and a guerrilla army of poor and landless peasants on the other. For both sides it was more of a war over land than over national independence.

But it was not that simple, for the Communist leaders themselves were the children of landlords, businesspeople, and government officials. They wanted a strong, independent, socially just Vietnam. But they also wanted to be the new ruling class in that Vietnam, on the model of the people who ruled Russia and China. So at times they led the peasants against the landlords, at times they held the peasants back, at times they exploited the peasants, and at times the peasants forced them to fight. Chapter 1 chronicles the twists and turns of this contradictory struggle.

Chapter 2 is about why the American government intervened. The stated reason was to fight Communism, but after 1945 official American anti-Communism did three jobs at once. First, "fighting Communism" was the rationale for the Cold War competition with Russia about who would be the dominant power in the world. Second, it was the rationale for supporting the rich in poor countries against movements from below. Third, inside America, anti-Communism was in practice a pretext for persecuting radical shop stewards and union representatives.

So when it looked like the Communist-led guerrillas would win in Vietnam, the American government was afraid that it would make Russia more powerful, encourage revolts from below in other countries, and encourage radical tendencies in the American civil rights movements and the unions. It sent troops to Vietnam to stop that from happening.

Chapter 3 is about how the war was fought. The American government used bombs and artillery on a scale never seen before in the world. I argue this was because the Viet Cong had won the political war. The majority of Vietnamese supported them, and that meant the American combat troops were outnumbered. To put it in simple terms, there were more guerrillas than GIs, so the Pentagon's strategy was attrition—to kill very large numbers of Vietnamese until they were broken.

This strategy was carried out by American soldiers. But for them it was a working-class war.[1] It was not the children of the rich and powerful who were sent to Vietnam. For those who went, being there was part and parcel of their oppression at home, perhaps the worst part of it. And the killing and cruelty they found themselves doing were part of their oppression.

Chapter 4 is about the Vietnamese guerrillas. They fought with courage, and the main form of that courage was simply enduring the bombing. But the firepower ranged against them was such that by 1969 the local guerrillas had been beaten militarily. However, they still had the support of the majority of peasants. If the U.S. troops left, the guerrillas would win.

Chapter 5 is about the protestors in America. The main argument here is that from 1968 on, the rich and powerful in America wanted to withdraw from Vietnam because the protest movement was beginning to threaten their control at home. When push came to shove, power in America was far more important to the American leaders than power in Vietnam. But simply leaving Vietnam would weaken their position with many regimes in the world and weaken their control at home. So they chose a middle road, trying to wind down their involvement without leaving. Protest continued, and many more people on both sides died.

Chapter 6 is about the revolt against the war in the American armed forces. From 1968 on, the American troops killed many of their officers, and by 1971 most of the GIs were refusing or avoiding combat. In early 1973 the United States was forced to withdraw completely, and without the support of U.S. troops the southern government fell in 1975. I write about the soldiers' revolt at length because it is a part of the story that rarely gets told, and it is a part of the story that the Vietnam generation needs to have acknowledged. It is also something that people outside the United States, particularly in Vietnam, may know little about.

Chapter 7 is about Cambodia and Vietnam after the American War. Again, it concentrates on the class struggle in those countries. The horror of the killing fields in Cambodia was in part a consequence of the horror of the U.S. bombing that the Cambodians had already been through. But that horror also needs to be understood in terms of the struggle between a new, small, Communist ruling class in Cambodia and the peasants who turned against them.

Vietnam after 1975 was affected by an American-led boycott, Russian exploitation, and Chinese enmity. But Chapter 7 concentrates particularly on the attempt of the new Communist ruling class to build a modern economy by taxing the peasants heavily and sweating the workers, and on the attempts of peasants and workers to resist that exploitation.

Chapter 8 is about the consequences of the war for the United States and the world. The emphasis here is on the "Vietnam syndrome"—the insistence by the majority of working Americans, passed down from parents to children over the last thirty years, that the government may or may not be right about foreign policy, but the people will not send their children to die for Washington again.

This Vietnam syndrome makes it very difficult for the U.S. government to use ground troops. So the United States has become a strange kind of imperial power, effectively a superpower without an army. Chapter 8 traces how the limits imposed on American power by American workers have changed the nature of international relations in the last twenty-five years. It also traces the backlash in America against the movements of the 1960s. I argue that this backlash has been simultaneously an attack on the memory of Vietnam, on African Americans, on feminism, on gays and lesbians, on labor unions, and on the incomes and lives of working America. The backlash is part of the class struggle at home, and it is simultaneously an effort to win American workers back to dying abroad.

The book ends with the resurgence of American power in the world after September 11, and the rise of a new anti-war movement across the world.

I have tried to write in a straightforward, accessible style. This has forced me to think carefully. If you make all the steps in an argument explicit, you can notice the gaps, and so can the reader. Tony Cliff, the British socialist, once said that the more complex the argument you want to make, the simpler the language you should use.

Three things make this book complex. First, it was a complicated war, fought in four countries by soldiers from ten countries, with many twists and turns, and with complex roots and consequences. Second, there is a complex argument about class and war running through the book. Third, the standpoint adopted here is outside the mainstream. Noam Chomsky, the American anarchist, often says how much he hates giving one-minute answers to questions about American foreign policy on radio and television. The reason, he says, is that ideas outside the mainstream are often hard to grasp because people have not heard them before. Many mainstream ideas are complicated too, but because people have heard the arguments many times before they can be explained quickly.

I need to make two small points. The first is about "America." This is not an anti-American book. It is anti–American government, but then I think that the American government is anti–most American people. And so I have said "the American government" or "the United States" or "Washington" did this or that, because I don't want to assume that the policies of the government and the wishes of the people are the same. I am also aware that everybody in North and South America is American, and most of them say "North American" where I have used "American." I apologize for any offense.

Second, I'm American, and when I was 18 in 1966 I was a supporter of my country's role in Vietnam. If I had been drafted then, I would have gone. I wasn't drafted because my parents were middle-class teachers and I could go to college. By 1969 I was marching against the war. In 1970 I was refused conscientious objector status and decided to go to prison rather than the army. I was afraid of prison, but in the long run the people who went to prison had an easier time than the people who went to Vietnam and survived. Then my draft board gave me conscientious objector status on appeal and I did not have to go to jail.

If I had to do it over again, I hope I would go into the army and agitate against the war. I have written this book because I have mixed feelings about the anti-war movement. I am intensely proud of what we did and achieved, but we were ignorant about many things, and particularly about the class system in the United

States. Our passion helped to end the war, but our mistakes meant that the radical movements of the 1960s were eventually marginalized. I have written this book not out of nostalgia, but in the hope that another generation can learn from our experiences and act more wisely.

1

The Vietnamese

This chapter is about why the Vietnamese fought. To understand this, we have to begin with how French colonialism changed life for rice farmers.

The French conquest of Indochina began in 1859 and was complete by 1883. French Indochina was three neighboring countries—Vietnam, Laos, and Cambodia. Vietnam was overwhelmingly the most populous and important of the three. Vietnam had been independent of China for 900 years, but Chinese cultural influence was strong. Before the French, Vietnam, like China, had an emperor served by officials (mandarins) who were selected by examinations in the Chinese classics.

In 1888 most Vietnamese were rice farmers. There were two great centers of cultivation. In the north the densely populated Red River Valley was irrigated by an ancient system of dikes and canals. In the south the Mekong River Delta was the rice basket of Vietnam, with its thousands of small waterways and low-lying fertile land. North and south were connected by a long thin coastal strip in the center.

The French divided Vietnam into three zones for administrative purposes. The capital of the north was Hanoi, of the center Hue, and of the south Saigon. Eighty-five percent of the people spoke Vietnamese as their mother tongue. There were minorities of Chinese and Cambodian speakers, and mountain peoples speaking a variety of languages.

In the irrigated villages where most people lived, a small number of landlord families usually owned much of the land. A larger number of families owned enough land to get by, while a majority of the village had to rent land to live. But the emperors and the landlords knew they could only push the peasants so far—Vietnam had a history of peasant revolts. The main protection for the poor peasants was the institution of "village land." Part of the land in each village was owned by the village as a whole, and the village council rented fields to the poorer families at reasonable rates. The amount of village land varied from one-quarter of the total in some villages to two-thirds in others. In most Vietnamese villages in 1888, the rich were rich but the poor could live.

French colonialism didn't make much difference to this at first. But from 1900 on, the colonial government began to transform the village economy into part of the world capitalist system. It did this in four ways. First, the government took much of the land and gave it to French businessmen to run plantations and mines. Second, the government raised agricultural taxes to about a fifth of the crop so it could fund a strong, modern state.

Third, it needed workers for the expanded mines, plantations, and cities. But as long as the Vietnamese peasants could grow enough rice to live, they did not have to work for the low wages that business and industry wanted to pay. This was a common problem for colonial governments in many parts of the world in this period. The solution, particularly in French and British Africa, was usually a head tax that had to be paid in cash. Then the country people had to send their sons to the city to earn money, even if they grew enough food to survive. Traditional Vietnam already had a head tax, but it was paid in rice and the emperor cancelled it in years of bad harvest. The French doubled the tax, refused to reduce it in bad years, and insisted on cash.

Fourth, and most important, the French government increased the power of the landlords in the villages. This had both political and economic advantages for the colonial authorities. Politically, the French, like all colonial governments, faced a constant problem because there were so few French in Vietnam and so many Vietnamese. The French encouragement of the landlords led the landlords to support the French—it gave colonialism a real social base in the villages.

Economically, the power of the landlords meant that more rice went to the cities. As the landlords became more powerful, they took more and more of the rice produced in the villages and the peasants took less. This meant that more peasants had to become workers in the "modern" parts of the economy. But it also meant that the landlords could not eat all that rice, so they sold it on to the cities in return for industrial goods produced there and in France.

Inequality in the villages thus strengthened the colonial government, and sent workers and rice to the cities. But at the same time bitterness grew in the villages, followed by resistance. *Village at War*, a book by James Trullinger, traces this process in detail in the village of My Thuy Phong (Beautiful Waters), just south of Hue in central Vietnam.[1] During the war Trullinger worked for an American aid agency with shoeshine boys in Hue. Late in the war, in 1974–75, after the last American troops had left but before the South Vietnamese government fell, Trullinger returned to Vietnam as a graduate student and did six months of research in Beautiful Waters. His book is a stunning piece of work because he was brave—and smart—enough to talk to both sides. He had permission from the local South Vietnamese commander to do his research. Unlike all other American researchers, he also applied formally to the National Liberation Front for research permission. Supporters of the South Vietnamese regime talked to him in the village, and local Communists talked to him at secret meetings near the village or in Hue.

When Trullinger asked the old people about the origins of Communism in the village, they explained it to him by telling him about what the French had done.

Before the French came, two-thirds of the land in Beautiful Waters was owned by the village as a whole, an unusually high proportion. As in the rest of Vietnam, the richer landlords had always dominated the village council that rented out the land to poor villagers. But the villagers said that the council had "operated more or less fairly and consistently within the expected bounds of hierarchy. . . . It never demanded in taxes more than what people, perhaps in patient submission, accepted."[2]

Under French rule after 1900, and particularly after 1920, the village councilors found they could charge more for village land, take more rental contracts for themselves, and charge larger bribes for distributing land. Some of the councilors were unhappy with this new corruption, but they tended to resign from the council and leave the less scrupulous landlords in charge.

By 1940 five or six families controlled 30 to 40 percent of the land in Beautiful Waters, and the poorest 90 percent of the villagers controlled roughly a third of the land. The 90 percent now had to rent land from the landlords or find wage work. The usual rate for renting land, as throughout Vietnam, was a sum of money equal to half the crop in a good year. In a bad year the rent could be as much as the whole crop, but the tenant still had to pay.

It is important to understand what that meant in human, physical terms. The relationship between peasants and land is not mystical. Vietnam has a landscape of stunning beauty, of infinite shimmering greens, which any Vietnamese peasant can see. And of course people love the look, feel, and smell of the place in which they grew up. But the question of land, for peasants in Vietnam and anywhere else, is a matter of work, pain, and food. It is not an abstract question.

They know that the landlord takes half the rice and the government takes a share on top of that. Their exploitation is not mystified, nor is it hard to understand. They grow the rice, then somebody else comes, takes it away, and eats it. They feel their work, and their hunger, in their bodies all day every day. And they can see their children are weak and the landlords' children are fat.

That is the reality behind questions of land tenure in every peasant village. And in Beautiful Waters, behind the landlords who took half or more of the crop stood the colonial police. The old

Vietnamese imperial government had mostly left the village land-lords to deal with the peasants on their own. Under the French, however, there were police in the village. One man told Trul-linger:

> The policemen came round with the landlords to force us to pay the rent. Once we had a very bad flood, and the crop was lost, but the policeman came anyway. He said that if we did not pay he would arrest us, or take the land and rent it to someone else.[3]

Another peasant was arrested when he could not pay:

> I was held for a week in the (village) office. They made me sit in a corner, and my family had to bring me potatoes to eat. Finally, my son borrowed money from friends, and they let me go. But I had to give the policeman some money for himself, even after I had paid the rent.[4]

One incident in 1944 stood for many in the preceding decades. That year a few landlord families realized that their fields surrounded the fields of several poor peasant families. They refused the poor peasants the traditional right to walk across their land. The poor peasants could not farm, and they complained to the village council, which backed the landlords. The police backed the village council, and the small farmers had no choice but to sell their land cheaply to the big landlords.

Behind the police stood the colonial courts, which always ruled in favor of the landlords. Poor peasants who could not meet the rent had to borrow from moneylenders in the city at interest rates of 50 percent or more a year. The peasants were caught in a spiral of debt, and more and more of them lost their land.

The same thing was happening throughout the country. In the south, by the late 1930s, 6,200 landlords owned 45 percent of the rice land. In the north of Vietnam, in the Red River Valley, 2 percent of households owned 40 percent of the land.[5]

French colonialism was also transforming the old class of feudal landlords and imperial officials into a new class of capitalist landlords and colonial officials. The children of this class became government officials and junior officers in the army and police. They went to the new government schools—usually for three years or less, but they learned to speak French and honor French culture. Moreover, they knew that they owed their increased wealth to French power.

So, in about 1935, five men in the village of Beautiful Waters began to meet and talk. One, about 50 years old, ran a small shop in the village. Another was a low-level clerk for the colonial government in nearby Hue. In his thirties, he owned a bicycle, a little bit of land, and a small wooden house. He was poor but educated, and "always full of opinions on everything."

The third man, Truong, was a peasant of about 40. He could not read, but "reveled in the long rambling conversations that he sought out and dominated in the village. Many remembered Truong's inquiring mind and quick sense of humor."[6]

The fourth man was a poor peasant who spent much of his spare time maintaining the village shrines and pagoda.

The fifth man, Minh, was about 30. He was the son of one of the big landlords. Trullinger writes:

> Minh was somewhat estranged from his father, and for some reason rejected his father's wishes that he behave as a subservient son, loyal to the large landholding class. Minh had received some schooling, perhaps at a private school in Hue. He was good-humored and, in the words of a peasant related to him, "frighteningly intelligent". . . . One elderly peasant said: "His father was a typical rich man, and did not care about the people. But the son was completely different. He seemed to be interested in the poor people, and always had ideas about how poor people could live better."[7]

When he was in his twenties, Minh left his father's house and became a tradesman. The five friends met regularly for years:

Usually the conversations among the five men were after dark, when work was done, and when gatherings were not as obvious to the unfriendly eyes of colonial security agents. The men met over small glasses of rice wine, beer, or tea. They all gathered as frequently as possible, but often only two or three could come. Those who attended passed on opinions and reactions to those who could not come or dared not attend. A peasant described the conversations among the five: "First they talked about the problems and difficulties of life—like taxes, land problems, and corruption among local authorities. They talked about their own personal problems, their families' problems. But that was not all! After a little while they also talked about the village, then after about the problems outside this place. They talked so much, and after much talk they clearly understood all about the Westerners. They knew what France was doing in our fatherland. They understood why Westerners were here."[8]

In 1939, after years of meeting, those five men began to look outside the village to nearby Hue for ideas about how to fight the French and the landlords. The people they found with those ideas were Communists.

VIETNAMESE COMMUNISM

The Vietnamese Communist Party had been founded by Ho Chi Minh, the son of a mandarin. The majority of mandarins and landlord families supported French colonialism, but a minority always opposed it. This reflected a contradiction in the lives of this class. French colonialism made the landlords stronger in relation to the peasants, but weaker in relation to the French colonial government. So, many landlord families were split between supporters and opponents of colonialism, and many mandarins were torn inside themselves.

Ho Chi Minh's father, for instance, was a highly educated young man when the French first came. In 1885 there was a rebellion against French rule, called the Scholars' Revolt because it was led by mandarins. Ho Chi Minh's father was part of that revolt. When it failed the French ruled north and south Vietnam directly, but left a puppet emperor in Hue in charge of central Vietnam. Ho's father eventually took a job in the puppet emperor's court under the French, but he hated it and used to say, "Being a mandarin is a form of slavery."[9] His opinions finally cost him his job. Then Ho's father left his family and wandered across Vietnam and the neighboring French colonies of Laos and Cambodia, working as a story teller, a setter of bones, and a letter writer.

Ho Chi Minh himself left Vietnam at the age of 21, in 1911, as a mess boy on a ship. He worked at various jobs, mostly cooking, in the United States and Europe. In 1919 he was in Paris. Fired by American President Woodrow Wilson's rhetoric about the rights of nations, Ho went to the Versailles peace conference to argue for freedom for Vietnam. They showed him the door. Wilson's freedoms were not meant for the colonies.

Ho Chi Minh was already a member of the French Socialist Party. The next year, 1920, he joined the newly formed French Communist Party.

The party he joined was a revolutionary organization, inspired by the Russian Revolution three years before. In 1917 the Russian soldiers had refused to fight in World War One. The workers had taken over the factories, and the peasants had burned down the landlords' mansions and divided up the land. The Russian Communists, the Bolsheviks, backed all this—their slogan was "Land, peace, bread." The Russian workers elected committees, called soviets, in their workplaces, and the soldiers elected similar soviets in their barracks. Because the Bolsheviks were the only party backing all the struggles, the workers and peasants elected them to these soviets, and in October 1917 a national congress of all the soviets elected a Communist-led government.

That government took Russia out of the world war, gave full rights to women, legalized homosexuality, and appointed women ministers, which were unusual things to do at the time. In a country where anti-Semitism was the main form of racism, many of the Communist leaders were Jews. The new government declared that all parts of the Russian Empire had the right to secede, and announced its support for every anti-colonial movement everywhere in the world.

That revolution lit a fire in the minds of men and women in Europe and the colonies. The Russian Revolution is now usually presented as a coup. At the time, however, everybody, left and right, thought that the working class had taken power in Russia.

That was the cause Ho Chi Minh joined. By 1923 he was in Moscow working for the Communist International, trying to spread revolution in Asia.

But by 1923 Russian Communism was changing. There is much debate about what happened in Russia in those years.[10] To put it simply, by 1923 what had been workers' power was becoming a dictatorship of the bureaucrats. A bitter civil war had devastated the economy, and there were now more bureaucrats than factory workers. The Communists had always said Russia was a poor country and they could only build socialism with help from revolutions in the developed West. Now, after the civil war, surrounded by hostile capitalist powers, they needed revolutions abroad or they were finished. But revolutions were smashed in Hungary, Germany, and China.[11] Russia stood alone.

The new bureaucracy saw their task as survival. Their spokesman, Joseph Stalin, argued that sooner or later the great capitalist powers would invade. When they did, Russia would need modern industry, the basis for a modern army. They had to build that industry in a hurry. The Russian government had to push the workers and peasants, make profits, invest those profits, push the workers and peasants harder, make more profits, invest them, and so on. This had happened during the Industrial Revolution in England over a hundred years ago. The Russian state had to catch up in a decade, so they pushed their people to the limit.

In effect, Russia became a state capitalist economy. It was capitalist because the driving dynamic of the system was to make profits and invest to compete with other countries, just as the driving dynamic of private capitalism is for companies to make profits to invest to compete with other companies. But Russia's was "state" capitalism, not privately owned.

Stalin's government broke strikes and made independent unions impossible. By 1926, working in a Russian factory was just like working in a factory in any other police state. And in 1929, the government took back control of the land the peasants had won in the revolution. To do that, it had to arrest millions of peasants and kill hundreds of thousands. But the peasants' grain now fed the workers in modern industry.

Stalin's state capitalism worked—when Nazi Germany invaded in 1941, Russia had enough modern industry to resist—but it was built on brutal work and terror.

During the 1920s and early 1930s, most of the old Bolsheviks broke from Stalin's state. At some point each of them realized the dream had become a nightmare, and they could collaborate no longer. Those who spoke out were arrested in the 1920s. They were shot in the 1930s, and so too were almost all those who kept quiet, because Stalin and the new bureaucrats saw in them the memory of the revolution.

During these years Ho Chi Minh worked for the Communist International. It was a contradictory organization. The people who joined Communist parties wanted revolution, and the International openly said it did too. But after 1926 the Stalinist machine would not tolerate a democratic workers' revolution anywhere. The example would be too much of a challenge to the Russian regime.

Stalin sacrificed foreign Communists to make deals with their rulers. In China, for instance, a joint army of Communists and the nationalist Guomindang (Kuomintang) marched north in 1926 to take Beijing and Shanghai. In Shanghai there was a general strike and armed workers took power. But the nationalist Guomindang was one of Stalin's few allies in the world. The Communist

International told the Communists and workers to turn their guns over to the Guomindang when the army arrived in Shanghai. They did. The Guomindang then killed tens of thousands of workers and Communists, and the few surviving Communists fled to remote rural areas.[12]

Similar things happened in many countries. But the local Communist parties did organize, and they led strikes and peasant movements. After all, people became Communists because they wanted to change the world, and Stalin would have nothing to bargain with in international politics if he did not lead a movement.

Ho Chi Minh was in China working for the Communist International for much of the 1920s. In 1924 he founded the first Communist party in Indochina at a meeting of Vietnamese exiles in China. There are conflicting accounts of what he did in the 1930s. For much of the time he lived in Russia and kept his head down, scraping a living by teaching Vietnamese. He also went back to China for the International at some point; he was still part of Stalin's machine. But then in 1939 he left Russia for China, probably on his own account, to build an anti-colonial revolution in Vietnam. He finally got home in February 1941, after thirty years abroad, and found the Communists hiding in small camps in the jungle. They welcomed him. Almost everyone who ever met Ho agreed that he was a nice man—humble, gentle, and kind.

His project was to build a state capitalist regime in Vietnam like Stalin's Russia. Ho wanted a proud and independent state with modern industry. The Communists would rule, and the workers and peasants would work, and be arrested if they talked back. Ho wanted, in short, what the Vietnamese now have.

The Communist Party he returned to in Vietnam was a nationalist party with socialist roots. Its members were mostly, like Ho Chi Minh, the educated sons and daughters of landlords and government bureaucrats, but the decent and honest minority among those people. Only the rich got any education in French Vietnam, and they did not get much. In the 1930s only eight

Vietnamese in 1,000 had three years of school. These men and women were the majority of the Communists, and the great majority of the leadership of the party.

So when the five men from the village of Beautiful Waters contacted the Communists in Hue in 1939, the party recruited Minh, the radical landlord's son, first. After it trained him, the other four men were allowed to join the party cell in the village: "Many years later, one of the five men told two friends that the five had considered themselves equals within the cell, but that Minh had served as chief contact man with district and provincial (party) organizations."[13] This was how the Communist Party worked. First it recruited educated men like Minh. Then those people recruited and led the villagers they knew.

This produced a party in the image of people like Minh. They were the decent minority of the landlord class. They hated the corruption and brutality of their class. They wanted to sweep aside the old order and replace it with a modern industrial state. They saw that state not in terms of democracy, but in terms of a better world led by people like them. They were in daily, intimate contact with poor villagers and saw themselves as tribunes of the oppressed. They were honest men and women, worthy of respect. You cannot build an underground revolutionary organization in a village unless the people who have known you all your life trust you. But men like Minh were not themselves the oppressed.

This meant the Communist Party was always deeply ambivalent about land reform. Building a new society would mean breaking the old landlords. The rank and file of the party in the villages, the other four men in the party cell in Beautiful Waters, would have no problem taking the land from the landlords and shooting them if necessary. But men and women like Minh would always be torn. They themselves would come out of such a revolution as rulers in the cities, but their families would be impoverished and many of them killed. So the Communist Party was always torn between the leaders and the led, and the leaders were torn between their families and their vision of the future.

For some this suffering increased their resolve. Vo Nguyen Giap, for instance, was a Communist and the son of a mandarin. In the 1939 crackdown the French government jailed his wife, daughter, father, sisters, brother-in-law, and sister-in-law. Between 1941 and 1943 all of them were killed in jail.[14] Giap escaped arrest and remained a revolutionary all his life. He went on to become the military leader of the resistance against the French and then the Americans.

THE VIET MINH

Ho returned to Vietnam in 1941 with a plan, and he persuaded the other Communist leaders to agree to it. They set out to build a mass organization to fight for independence, the Viet Minh (Vietnamese League). This organization would unite everybody— workers, capitalists, peasants, and landlords—who wanted to fight the French. The Communists would be the organizers and political leadership of this alliance. This was not a trick. Everybody knew the Communists led the Viet Minh. But the structure of the Viet Minh allowed people to say to themselves, "The choice is between working with the Communists and working with the French. I am not a Communist, but I do want to fight colonialism. I will join the Viet Minh."

The structure of the Viet Minh also allowed the Communists to build a mass movement without recruiting too many people to the party. They could pick and choose people they trusted to follow their discipline.

The Viet Minh faced a complicated political situation in the middle of World War Two. Vietnam was a French colony, but Germany had conquered France in 1940. France was then occupied by German troops who set up a puppet French fascist government, the Vichy regime. The French colonial government in Vietnam declared itself loyal to Vichy. Later in 1940 the Japanese army invaded Vietnam. A French colonial government loyal to Vichy remained in place, backed by Japanese military power.

In 1941 the Vietnamese Communists were in no position to launch a general resistance against the Japanese army. They had been shattered by the French crackdown of 1939. They had no arms and few members (four years later, after considerable growth, they would still have only 5,000 members). For the moment, they survived in a few small guerrilla camps in the mountains in the north, near the Chinese border, but they were unable to launch a guerrilla war. Where they had members, they concentrated on talking to people and trying to build an underground organization.

But then the Allies drove the German army out of France. General Charles de Gaulle's Free French Party took power in alliance with the French Communists. De Gaulle wanted to hold on to the colonies. The colonial government in Vietnam could see the Allies were winning. It wanted to come out of the war on the winning side and hold Vietnam for France. It began secret talks with de Gaulle's new government. The Japanese army could no longer trust the French colonial authorities, and on 9 March 1945 the Japanese army took over the government directly and interned all the French.

Now Ho's Viet Minh could present themselves as part of the Allies, along with America, Russia, France, and Nationalist China, against Germany and Japan. The American Office of Strategic Services (OSS, the forerunner of the CIA) sent a few agents to Ho's camp in the mountains.

One man in Beautiful Waters remembered:

> We knew the war was coming to an end, and we knew the Japanese were going to be defeated by the Americans. We were also sure that the Americans would not let the French come back to Vietnam. We were all hopeful that Vietnam would be independent soon.[15]

A woman in Beautiful Waters said:

> I was a little girl at the time. But I can still remember how much everyone liked the Viet Minh. In my family, my mother and sisters

and I spent our time late at night making little Viet Minh flags. We worked on them together. We sewed all the flags with the yellow star, because we knew that the people would want them to celebrate the Viet Minh victory. And we were pretty sure that the Viet Minh was going to take over the country.[16]

Then in the spring of 1945 there was famine in the north. The Mekong Delta in the south had always been the rice basket of Vietnam. From the fall of 1944 on, it was clear that famine was coming to the north. But the only way to get rice north from the Mekong Delta was one two-lane highway and one slow railway line. The Japanese army needed what transportation lines Vietnam had to move rice and war materials for its own troops. The rice did not get through to the northern Vietnamese. Of the 10 million people in the north, 1 million starved to death.

There is always food for some during a famine. During 1943, for instance, the British colonial authorities in India had presided over a similar famine in Bengal, in which between 2 million and 3 million people died. The priority for the British, as for the Japanese, was supplying the front. And in both Bengal and north Vietnam, as in all famines, the rich, the soldiers, and the police had enough to eat. In north Vietnam, the French colonial police and Japanese army guarded the rice stockpiles from the hungry. The government continued to send troops into the villages to collect taxes—in rice.

The Communists and the Viet Minh told people to attack the rice warehouses and refuse to pay the taxes. They had almost no arms, so they also encouraged people to petition local officials not to collect taxes. According to historian David Marr, unsympathetic officials

found themselves surrounded by angry compatriots wielding bamboo spears, machetes, or knives, escorted to the village ceremonial house, and compelled to apologize publicly for abusing their powers and denigrating the Viet Minh. If the village possessed a small stock of "charity grain," officials might be persuaded to release it. Grain already collected and about to be turned over to private syndicated tax collectors . . . sometimes had to be returned. . . . When the district mandarin arrived at Phu Ninh village to collect taxes escorted by a Japanese squad, the alert drum sounded and hundreds of villagers surrounded the party. After a standoff lasting all day, the Japanese fired a volley that killed two people, then withdrew. . . . The district mandarin or An Thi (in Hung Yen) reported that most village officials were now more afraid of being killed than of disobeying repeated orders from superiors to collect taxes. . . .

Sometimes people broke into grain warehouses owned by the government or big landowners. Most commonly a small group of young men armed only with spears and machetes would over-power two or three guards in the middle of the night, break the locks, then urge a much larger group to grab sticks of paddy [threshed, unmilled rice] and disperse as quickly as possible. In other cases, large crowds were mobilized first to cow guards and provide a screen against outside interruption as the warehouse was emptied. Occasionally, it was possible to take advantage of Allied air attacks, when warehouse guards ran for shelter, to seize a quantity of paddy and rice.[17]

There were hundreds of tax refusals and about seventy-five to one hundred warehouse raids. These definitely saved lives, perhaps 100,000, maybe more. But without arms they could not stop the famine.

Famines change whole societies. Poor people beg from the rich and are refused. People refuse to share with their neighbors and their kin. They have to sell their land and their daughters. Decisions are made inside families about who will eat. The children or the old people do not get their share and they die. This is a daily event, something unspoken, but clear every time people eat. People are ashamed of what they do, and do not talk about it much afterwards. But they do not forget or forgive. The Viet

Minh had established themselves as the people who fought the famine. After the famine, the Communists and the Viet Minh were always strongest in the north.

The new harvest began to come in that summer of 1945. Then the American government dropped atomic bombs on Hiroshima and Nagasaki, and the Japanese government surrendered. Nobody in Vietnam had expected the war to end so quickly and there was a sudden power vacuum. The Japanese had been defeated and the French were still interned. The Viet Minh units in the north marched towards Hanoi, exulting in walking openly in daylight. They were largely unarmed. The main Viet Minh unit in Hanoi had only 800 fighters with ninety firearms, but they had the support of the people. The Japanese army stayed in their barracks, waiting to surrender to the Allies. If the Viet Minh did not attack them, they would not fight.

On 16 August, 20,000 people attended a rally in the square facing Hanoi Opera House. A Viet Minh flag was unfurled, the crowd cheered, and the police did not dare open fire. Three days later a Viet Minh–led crowd of 200,000 seized the palace, the city hall, the civil guard barracks, and power.[18]

On 2 September 1945 Ho Chi Minh declared Vietnamese independence in front of a crowd of half a million in Hanoi:

> [He began] "All men are created equal. The Creator has given us certain inviolable Rights: the right to Life, the right to be Free, and the right to achieve Happiness." At this point he looked out over the crowd, and gently asked, "Do you hear me distinctly, fellow countrymen?" And the crowd answered that they did indeed hear him.[19]

Ho was using the words of the American Declaration of Independence. It was a direct appeal for American support against French colonialism. He didn't get that support.

THE SUPERPOWERS

The leaders of the great world powers had already agreed what they were going to do with Vietnam. As World War Two came to an end, the leaders of Russia, the United States, and Britain held summit meetings in Yalta and Potsdam. There they agreed how to divide up the postwar world into spheres of influence. Russia got Eastern Europe, the United States and Britain got Western Europe, and they split Germany. The United States would dominate the Americas, of course, and Britain and the United States together would dominate the Middle East.

The British prime minister, Winston Churchill, insisted that France should keep its three colonies in Indochina: Vietnam, Laos, and Cambodia. Churchill was dedicated to retaining the British Empire, and was worried that Indochinese independence from France would strengthen the case for Indian and African independence from Britain.

In 1945 France mattered more to America than Vietnam. In March de Gaulle called in the American ambassador to France. General de Gaulle was a right-wing nationalist and the leader of a new coalition government with the French Communists. The Communists had been the core of the French resistance to the Nazis, and it was not clear then if they would take power in France, or in all Europe. So de Gaulle threatened the American ambassador:

> What are you driving at? Do you want us to become, for example, one of the federated states under the Russian aegis? The Russians are advancing apace, as you well know. When Germany falls, they will be upon us. If the public here comes to realize you are against us in Indo-China, there will be terrific disappointment and nobody knows to what that will lead. We do not want to become communist; we do not want to fall into the Russian orbit, but I hope you will not push us into it.[20]

De Gaulle was bluffing, but the American ambassador took the point. The Russian, American, and British governments agreed that Vietnam, Laos, and Cambodia would remain French colonies.

However, they all knew that in 1945 the French government did not have the soldiers, the guns, or the ships to retake Indochina. So Russia, Britain, and the United States agreed that the British army would receive the surrender of the Japanese troops in southern Vietnam, restore order, and then hand the country back to the French. The Nationalist Chinese army would do the same in the north.

The French War

The Viet Minh took power in Hanoi on 19 August 1945. Two days later there was a mass demonstration in Saigon, in the south, led by the Viet Minh. Ngo Van Xuyet was there.

Ngo was a Trotskyist. Leon Trotsky, one of the leaders of the Russian Revolution, had been the leader of the Communist opposition to Stalin's government in Russia. He was arrested and went into exile, where he spent the 1930s trying to build an international movement of socialists opposed to both Western capitalism and the Stalinist dictatorship. When Trotsky was killed by Stalinist agents in Mexico in 1939, he left behind small groups in many countries.

The Trotskyists in Vietnam had a few hundred members in the south, mainly workers on the plantations and workers and intellectuals in Saigon. In the 1930s they won local elections in Saigon and were central to a general strike there in 1938. But the crackdown of 1939 destroyed them, just as it did the Communists. Ngo Van Xuyet and the other survivors began to get released from prison in 1944.

In August 1945 Ngo was worried about the demonstration because it was led by the Viet Minh, who were telling people to remain calm while they negotiated independence with the French.

He was sure the French were about to return, in blood. But the demonstration affected him deeply:

> For the first time in the political life of the country, from the morning onwards, veritable masses of people assembled like ants and filled the Norodom boulevard, then the Botanical Gardens near the governor's palace, and then crossed the major arteries chanting slogans. . . .
>
> The Vietnamese police at the service of the occupation no longer knew from where to take its orders: it remained passive in the presence of the procession crossing the city on strike. . . . The demonstration, which owed its initiation to the Viet Minh, was the classic tactic preparatory to the seizure of power—it represented the seal of general approval. But in fact everybody went down the street with different aspirations. The only common but overwhelming sentiment was "never to see the French back in power." . . .
>
> The first awakening of these masses, who had been forever in "chains and gags," emanated an electric tension amid an unusual calm, the calm that precedes a storm. All constraint was broken, and everybody seemed to live in a moment of total liberty. . . .
>
> [But] Roosevelt, Churchill and Stalin had decided our fate at Yalta and Potsdam. We were not to be cast body and soul into a future without a tomorrow. Faced with the imminent arrival of British troops, and faced with the threat of the return of the old colonial regime (Colonel Jean Cedile, the special envoy of the "New France," was already in the governor-general's palace in Saigon), everybody decided to look for and obtain weapons; everyone lived in the same electric atmosphere.[21]

In September British troops, mainly Nepali Gurkhas under the command of British officers, arrived in Saigon. The British government was now Labour and Churchill was no longer prime minister, but this made no difference to imperial policy. The British did not have enough troops to attack the Vietnamese on their own. So they released and armed both the Japanese troops and the imprisoned French colonials. On the night of 22 September, Nepali, French, and Japanese troops under British command occupied the main buildings in Saigon.

The Viet Minh called for restraint and negotiation with the allies. But Saigon rose—the Trotskyists, the Buddhists, the religious sects, the many Communists who could not stomach the party line, and above all the workers. It was spontaneous. A hundred and fifty French civilians were killed, and the rebels held the working-class suburbs for several days. But the Viet Minh withdrew from Saigon and the rising was crushed.[22]

The French army replaced the British and slowly reasserted its power in the south. As they all retreated, the Communists hunted down and killed almost all the Trotskyists. For the moment the French were not strong enough to take all of Vietnam, and the Viet Minh still held power in the center and north.

In Beautiful Waters it was a good time. The local Viet Minh held power for eighteen months. They did not punish their enemies, and they did not take the land from the landlords. But they lowered many rents and gave the communal land back to the poor peasants. They abolished the land tax on smallholdings and the head tax. They set a ceiling for interest rates of 30 percent, and made strenuous efforts to hold back corruption in their ranks.[23]

It was what the Communists had promised, and what men like Minh had devoted their lives to. It was an attempt to satisfy the poor peasants without losing the support of the landlords and the businessmen in the cities. At the same time Ho Chi Minh was desperately negotiating with the French. The first and last fair elections in Vietnam were held in the center and north in January 1946. The Viet Minh won overwhelmingly. But they did not have the arms to fight. To the north, in China, there was civil war between Communists and nationalists. The Viet Minh could get no arms from there. And the Vietnamese Communists were still part of an international movement run from Moscow. The line from there was to negotiate with the French.

So Ho agreed to the landing of French troops in Hanoi in March 1946. In November, the French struck and drove the Viet Minh out of Hanoi. In Beautiful Waters, the Communists went underground again, but the Viet Minh kept the support of most of the villagers. The guerrilla war against the French lasted eight more years.

The main highway in the country ran through the fields of Beautiful Waters, and the Viet Minh in the village became snipers, firing at French convoys from their hiding places and then running away. The French army made many sweeps through the village looking for rifles, Marxist pamphlets, or entrances to tunnels. In the search they would stick their bayonets into the rice storage jars, searching, and the villagers would stand very still and say nothing. They saw the French as cruel and unpredictable. Every sweep took prisoners, and some of them never came back. As the war went on, the Viet Minh grew stronger in Beautiful Waters, and at night small units began to stand and fight the French in the dark.

But not all the villagers in Beautiful Waters supported the Viet Minh, and not all the French supported colonialism. The French Communist Party had supported colonialism as long as it was in the government, but after it left de Gaulle's coalition in 1947 it began to organize against the war. Even before that, the French government had assumed it would be politically impossible to use French conscripts in Indochina. So they used 80,000 French career soldiers, 20,000 French Foreign Legionnaires (half of whom had fought for the Nazis), and 48,000 troops from the French colonies. It was not enough, but they also had 300,000 Indochinese troops.[24]

The sergeants and officers among the Indochinese troops were mostly the children of the landlords, the government officials, the moneylenders, and the businessmen in the cities. So were the police. The Communists were trying to build an alliance with that class. But the majority of the landlords figured their future was safer with the French. In Beautiful Waters the same few families who had controlled the land in the 1930s now leaned on French support.

Back in the hills, particularly in the north, the Viet Minh were building larger units in the jungle. The war spread across the whole of Indochina. The Vietnamese Communists had called themselves the Indochinese Communist Party. Now they formed separate parties in Cambodia and Laos, which built mass guerrilla organizations modeled on the Viet Minh—the Pathet Lao in Laos and the Khmer Serai in Cambodia. These movements diverted French attention and resources, but the crucial battle was in Vietnam.

In 1949 the Communists in China won their civil war, and the Viet Minh could finally obtain arms from over the border. The Vietnamese Communist Party expanded massively, still favoring people from rich backgrounds but also recruiting more widely.

This seemed natural and right to the educated Communists. Le Van Tiem, for instance, became party secretary in the village of Son-Duong in the north in 1948:

> The three members of the modern intelligentsia, [elementary school graduates] like myself, all became party members because, with our prestige, our advice to the other villagers was frequently followed. Similarly, many other teachers were also recruited into the Party because of their education, their speaking skills and the prestige they commanded as members of the teaching profession. I can recall only a few cases of teachers who were not invited to join the Party: one because of his competitive and argumentative style of interaction and two others because of their distance from other villagers.[25]

However, the war was making landless peasants more important to the party. The party secretary in Son-Duong village was a teacher, but the commander of the village guerrillas, Te, was a landless laborer. When Te was a boy and his father lay dying, very few of the villagers had come to say goodbye to the old man because the family was poor and of no account, and because there was a rumor his father had tuberculosis. Even in that poor household, Te had been at the bottom of the hierarchy because his mother was not his father's favorite wife. From the age of five he had worked for wages. As a teenager he became a plowman for the mayor of a nearby village:

> On the first day he beat me right and left with a bamboo rod in the field as I tried to plow. The following morning, weeping and holding the plow but determined to master the technique, I succeeded at the task. . . . I always went to work hungry. Even at their family celebrations, I ate the leftovers when I returned from the field.

Te worked for the mayor for six years, and "for all those years, my [widowed] mother remained a hired laborer in Son-Duong."[26] When the war against the French came, Te joined the guerrillas. By 1952 he was the commander in the village where his father and mother had been treated as nothing. In the war, what a person did mattered as much as who they were.

After 1950 Viet Minh propaganda and speeches in Son-Duong and Beautiful Waters, and across Vietnam, began to emphasize class differences and land reform. The war was hardening the Communists. They could see that the landlords were dragging their feet and looking to the French for support. The Communist Party had been founded by revolutionaries. They understood class, and they knew how to mobilize the energy and passion of the oppressed. So in 1953, after eight years of war, they began a thorough land reform in the areas they controlled in the north (but not in their areas in the center and south). In the north, the party organized landless peasants to haul the old landlords in front of village meetings, humiliate them, make them apologize, take their land, and sometimes kill them. The accounts we have of the land reform are mostly hostile.[27] They all agree that the reform was led by the lowest of the low, and that those people had a lifetime of bitterness to avenge.

Once the landless began, they attacked both the "feudal" landlords who had supported the French and the "progressive" landlords who supported the Viet Minh. As we have seen, many Communist leaders came from landlord families. Now, with land reform, the class tensions in the Communist Party came to the surface in stark form. Communists from landlord families found their fathers publicly humiliated and their families reduced to ordinary poverty. When they went home, their mothers looked at them in sullen judgment over the rice bowl. The landless could simply hate exploitation and want their fair share. The Communist Party cadres were torn.

The party dealt with this in two ways. At first, people from landlord families who protested too loudly were expelled. But in 1955 Ho Chi Minh himself announced that there had been many mistakes and injustices in the land reforms. There were investigations, village by village, many apologies, and some people got some of their land back.

However, the deed was done. The power of the old order in the countryside was broken in the north. And that released, as Ho and the other leaders had known it would, the ferocious energy of the landless. In 1954 the French army dug themselves into the valley of Dien Bien Phu in the mountains near the Laotian border. They built their base in a valley because they knew the Viet Minh in the hills above them had no heavy artillery. But the Viet Minh had organized a civilian transport force of a quarter of a million people, most of them landless peasants, who had carried Chinese heavy artillery, broken down into many pieces, on their backs along paths through the jungle and over the mountains. The French were cut off at Dien Bien Phu and pulverized by that artillery. They surrendered.

The Viet Minh had won the war. But not quite the peace.

The Geneva Negotiations

After Dien Bien Phu, the French and the Viet Minh sat down to negotiate in Geneva. It was clear to all that the Viet Minh could defeat the remaining French units and take over the whole country within a year. So there was no question that Vietnam would become independent. The question was whether it would be Communist.

The talks in Geneva were part of larger negotiations between America, Russia, and China over the end of the Korean War. Vietnam was a sideshow for these powers, but a sideshow they wanted settled. The big powers agreed that Laos and Cambodia would become independent kingdoms, formally neutral in the Cold War but in practice leaning towards the Americans. Vietnam would be partitioned like Korea and Germany. The Communists would get north Vietnam, and south Vietnam would become a separate state aligned with the Americans.

The Viet Minh wanted the country divided at the 13th parallel, just north of Saigon. More important, they insisted the partition had to be temporary, with elections within six months. The American president, Dwight D. Eisenhower, later wrote, "I have never talked with or corresponded with a person knowledgeable in Indo-Chinese affairs who did not agree that if elections had been held as of the time of the fighting, possibly 80 per cent of the population would have voted for Ho Chi Minh."[28]

The French insisted on the 18th parallel, just south of Hanoi, and no elections. The Russian foreign minister, Vyacheslav Molotov, proposed the 17th parallel, north of Hue, and elections in two years. Everybody involved knew that two years would give the new southern regime enough time to consolidate power and prevent free elections. So Ho Chi Minh flew to China and personally appealed to Zhou Enlai, the Chinese foreign minister, to overrule Molotov. Zhou told Ho to accept the Russian settlement.[29]

For the Russian and Chinese governments, Vietnam was not

worth upsetting the larger deal between the Americans and Russians over Korea and the world. The Viet Minh were dependent on China for weapons, and the Vietnamese Communist Party was still very much part of a world movement led by the Russians. Moreover, the Vietnamese were aware the American government was considering sending troops to Vietnam.

So the Viet Minh accepted partition at the 17th parallel and elections in two years' time. The American government refused to sign the final peace settlement so it would not be bound by the promise of elections. North Vietnam and South Vietnam became separate countries. In North Vietnam, the Communist Party began to build a state capitalist economy modeled on Stalin's Russia and Mao's China. They wanted a modern, industrialized economy in North Vietnam, ruled by the leadership of the Communist Party. South Vietnam became a corrupt American client state.

The Republic of South Vietnam

The new Republic of South Vietnam was headed by Ngo Van Diem, a Catholic mandarin. Diem had gone into exile during the French war—he hated the Communists yet could not bring himself to support the French. Now his government was the old colonial government, his officials the Vietnamese who had served the French. His army officers had almost all fought for the French against the Viet Minh. A million Catholic refugees came down from the North. Some Catholics had fought for the Viet Minh, but the Catholics who had become refugees had supported the French. Diem was a Catholic too, and now they were his strongest supporters in the South. The big businessmen in the cities were largely Chinese, and they too supported Diem.

In the villages the landlords supported Diem's government. Hue and central Vietnam were south of the 17th parallel, so Beautiful Waters was now part of South Vietnam. The same families who had dominated the village council under the French now dominated it under Diem. The individuals differed—under the

French it had been one brother, now it was the other brother or a nephew. But the policies continued. The same few families still controlled 30 to 40 percent of the land in Beautiful Waters. And "many abuses of council authority common under the French became virtually routine" under Diem.[30]

The Communists had accepted the Geneva peace agreement in 1954. They had had 60,000 political activists in the South, and all but 15,000 were withdrawn to the North. Of the 100,000 Viet Minh soldiers in the South, 90,000 left for the North, taking almost all the modern weapons with them. The 10,000 soldiers left behind lived secretly in the jungle because their presence was an open violation of the Geneva peace deal. Vo Van An, a Communist activist, defected to the Americans in 1965 and told his interrogators that after 1954:

> These units lived deep in the jungle, "fleeing from people as if they were tigers." . . . They maintained no bases, no camps. . . . Each soldier had a hammock which was his home. . . . They were constantly on the move, avoiding contact with anyone, using every means of camouflage, covering their tracks, leaving absolutely no sign at all.[31]

The Communist Party was now run from the North. The strategy was that the party in the South would try to build support for elections. It is unlikely that the Communist leaders believed the elections would actually happen. It was pretty obvious that Vietnam was being divided as Germany and Korea had been divided. Moreover, the Communists had withdrawn three-quarters of their political activists from the South. Had they expected democracy and elections, they would have left those people in place. Vo Van An, the Communist defector, told his interrogators that higher level cadres like him had been

> certain that general elections would never take place, although this was not discussed at lower levels to maintain morale and so as not

to conflict with the Party's public stance that the Geneva Accords were a great victory for the Party. By the summer of 1955 it became apparent to everyone what the higher echelons in the Party had felt all along: there would be no general elections and no steps toward reunification talks. The leadership was not surprised. "We just considered Diem as a debtor who refused to pay—we would make him pay."[32]

When the elections did not happen the Communist Party told its members that a revolution might be necessary later. For the moment the task was to build the party, organize, and agitate for elections. This was in line with what Communist parties were saying in Europe and India at the same time—don't try to take power, organize campaigns and unions, try to win elections. This line fitted with Russian foreign policy. The Russian government had effectively decided that if the Americans did not challenge its rule in Eastern Europe, it would not challenge American influence in the rest of the world. But it also fitted with the exhaustion of the party in North Vietnam. It felt it needed time to rebuild a working economy in a ravaged land—and for that it needed Russian aid.

But the party cadres left behind in South Vietnam found themselves in desperate times. Diem's new government was a police state. In a sense, Diem had no choice. In the class struggle one side always feels it is on the advance, while the other feels it is on the retreat. The majority of the peasants and workers had supported the Viet Minh. If Diem did not push them back, hard, with repression, they would only become more confident and his government would fall.

And the issue of land remained. The Communist Party in the South had not redistributed all the land as it had in the North. But what the party did in Beautiful Waters it had also done in most of the Mekong Delta. It had rented more communal land to the poor and less to the landlords, and it had reduced rents and controlled debts. Now the landlords were back, but facing tenants who had felt their own power for years. In South Vietnam in 1954, the landless and the peasants could imagine freedom from economic slavery.

The landlords could only claw back their rents in that situation through great fear, and therefore great cruelty. But if they did not take their land back quickly, they might lose it forever.

Diem's American advisors urged him to implement land reform to weaken the Communists. The Americans had recommended this strategy in Japan, Korea, and the Philippines, and there it had largely worked. But in those countries there had been a powerful native ruling class in the cities, for whom land reform had made sense. They would sacrifice some of their land in the countryside to consolidate the power of their businesses in the city. They could do this because land was not their most important possession.

South Vietnam was different. There the Vietnamese who backed the government relied on their land ownership. Under French colonialism, the big businessmen and plantation owners had been French and Chinese. After 1954 they were mostly Chinese. (This does not mean that most Chinese in Vietnam were rich. Most Chinese were poor workers, but most big businessmen and traders were also Chinese.) These Chinese capitalists supported Diem's government, but they were not its core, its officials, or its officers.

The U.S. government bankrolled Diem's government by supplying large quantities of American consumer goods. Diem's government then sold licenses to import these goods cheaply to local capitalists, often Vietnamese ones. (The local capitalists also had to pay large bribes for the licenses.) The government used the money from the sale of the licenses to fund government expenditure, the capitalists got a windfall, and the ministers became hopelessly corrupt.[33]

It is probably true that Diem's government would not have lasted a month without American support. Even with that support, it also would not have lasted a year without a real base in the country, among a real class. That base was the landlords and their children in the army. Diem had to defend them. So Diem agreed to the American idea of land reform and passed a law, but in fact little changed. And he attacked the Communists. In 1956 anybody who had agitated for elections was arrested—about 50,000 people, of whom roughly 12,000 were executed.[34] This is an extraordinary number given that there were probably only 15,000 Communists left after so many withdrew to the North in 1954. The terror smashed half the Communist cells in Tay Ninh province by late 1955, and 90 percent of the party cells in Tay Ninh were gone by the end of 1956.

The Communists left alive in the villages knew what to do in this situation. They had to kill a few government informers and landlords in the village—that would drive the rest into the provincial towns. The army might come back in sweeps, but the Communists could hide. That is what the Viet Minh had done in the war against the French. The guerrillas fighting the French in the nineteenth century had done it too. It was the obvious thing to do. And there were still a few thousand armed guerrillas in the jungles, hunted, living like animals, under orders not to fight, but desperate.

The southern Communists in the villages begged their provincial party committees to let them fight. The provincial committees said no, and simultaneously begged the leadership in Hanoi for the order to fight.

The leadership in Hanoi was torn.[35] The southern Communists had great moral force on their side. The southerners who had gone North wanted to fight, but most of the leadership was from the North. More important, they were trying to build state capitalism in one poor country, North Vietnam. They wanted time.

During that time the southern party was dying, and North Vietnam was part of a world Communist movement undergoing considerable change. Stalin was dead, and in 1956 Nikita Khrushchev attacked the worst of Stalin's crimes and announced that the foreign policy of the Communist states would now be peaceful coexistence with the West.

For the Russian leaders, anxious about nuclear armageddon and concerned for their own dictatorship, peaceful coexistence made sense. But when the leadership in Hanoi said "peaceful coexistence" to its comrades in the South, it was an impossible joke. The southern regime was killing them all, not offering coexistence.

Still, in 1957 and 1958 the underground party began to recruit again, as Diem's government restored more and more land to the landlords. But then in 1959 repression intensified. "Le Van Chan" (a pseudonym) was a senior party official then. He was captured in 1962, and later told his American interrogators about the

period toward the end of 1959, when if you did not have a gun you could not keep your head on your shoulders. . . . There was no place where Party members could find rest and security. Almost all were imprisoned or shot. . . . Some village chapters, which had had four or five hundred members during the Resistance [to the French] and one or two hundred members in 1954, were now reduced to ten members, and even those ten could not remain among the people but had to flee into the jungle to survive.

In the face of such activity by the Diem government, the demand for armed activity by Party members increased daily. . . . Party members felt it was no longer possible to talk of political struggle while looking down the gun barrels of the government. Yet, despite the bitterness within the Party and their anger at the Central Committee, the Regional Committee, the zone committee and the village committee, party members were unable to break away from the organization that was killing them. There never were clear factions or groups within the Party demanding armed activity, which might have broken off from the Party organization in the South, or from the Central Committee in Hanoi—that could never happen. Nevertheless, there were individuals—say, draft-age youths—who became so angry that they took the weapons the Party had hidden and came out of the jungle to kill the officials who were making trouble for them or their families. They did this, not because the Party had condemned those officials, but to preserve their own lives or to defend their families. Sometimes those individuals were so angry at the Party that they allowed themselves to be captured afterwards—just to spite the party.[36]

The Communists in the South were screaming at the North. Their voices had great moral weight. Diem's regime was winning. As Le Van Chan said to his interrogators, "The Central Committee kept calling for political struggle. If they had kept that up, where were they going to find the cadres to carry it out?"[37] And the movement in the South was beginning to fight on its own. The Communist leaders in the North faced the alternatives of total defeat in the South, or a peasant movement fighting against their orders and outside their control.

In late 1959 the party in the North decided to back the killings of government agents that were already happening in the South, and to organize and broaden them. At Vietnamese New Year in January 1960, the Communists launched an assassination offensive against secret policemen and village chiefs. In Long An province they had a list of hundreds of names. By the time they had killed twenty-six, the others had all fled to the towns and cities.[38] In Ben Tre province in the Mekong Delta, the party organized an uprising as an experiment. According to the historian Gabriel Kolko:

> Virtually unarmed masses briefly took over much of the province; land was distributed during the uprising itself. The formula worked virtually everywhere and soon gave the Party a vast presence and power despite the ARVN's [Diem's Army of the Republic of Vietnam] ability to quickly retake public buildings. Within months a major power shift had taken place in Vietnam.[39]

As in Ben Tre, everywhere the Communists began to share out the land as they drove out the officials and the secret police. The party in the North had been dominated by the educated class and torn over land reform. The party in the South was different now. When the party took most of its activists North in 1954, those left behind would have been, by and large, less important in the party. To put it another way, they were less likely to be educated or from landlord families. The Southern party's recruitment since had been among peasants who were angry at the return of the landlords under Diem. And by 1960 the Communists had an ocean of grief to avenge. They were mostly poor men and women, they did not care if they kept any "progressive" landlords on their side, and they knew that handing out the land would unleash the whirlwind.

A landless peasant who joined the resistance in Long An in 1961 put it this way:

> I was poor. I had lost my land. I didn't have enough money to take care of my children. In 1961 propaganda cadres of the [Communist-led National Liberation] front contacted me. . . . They came to all the poor farmers and made an analysis of the rich and poor classes. They said the rich people had always served the French and had used the authority of the French to oppress the poor. . . . Without any other means to live, the poor had become the slaves of the landlords. The cadres told us that if the poor people don't stand up to the rich people, we will be dominated by them forever. The only way to ensure freedom and a sufficient life was to overthrow them. . . .
>
> In my village there were about forty-three hundred people. Of these, maybe ten were landlords. The richest owned five hundred hectares, and the others had at least twenty hectares apiece. The rest of the people were tenants or honest poor farmers. I knew that the rich oppressed the poor. . . . So I joined the Liberation Front.[40]

For many it had become a matter of human dignity. Chan, the captured Communist, told his American interrogators:

Previously, the peasantry felt that it was the most despised class . . . particularly the landless and the poor peasants. . . . At a celebration, they could just stand in the corner and look, not sit at the table like the village notables. Now the communists have returned and the peasants have power. The land has been taken from the land-lords. . . . Now the peasants can open their eyes and look up to the sky; they have prestige and social position. The landlords and other classes must fear them because they have the power: most of the cadres are peasants, most of the Party members are peasants, and most of the military commanders are peasants.[41]

2

Why America Intervened

The U.S. government became involved in Vietnam because it looked like the Communists were going to win. The U.S. government was heavily committed to anti-Communist regimes in other parts of the world, and the rich and powerful in the United States had found anti-Communism essential to weakening the unions and socialism at home. So they intervened in Vietnam for reasons that came from outside Vietnam—and some of the reasons came from the class struggle between business and unions in the United States.

This is hard to grasp. In universities and the media, phenomena that form an organic whole are always divided into compartments. So economics is separated from politics, society from individual psychology, culture from history, science from religion, policy from morality, mental work from manual work, and the body from the mind. In the same way, we are used to thinking that international relations and class struggle are as different as cabbages and goldfish.

And within the United States, foreign policy is almost always explained in terms of what is happening in the other country. So, for instance, during the war between the United States and Serbia in 1999, even anti-war Americans looked for an explanation of the war in terms of what was happening in Serbia. They asked why the Albanians and Serbs were fighting. On the television, they could see American bombers and Serb targets. They saw war between the United States and Serbia, and asked for its roots in Serbian history, not American history.

There were some on the left, myself included, who suggested to them that the American government was bombing Yugoslavia because Saddam Hussein had successfully defied American bombs in Iraq a few months before. Now the United States had threatened the Serbian government with force, the Serbs had defied it, and the American government wanted to demonstrate it could not be defied. This was important to maintaining American power in Europe and the Middle East.

Yes, people would say, that's probably true, but why are the Albanians and Serbs fighting?[1]

For Americans to understand U.S. policy towards Vietnam requires a similar stretch. For the U.S. government, what happened in Vietnam was not the point. It was the effect Vietnam would have in the world, and in America.

After all, although academics and news programs may treat the struggling world as unconnected bits, the people who run American foreign policy do not. They deal, at the top, with Yugoslavia and social security and the death penalty and Iraq and abortion and Monica Lewinsky and China and Teamsters' strikes, one after another, their minds dancing. In their actual lives, and in the world, these things are integrated. If we are to explain them, we have to understand this integration. So the first half of this chapter is about anti-Communism and the rich and powerful in America.

The Ruling Class

The journalist David Halberstam describes a meeting in 1960 between two ruling-class men: president-elect John F. Kennedy and Robert Lovett. Lovett was from Texas, the son of a lawyer for the Union Pacific Railroad who became a judge and a member of the Union Pacific board. Lovett went to a private school and Yale, joined the Skull and Bones club there (like George Bush Sr.), and married a banker's daughter. He was one of the Yale pilots who volunteered for World War One and was commander of the Naval Air Squadron. After the war, he rose high in his father-in-law's bank. In World War Two, Lovett was a staff man at the Pentagon, and after the war he was undersecretary of state at the Department of Defense. Now he was advising the new president.

Halberstam says that Lovett:

was the very embodiment of the Establishment, a man who had a sense of country, rather than party. He was above petty divisions, so he could say of his friends, as so many of that group could, that he did not even know to which political party they belonged. He was a man of impeccable credentials, deciding who was safe and who was sound, who was ready for advancement and who was not. . . .

Robert Lovett understood power, where it resided, how to exercise it. He had exercised it all his life, yet he was curiously little known. . . . [He was the] financier who is so secure in his job, the value of it, his right to do it, that he does not need to seek publicity, to see his face on the cover of a magazine or on television, to feel reassured. Discretion is better, anonymity is safer: his peers know him, know his role, know that he can get things done. Publicity sometimes frightens your superiors. . . .

He did not need to impress people with false images. He knew the rules of the game, to whom you talked, what you said, to whom you did not talk, which journalists were your kind, would, without being told, know what to print for the greater good, which questions to ask, and which questions not to ask. He lived in a world where young men made their way up the ladder by virtue not just of their own brilliance and ability but also of who their parents were, which phone calls from which old friends had preceded their appearance in his office. In a world like this he knew that those whose names were always in print . . . were there precisely because they did not have power, that those who did hold or had access to power tried to keep out of sight. . . .

They were men linked more to one another, their schools, their own social class and their own concerns than they were linked to the country.[2]

John F. Kennedy was of this class too. His grandfather had not been. But JFK's father, Joe Kennedy, had been a Wall Street trader, a Hollywood executive, Franklin Roosevelt's head of the Securities and Exchange Commission, and then ambassador to London. The other rich men did not trust Joe Kennedy—it was said he had been a bootlegger, too friendly to Hitler, too dishonest and personally cruel. But his son John was rich, Harvard-educated, personable—he belonged.

Now JFK was looking for men like Lovett to run the country for him. He offered Lovett the position of secretary of state. Lovett thanked him, but said he was too old. The office went to Dean Rusk, the head of the Rockefeller Foundation.

Kennedy filled his cabinet with such men. Most were Republicans, which was only natural for bankers, lawyers, and Wall Street men. Kennedy, a Democrat, was surprised that Robert McNamara, the president of Ford, had voted Democrat, but Kennedy would have made him secretary of defense anyway—everybody spoke well of him. McNamara had voted Republican only once, against Governor "Soapy" Williams of Michigan, because Williams was too friendly to the United Auto Workers Union.

These men were the class who took America into Vietnam. We need to be specific about this ruling class. They include the owners of corporate wealth—not pension funds or houses, but enough shares to make a difference to how companies are run. They also include the senior management of the corporations, the armed forces, the federal, state, and city governments, and the major institutions. To put it differently, the ruling class includes both those who own the system and those who run it. The latter, of course, can hope to become rich in return for running the system.

This class is not a closed group. Some people fall out of it in every generation. Some join it—at different times, for instance,

John D. Rockefeller, Andrew Carnegie, Lyndon Johnson, Harry Truman, Colin Powell, and Bill Gates. And the edges of the class are fuzzy. An undersecretary of state is certainly part of this class, the mayor of New York probably is, and so is the Los Angeles chief of police.

I am not here defining the ruling class by culture or background. I am defining them by their relationship to the rest of society. They are the rich and powerful, who own and run the system. They have a sense of their collective interests. In public, and often in private, they identify these interests with "America." "We," they say, identifying the interests of the corporations, the government, and the people as one. (Most Americans call the corporations and the government "they.")

The rich and powerful have social networks built around schools, colleges, charities, balls, and vacation homes. But, more important, the boards of the largest 500 corporations are interconnected, because most members of any one board will sit on several others. This means that many small conversations in many cities can form collective opinion and corporate action over the course of a month. Money gives businessmen access to politicians, and increasingly allows the rich collectively to choose political candidates. There are lawyers who exist to put people in touch with other people, to knit the system together. And there are the people, like Robert McNamara—first president of Ford, then secretary of Defense, then head of the World Bank—who knit the system together in their careers.

It was this class who took the decisions to intervene in Vietnam and eventually to withdraw from Vietnam. To understand why, we need to begin with how they saw the world in 1945.

Foreign Policy

As World War Two began, the great powers in the world were the United States, Britain, France, Germany, Russia, Japan, and China. When it ended, Germany and Japan had been decisively defeated, France was no longer a world power, China was locked in civil war, and the Russian and British economies were exhausted. But in America industrial production doubled during the war. In 1945 the United States produced half the coal in the world, over half the electricity, and two-thirds of the oil. And in 1949 the United States had military bases in fifty-six countries. It was the greatest power in the world, with Russia the only serious challenger.[3]

The American ruling class accepted their new mission. As the economic and political victors of the war, they would make the world safe for American influence and American business. They were not embarrassed about this. They genuinely thought their way of life was better. They also talked of freedom. Sometimes they sponsored democracy and sometimes they sponsored dictators, as the occasion demanded. The bottom line was business freedom.

That meant supporting the rich in every country against the people who worked for them. In Vietnam, for instance, from 1954 on they supported the government and therefore sided with the landlords against the peasants. This was not an accident or a mistake. The U.S. government abroad always supported the owners. That was the only way they could make a foreign country safe for business.

But this did not always mean supporting the landlords. Where the businessmen in the cities were the real power, the American government could support them and help them give the peasants land reform. And it did not always mean supporting dictators. In Britain both the Conservative Party and the Labour Party did a reasonable job of running the country for business, and the same was true in many other countries. But particularly in the Third World, where people were desperate and the ruling class was often weak, the United States regularly supported dictators because they were the only people who could keep inequality safe.

In 1945 the United States appeared to be the dominant superpower. By 1948 the Russian state seemed to be gaining ground.

In 1945 only the United States had the atomic bomb, and the destruction of Hiroshima and Nagasaki had been a very public warning to the rest of the world of what American power could do. Three years later Russia had the bomb too. In China, the Red Army defeated the nationalists and took power in 1949. In Eastern Europe, Communist parties with far less popular support than the Chinese also seized power and began to turn Czechoslovakia, Hungary, Romania, Bulgaria, and East Germany into state capitalist copies of the Soviet Union.

These state capitalist countries were a threat not so much because they called themselves "socialist," but because they were competing capitalist powers and their markets were largely closed to American business. Whereas Russian domination of Eastern Europe had been agreed on as the quid pro quo for American domination of Western Europe, China and the bomb had not been agreed on. Moreover, the ruling classes in America and Western Europe had not forgotten that a wave of revolution had followed the First World War.

In short, anti-Communism seemed to fit for the American ruling class abroad. We can now begin to look at how it suited them at home.

McCarthyism

A wave of anti-Communism swept through America between 1947 and 1960. In what follows I will take issue, in some detail, with the received wisdom about this period.[4] Because what happened then was shameful, liberals have since popularized a series of myths about anti-Communism. The wisdom says that anti-Communism was invented and led by Senator Joe McCarthy, when in fact it was organized by President Harry Truman and FBI Director J. Edgar Hoover. It says "McCarthyism" was Republican, when it was in fact started by Democrats. The myth depicts a witch-hunt, the persecution of people who were innocent of any involvement with socialist ideas or activities. In fact, an overwhelming majority of those punished were people who had been socialists or Communists, or had worked with them or spoken out in their support. The myth also says that the anti-Communist "hysteria" came from the American people. In fact, it came from the top—the federal government was the prime mover, and people were mostly punished by their employers.

The force driving this anti–Communism was the opposition of business leaders to labor militancy. In the 1920s business dominated the United States. But then the Depression came, and it hit America harder than Europe. In 1933, the year Hitler came to power, unemployment was higher in America than in Germany. People were becoming increasingly desperate. A new president, Franklin Roosevelt, was elected in 1933. He promised people a New Deal, which mainly meant government pensions (social security) and workfare for the unemployed. The government also made kindly reference to unions, particularly in the National Recovery Act. It is unclear how serious this was, but working people took it as a green light.

The union leaders were more cautious at first, but by 1936 some unions were recruiting aggressively in the large factories and steel plants where there had been no unions before. The turning point came in Flint, Michigan, early in 1937. The auto workers at the General Motors plant went on strike for union recognition, and sat down inside the plant to stop scabs from coming in and taking their jobs. The police came to remove them, but the strikers' wives and other workers in Flint fought the police in the street and defeated them. The new union, the United Auto Workers (UAW), won recognition at the plant, and the sit-down movement spread across the country. By the end of the year, the number of workers in unions had doubled. By 1941 the unions had won recognition in auto, rubber, steel, electrical manufacture, airplane manufacture, the docks, the ships, and most mines.[5]

During World War Two, the federal government obliged business by regulating wages and outlawing strikes, but obliged labor by insisting the corporations recognized unions. When the war ended in 1945, union members were confident. They felt the war had been fought against fascism and for people like them. Their wages had been held down during the war, but there was full employment now. In late 1945 and early 1946 there were long national strikes in rubber, steel, and the mines, and at General Motors. These were seen as trials of strength both by the unions and by the corporations, and on balance the unions won.[6]

Measured in person days on strike, this was the largest strike wave the world had ever seen. This is important. In 1938 American industry had gone from mostly non-union to mostly union. In 1945–46 there was no revolutionary political movement in America, but American business faced the largest challenge from labor in its history. This was not the most numerous movement against American influence in the world: the Chinese Communist movement was bigger. But it was the largest union movement, the largest movement of workers, facing the American ruling class. And the momentum of the last ten years had run against the ruling class.

American business leaders knew they had to turn the momentum around. They did this by using the law and anti-Communist propaganda. The crucial law was the Taft-Hartley Act in 1947, which effectively made solidarity illegal. It forbade strikes in support of workers in other companies, and it made it illegal to honor their picket lines or refuse to work on goods made by scabs. Workers could only take action against their own employers. Most important, the unions were fined for wildcat strikes. Philip Murray, the new head of the Congress of Industrial Unions (the CIO, the militant breakaway from the old AFL, the American Federation of Labor) testified to Congress in 1947:

> If the financial responsibility of the union is to be expanded to include liability for actions of all these "agents" even when the acts are not authorized or ratified, then this bill is precisely en-

couraging and insisting that, in self-protection, the unions impose greater centralization so as to confine authority and agency only to the highest and most restricted levels of leadership.[7]

Precisely—that was the point of the bill. As Senator Robert Taft said, "I think the men are more radical than their leaders in most cases."[8] His bill also required unions to make all full-time officials swear that they were not members of the Communist Party. This was part of the anti-Communist crusade, which was at its base an attack on militants in the unions.

The American Communist Party had a few thousand members when the New Deal started. By 1945 it had somewhere in the region of 100,000 members. Even then, it was much more important than its numbers might suggest. It had built the party by building the unions, particularly the CIO. In many cases, small party cells had organized for unions in a plant for months or years before the union finally won recognition. Communist Party members were often rank and file leaders of strikes. The CIO had also employed hundreds of party members as full-time organizers in the 1930s. By 1945 the Communists led lively left-wing oppositions in many unions. In the United Auto Workers and the Steelworkers Unions, they seemed to stand a real chance of election to run the union. In the Electrical Workers and several smaller unions, they had won the leadership.

Besides unions, the Communist Party had built on two other issues. Its members had been staunch anti-racists, campaigning for integration and running an integrated party. And it had been the organizing core of the American movements protesting against European fascism in Germany and Spain.

The Communist Party was not led by revolutionaries. When Stalin signed a pact with Hitler in 1939, the Communist Party supported it. When Hitler went to war with Stalin, the Communist Party was suddenly against all strikes in America because they would disrupt the war effort. It said, "Communism is 100 percent Americanism," and it meant it. But from the point of view of the business leaders in 1946, the Communists were the core of the militant network in the unions, and the clearest socialist voice.

So the ruling class—the federal government and the employers—launched an attack on Communists in America. The organizing force behind this was the Federal Bureau of Investigation (FBI).[9] Every country has a secret police force that watches the political opposition—the Special Branch in Britain, the Sûreté in France, and so on. The FBI is the American secret police, but it is a secret police that does other things as well, and it is never publicly referred to as the secret police. The FBI was founded at the end of World War One, just after the Russian Revolution and during a large strike wave in America in 1919. At this point it was a purely political police, a "red squad" whose job was to spy on, harass, prosecute, and deport socialists, anarchists, and Communists in America. But by 1924 the socialist and Communist movement was in disarray, and the attorney general forbade domestic spying by the FBI. J. Edgar Hoover, the director of the Bureau, continued spying secretly, but he also added a public face of ordinary law enforcement, with FBI agents chasing car thieves and a few bank robbers. This public face legitimated the FBI, and gave a cover for its continuing existence. In 1939 the federal government allowed the Bureau to spy legally on Nazis and Communists. That year the FBI had 851 agents. Four years later it had 3,500. In 1945 Hoover and the FBI were ready and waiting, with the lists of Communists they had been keeping for years.

From 1947 on, the usual procedure was for the Un-American Activities Committee of the House of Representatives, or some other arm of the government, to name somebody as a Communist, or former Communist, mostly using FBI lists. The accused person's employer then fired them, their landlord often evicted them, and they usually had a lot of trouble finding another job. Most of the accused were workers and union activists—partly because that is who the Communists were. Under Democratic President Truman, there was a clean-out of Communists in government. The department of the federal government with the smallest percentage of employees fired was the State Department, because few of the elite Ivy League types who worked there were Communists. The department with the highest percentage of employees fired was the U.S. Postal Service, because so many of the people who worked there were ordinary letter carriers, many of them black, and the union was strong.[10]

When people were accused of having been Communists they could go and testify before the House Committee, say they were sorry, and name the names of other Communists in public. They thus became informers and got other people fired, but were allowed to keep their own jobs. The great majority of accused Communists refused to do this. But the few who did had their testimony widely publicized to make Communists look like people without integrity.[11] (Part of the anger in Hollywood about the 1998 Oscar for Elia Kazan was because he was one of the few in Hollywood who informed, while the many who did not inform lost their careers and got no honors.)

The support of union leaders was critical for the attack on Communists. Like the Taft-Hartley Act, anti-Communism divided the union leaders from the militants at the base. The United Auto Workers (UAW), for instance, had been the most important union in the upsurge of 1938 and the strikes of 1945–46. In 1947 politics inside the union were split between a left wing, led by the Communists, and a right wing, led by Walter Reuther. (Reuther was right-wing in the UAW, but any leader in the UAW was still left-wing in terms of national politics.) Reuther used anti-Communism to break the left wing in the car plants. Some Communists and ex-Communists managed to keep their heads down and hold their jobs in the plants, but no Communists could be officials in the UAW.

A similar alliance between employers, union leaders, and the federal government operated in Hollywood.[12] There the leaders of the anti-Communist crusade were Walt Disney and Ronald Reagan. Communist activists had played a central part in the unionization of Hollywood in the 1930s. A strike by the animators at Disney had been an important early victory for the unions, and Walt Disney never forgave the Communists. Ronald Reagan, on the other hand, was the leader of the right wing inside the Screen Actors Guild, probably the most important single union in the country. He was also a secret informer for the FBI.

The persecution began when ten men were hauled before the House Un-American Activities Committee in Washington and accused of being Communists. They denied it, and the committee produced copies of their party cards. They lost their jobs, were blacklisted by all Hollywood employers, and eventually went to prison. After that many more Hollywood Communists and ex-Communists were blacklisted. The federal government was using show trials. The message was, "If they can do this to people in Hollywood, think what they can do to you."

But in Hollywood, as in Detroit, the persecuted Communists were also union activists. Eight of the original Hollywood Ten were writers, and all eight had been activists in their union, the Screenwriters Guild.

In short, the targets of anti-Communism were militant workers, not intellectuals. Of the roughly 20,000 people who lost their jobs in the anti-Communist crusade, the largest single group was 3,000 maritime workers. Again the crusade on the docks was organized by an alliance of the federal government, the employers, and some of the union leaders.[13]

Not all the militant workers under attack were Communists. Trotskyists and other revolutionaries were persecuted, and people who supported the Communist Party found themselves in trouble too. Many Communists, understandably, had kept their party membership secret for fear of losing their jobs. So the government investigators used what they called the duck test: "If someone walks like a duck and swims like a duck and quacks like a duck, he is a duck."[14] Consistent support for Communist-led campaigns became proof of Communism. These campaigns included the Soviet-American Friendship League during World War Two, support for the anti-fascists in Spain, and writing letters to the American Red Cross to protest its policy of segregating the blood of white and black donors. Many people who had not actually joined the party lost their jobs because of the duck test. Communists or not, all of them had been guilty of supporting social justice, and social justice was what was under attack.

However, that was not what the government said. It focused on the fact that Communism in Russia was a brutal dictatorship and the American Communist Party was a tool of the Russian government. It claimed that some members of the party were spies, all of them followed Moscow's line, and all of them wanted to replace American freedom with a dictatorship like Russia's.

This paralyzed the Communist Party. Very few of them were spies, but they did follow Moscow's line. More important, they thought the system in Russia was socialist, whereas everybody outside the party knew it was a brutal dictatorship. And, although unable to admit it, many people in the party knew it too. So they could not defend themselves properly. They could not hold public rallies and shout, "Yes, I am a Communist, from the hair on my head to the soles of my feet, and I want for us what they have in Russia, and I'm proud of it." Instead they defended themselves on the technicalities: "I didn't break that law," "The Fifth Amendment says I don't have to testify," "You have no proof I was ever actually in the party."

That was what made anti-Communism so ideal for the ruling class. The Communists who lost their jobs were not as important as the people who worked with them, watched them go, and didn't defend them. The fear and the shame of those people were what broke the left wing in the unions.

This process had been the joint creation of the employers, the FBI, and the liberals in government. The persecutions began in 1947 under President Truman, a Democrat. The liberal Democrat Hubert Humphrey, later Lyndon Johnson's vice president, said the Communist Party was "a political cancer in our society." Adlai

Stevenson, Democratic candidate for president in 1952 and 1956, said Communism was worse "than cancer, tuberculosis and heart disease combined."[15]

Later the liberals were ashamed of what they had done. They renamed their crusade "McCarthyism" and blamed it on Joe McCarthy, a Republican senator from Wisconsin. McCarthy did not get in on the act until 1950, long after anti-Communism started. But he introduced a new twist—he blamed the Democratic Party for shielding Communists in government. Since the Democrats were in fact persecuting all the Communists, McCarthy had to make up phony lists of Communists and accuse wholly innocent people, whom the Democrats had not fired precisely because they had not done anything. This was not the style of FBI, the employers, or the Democrats, who were all trying to destroy a real social force. But the Democrats had been so hysterically antiCommunist that they had trouble attacking McCarthy at first. And for a time the Republican Party under Taft and Eisenhower used McCarthy as a weapon to smear the Democrats. But after Eisenhower became president in 1953, McCarthy publicly attacked the army for harboring Communists. The establishment could not allow this, and the U.S. Senate censured him.

This was possible because anti-Communism had already achieved its purpose. The campaign had been remarkably successful. In all, two Communists were executed, a few hundred people went to prison, and just under 20,000 lost their jobs.[16] As political persecutions go, it was not that bad (particularly when compared with what the Communists faced in South Vietnam in the same period). But because so few people defended the Communists, and because the Communists could not defend themselves, the persecution seemed terrible. There was a great fear of speaking socialist ideas, of even using words like "working class" and "ruling class." Then in 1956 the Russian leader Khrushchev revealed that Stalin's crimes were all true, and the majority of the American Communist Party, the people who had stayed in it through the persecution, left the party.

The attack on the Communists had not destroyed the unions. The ruling class strategy had been to accept the unions and work with the union leaders to weaken the extremists on the shop floor. They were able to do this because the American economy expanded massively between 1939 and 1960, so union workers in industry won real wage increases of 75 to 100 percent or more over that period. They won medical coverage, pensions, and holidays— none of which they had before. The union leaders were able to deliver to the rank and file at the same time as they broke the Communists. But in the long run the attack on the Communists weakened the whole militant left, local democracy in the unions, and the power of union locals against their own management. With that came increasing union corruption.

The unions had not been smashed. But from the point of view of the ruling class, they had driven back the increasing workers' power they had faced between 1938 and 1946, and they had silenced the voices for socialism in the working class.

That was an important victory, and they would do a lot to defend it. One reason they intervened in Vietnam was that if they simply accepted a Communist victory there it would have weakened anti-Communism at home.

KOREA AND VIETNAM

Now we turn to anti-Communism in the world. After 1948 the Russian and U.S. governments basically tried to observe the status quo. Neither had much choice. The United States was vastly stronger than Russia in military terms, and they both had the H-bomb. The Russian government was on the defensive, but the United States could not go in for the kill.

In practice, the Russians did not support the Communist army in the Greek Civil War. The Americans did not support the Hungarian workers when they rose against Russian tanks in 1956. When the Shah of Iran sought to arrest the Communists in that country, the Russians caught fugitives at the border and sent them

back to the shah. And so on, endlessly. Both sides observed their
spheres of influence almost everywhere.

But not quite. The Communists in China took power independently of the Russians. And at the end of World War Two,
Korea, like Germany, had been divided into Russian and American sectors. In North Korea the Russians backed a Communist
dictatorship, and in South Korea the Americans backed a right-
wing dictatorship. In 1950 the two Koreas went to war. Contro-
versy still rages about who attacked first. It matters not—both
sides were ready to fight. The North Korean army swept all before
it, driving the South Korean army and its American allies into a
corner of the peninsula. The Americans persuaded the United
Nations to back retaliation. A UN force, with largely American
troops, then invaded and drove the North Korean army back,
almost to the Chinese border. General Douglas MacArthur, the
American commander, was a well-known leader of the lobby in
America for returning the nationalist Chinese to power by force.
The Chinese Communist government, expecting an American invasion, struck back across the border and rapidly drove the American forces halfway down the Korean peninsula, roughly to the
previous line of division between North and South. And there
the Chinese and American armies stayed, grinding each other up.

The Korean War lasted three years. It started under President
Truman, a Democrat. Eisenhower, a Republican, was elected
president in 1952, in part because of his promise to end the Korean War. At no point did the American people vote for the war.
There was little public criticism—people were either patriotic or
afraid—but they wanted the war over. Eisenhower in fact ended
it in 1953.

Four things about the Korean War were important for Vietnam.
First, 40,000 Americans, half a million Chinese, and 3 million
Koreans, the majority of them civilians, died in Korea. From this,
the American ruling class learned that it could conduct a blood-
bath in Asia with almost no protest at home.

Second, the Chinese army pushed the American army back and

held it back. It could be argued that the Chinese won, or that neither side won, but not that the Americans won. The American ruling class and the generals did not forget this. In America, the right wing now claims that the United States fought the Vietnam War "with one hand tied behind our back." They do not usually say exactly what that hand should have done, but the implication is that the United States should have invaded North Vietnam. However, from 1965 to 1973 China kept large numbers of troops in North Vietnam—170,000 at the high point in 1967. These troops did not fight in South Vietnam, and China refused to lend pilots to North Vietnam, but they did operate anti-aircraft guns. More important, they were there to signal to the U.S. government that an invasion of North Vietnam would mean war with China. They wore their own uniforms and made no effort to keep their presence secret, and the U.S. government knew they were there.[17] And after Korea the American generals feared the Chinese army would win a war with the United States. So whenever one or all of the Joint Chiefs of Staff proposed invading North Vietnam, they always immediately mentioned using the atom bomb if China came South. In doing so, they were sounding warlike but in effect ruling out war with China.

Third, the Korean War ended with Russia, the United States, and China all wanting a real settlement. They met in Geneva in 1954 and divided Korea again, with dictatorships in both North and South Korea. This was part of a general settlement. China was a poor country—it had lost half a million people. The Chinese government wanted to turn to economic development, and it was satisfied that the U.S. government would now allow it a safe place in the world. The United States could not win in Korea and was under pressure at home to end the war. Russia wanted peace and a general agreement among the great powers not to trespass in each other's spheres of influence. And what the Koreans wanted did not matter.

Fourth, from the beginning of the Korean War, the American government went from quiet support for France in Vietnam to massive backing. From Washington it all looked like one war. The Chinese Communists had won power in China's civil war. Now they were advancing in support of Korean Communists on their northeastern border and arming Vietnamese Communists on their southeastern border. So by 1953 the United States was supplying most of the French arms and ammunition, and paying about two-thirds of the cost of the war. And the negotiations to end the war between the Viet Minh and France were tacked on to the Korean peace negotiations in Geneva.

INTERVENTION

The last chapter dealt with the negotiations at Geneva and the history of South Vietnam up to 1960 from the point of view of the Vietnamese Communists. Here we pick up the story from 1960, from the point of view of the American ruling class.

In 1959 the Communist leaders in Hanoi took the decision to back the armed revolt in the South. The Communist cadres from the South who had been withdrawn to the North in 1954 were sent back down South to lead the guerrilla movement. The Communist policy now was to build a National Liberation Front of all classes like the Viet Minh. This also solved the problem of what to do with the hundreds of thousands of largely landless peasants flooding into the guerrilla army. They would be part of the front, but not the party.

The party in Hanoi thus kept control of the southern movement. But the Viet Cong guerrillas were southerners. At this point there were almost no North Vietnamese soldiers or arms in the South. The Viet Cong captured guns or bought them privately from soldiers of the South Vietnamese army.

In America, John F. Kennedy became president in January 1961. By then, the front could move in units of 1,000 in the Mekong Delta, and in September briefly took control of a provincial capital. Washington reacted by sending small but growing numbers of American troops: 3,200 by the end of 1961, 11,300 by the end of 1962, and 16,300 by the end of 1963. It also sent planes, pilots, bombs, napalm, and chemical defoliants. As presidential advisor Walt Rostow said in April 1961:

> We must somehow bring to bear our unexploited counter-guerilla assets on the Viet-Nam problem: armed helicopters; other Research and Development possibilities; our Special Forces units. It is somehow wrong to be developing these capabilities but not applying them in a crucially active theatre. In Knute Rockne's phrase, we are not saving them for the Junior prom.[18]

Rostow's confidence was typical of the Kennedy people at this point. They sent the first troops to Vietnam because they were needed, and that was what you did. Both the CIA and America's allies had a very good record of putting down insurgencies between 1945 and 1960. The Americans had not beaten the Chinese army in Korea, but there had been a Communist peasant movement in South Korea and they had smashed it. An American-backed government had also beaten the Communist Huk guerrillas in the Philippines. In Guatemala an elected reformist, non-Communist government under Jacobo Arbenz had come to power and challenged the American United Fruit Company. The CIA had organized a ragtag army of a few hundred and sent out false radio broadcasts saying a massive army was marching on the capital. Arbenz fled and the Americans were back in the saddle. In Iran a non-Communist, elected government under Mohammad Mossadegh had tried to nationalize the British and American oil companies, and the CIA had organized a coup that put Mohammed Reza Shah Pahlavi in power as the Shah of Iran. The Belgian Congo became independent in 1960 under a radical nationalist, Patrice Lumumba. African troops attacked white settlers, the UN invaded, and the CIA organized Lumumba's assassination and replaced him with its client, Mobutu Sese Seko.

That was how things worked. When they had to send the troops in, they did. The Kennedy people knew the French had lost in Indochina and the Dutch in Indonesia, but explained that by saying those were colonial powers. South Vietnam was not an American colony. Intervention should work.

It didn't. Between 1962 and 1965, the number of guerrillas in the National Liberation Front rose from 80,000 to 250,000. The South Vietnamese army (ARVN) fought less and less, not from cowardice, but because it was a conscript army that wanted peace and saw no point in dying for Diem.

Diem was already becoming increasingly isolated when Buddhist monks began organizing demonstrations for religious freedom. Vietnam was not a Buddhist country. A million Vietnamese were Catholics and many more were Marxist atheists. The Montagnard peoples in the hills had their own religions. Perhaps another million belonged to the Cao Dai religion, which borrowed from both Christianity and Buddhism. A majority of the rest worshipped at village shrines and honored their ancestors, but did not send their sons to the Buddhist monastery. Still, they were for certain purposes sometimes Buddhists.

Many people from all these groups, though, rallied behind the Buddhist monks. They were demonstrating for religious freedom and against the government. They wanted peace and a neutralist coalition government that included some Communists. The government fired on a Buddhist procession in Hue, killing nine. Ten thousand demonstrated in Hue, and monks began burning themselves alive on the streets in protest. Madame Nhu, Diem's sister-in-law, dismissed them as "barbecues." It looked bad on American television.

Diem was clearly losing control. Some of the Washington people, and some in the U.S. Embassy in Saigon, began to argue that Diem was too crazy, too isolated, too Catholic to save South Vietnam. And Diem was resisting the arrival of more American troops. He said they made him look like a lackey, made it harder for him to win support. Diem could feel American support slipping away, and his brother Nhu contacted Hanoi to talk about getting rid of the Americans and forming a neutralist coalition government. At that, the American ambassador in Saigon, Henry Cabot Lodge, organized a coup and the assassination of Diem and his brother in November 1963.

Later that month, John Kennedy himself was shot and Vice President Lyndon Johnson automatically became president. Many people now believe that Kennedy was trying to get out of Vietnam, and had he lived he would have done so. The evidence for this is what his friends and followers remembered him saying, after he was long dead and it was clear Vietnam had been a mistake. Most of them were remarks along the lines of, "This is a stupid insoluble mess," which were things that Lyndon Johnson, Richard Nixon, and everybody else involved also said privately. It is true that Kennedy threatened Diem with reducing the level of American troops in order to bring him into line. But once Diem was assassinated, Kennedy kept the troops coming.[19]

The Pentagon had been against the anti-Diem coup, so it had been largely kept in the dark. The new military government in South Vietnam under General Duong Van Minh, rather to Washington's surprise, turned out to have close ties to the Buddhists. General Minh began making moves to form a neutralist government. This time the Pentagon organized the coup—and they were hands-on organizers. There was an American officer in the room with the Vietnamese officers as they directed the coup, and the American called his boss every fifteen minutes.

This coup produced a South Vietnamese government led by another general, Nguyen Khanh. But the Front was still winning support in the villages, and those in the cities who did not support the Front wanted peace. General Khanh came to see that the only hope was a neutralist coalition government. He wrote to Huynh Tan Phat of the central committee of the Front, and in January 1965 Phat replied:

> I heartily approve of your determined declaration against American intervention and I congratulate you for having made it. You stated quite clearly in fact that "the USA must let South Vietnam

settle the problems of South Vietnam." In your recent press-conference your attitude was equally clear. . . . The road you have taken is a difficult one. . . . As you pursue this goal, you may rest assured that you also have our support, as we stated in our last letter.[20]

The Americans got hold of this letter and, in the next month, organized a coup against General Khanh. From this coup, the third one, General Nguyen Van Thieu, emerged as president and Air Marshall Nguyen Cao Ky as vice president. Both were corrupt in all the usual bribery and export-import ways. But both were also heavily involved in the heroin trade.[21] Finally the American embassy had found somebody at the bottom of the barrel who would do as they were told. Thieu and Ky would not talk to the Communists, favored the bombing of North Vietnam, and were prepared to accept a large number of American troops.

Many later American writers have said that the White House and Pentagon were foolish to be against a neutralist solution. But the politicians in Washington were clear that neutralism would not work, and they were right.

Hanoi may have been willing to live with a coalition. But the Communists and the Front had support on the ground. They were part of a land war, and there were a lot more poor peasants than landlords. A coalition government would find it hard to prevent elections, and the Communists would win the elections. In any case, the Communists were on the offensive. If it looked like American support for anti-Communism was faltering, the fence-sitters would jump to the Communists and it would be all over on the ground, in the villages. Although a compromise may be possible after an election, in a civil war over land somebody has to win.

During 1964 it became increasingly clear that Thieu's government in South Vietnam would soon fall. But that year Johnson was running for president against the Republican Barry Goldwater. Goldwater talked comfortably about nuclear war and was a warmonger ("hawk") on Vietnam. So Johnson ran against him as a peace candidate ("dove"), promising "no wider war" in Vietnam and implying Goldwater might start World War Three. But Johnson chose his words carefully in his campaign speeches. In Manchester, New Hampshire, for instance, he said of Vietnam:

> Some of our people—Mr. Nixon, Mr. Rockefeller, Mr. Scranton, and Mr. Goldwater—have all, at one time or another, suggested the possible wisdom of going north in Vietnam. . . . As far as I am concerned, I want to be very cautious and careful, and use it only as a last resort, when I start dropping bombs around that are likely to involve American boys in a war with 700 million Chinese.
>
> So just for the moment I have not thought we were ready for American boys to do the fighting for Asian boys. What I have been trying to do, with the situation that I found, was to get the boys in Vietnam to do their own fighting with our advice and our equipment. . . . We are not going north to drop bombs at this stage of the game.[22]

During the campaign, the Pentagon staged a phony incident in the Gulf of Tonkin between American naval ships and North Vietnamese gunboats. On that basis, the U.S. Congress passed a resolution saying the president could do more or less what he wanted in Indochina.

On 2 November, Johnson won the election, and Washington began serious planning for bombing North Vietnam. On 2 March 1965 the American bombing of North Vietnam began.

But the Pentagon and the U.S. Embassy in Saigon were clear they could not win without hundreds of thousands of American ground troops. There was real argument in Washington over this. It was secret, of course, and conducted in the National Security Council. It never occurred to anybody to involve the American people. But it was a debate, and the decision was not taken lightly. It was clear to many of the men involved that they had only a limited time to win in Vietnam. The American people had turned against the Korean War, and they might well turn against the Vietnam War if it went on too long.

But at the highest level only two men were against sending troops—George Ball, an undersecretary of state, and Lyndon Johnson, the president.[23] Ball and Johnson both said that the government in South Vietnam did not have enough popular support. Even if they sent troops, they would fail. Johnson was, of course, the only man involved in the discussions who faced reelection. He was also the only one who was not a Kennedy appointee. (Those who believe that Kennedy had said America should not be involved in Vietnam need to explain both why he sent troops there and why all his senior advisors except Ball wanted to send more troops.)

Kennedy and Johnson's senior officials had basically one argument for bombing North Vietnam and sending troops: the domino theory. President Eisenhower had formulated this in 1954, when he said in a speech that if French Indochina went Communist, the rest of Southeast Asia would "go over very quickly [like a] row of dominoes."[24] John F. Kennedy, in a speech as a U.S. senator in 1956, had used an architectural metaphor: "Vietnam represents the cornerstone of the Free World in Southeast Asia. It is our offspring. We cannot abandon it, we cannot ignore its needs."[25]

Anti-war protesters during the Vietnam War, and liberals since, have pooh-poohed the domino theory. The anti-war protesters felt hemmed in by anti-Communism, so they did not have the courage to say, "If other countries become Communist because that's what their people want, so be it." Instead they said, "What happens in one country does not determine what happens in another country."

Sometimes it does. Sometimes it doesn't. There are many examples of how the domino theory has worked in great social movements. The Russian Revolution of 1917 gave rise to revolutions in Hungary, Germany, China, Korea, Vietnam, and Yugoslavia. The victory of fascism in Portugal and Italy led to fascist governments in Germany, Austria, Hungary, and Spain. Indian independence from British colonialism in 1947 was followed by freedom for Indonesia and Vietnam, then Algeria and all of French North Africa, Malaya, and French and British Africa. That gave heart to the independence movements in Portuguese Africa, and when they won South Africa's African National Congress (ANC) knew its day would come.

The Islamist revolution in Iran in 1980 inspired mass Islamist movements in Turkey, Lebanon, Palestine, Jordan, Saudi Arabia, Egypt, Tunisia, Sudan, and Morocco. In 1989 Mikhail Gorbachev's reforms in Russia led to the fall of the dictatorships in Poland, Czechoslovakia, Hungary, Bulgaria, Romania, Yugoslavia, and finally Russia itself. That inspired mass movements for democracy, often victorious, in Nepal, Thailand, and across much of Africa.

Great social movements happen in a domino way. When people see other people like them win in other countries, particularly neighboring countries, they take heart. Politicians know this. The men who ran America in 1965 had seen it happen several times in their lifetimes.

Some people outside this inner circle argued against the domino theory in the Vietnamese case by saying that Ho Chi Minh was basically a Vietnamese nationalist. This was true, but it did not solve the American government's problem. Any victory for the National Liberation Front in Vietnam would be a defeat for American power. The American government was supporting regimes all over the Third World that looked like the governments in South Vietnam. Johnson's advisors were acutely aware that an American withdrawal from Vietnam would cause those regimes to look for other sources of support and would give heart to the people who lived under them. If it had been simply a matter of containing Russian Communism, the Russian leaders could have been persuaded to make a deal. But it wasn't. America's mission had become keeping the world safe for the rich, and that was more difficult than just containing Communism. In March 1965 Assistant Secretary for Defense John MacNaughton wrote a memo for his boss, Secretary of Defense Robert McNamara:

US aims:

70%—To avoid a humiliating US defeat (to our reputation as a guarantor).

20%—To keep SVN (and then adjacent) territory from Chinese hands.

10%—To permit the people of SVN to enjoy a better, freer way of life.

ALSO—To emerge from crisis without unacceptable taint from methods used.

NOT—To "help a friend," although it would be hard to stay if asked out.[26]

COMMITMENT

So in the spring of 1965 Lyndon Johnson gave in to his advisors. The United States sent in the Marines, beginning a build-up of troops that would soon reach 500,000. Four areas of the world bore particularly heavily on Washington's decision. First, Johnson's advisors kept saying that if South Vietnam fell Laos and Cambodia would follow. In fact, when South Vietnam eventually fell, they did follow.

The second area was Latin America. In 1958 the American government withdrew its support for Fulgencio Batista's corrupt regime in Cuba and accepted Fidel Castro as the alternative. On New Year's Day of 1959 the nationalist guerrillas, led by Castro, rode into Havana, greeted by a crowd of a million. Castro's new government was nationalist, not socialist, but it did drive the Mafia out of Cuba and nationalize some American businesses. The United States retaliated with trade and aid sanctions. Castro tried to negotiate with the American government and was rebuffed. He then declared that his revolution had been socialist all along and he was now a Marxist. He swung Cuba into the Soviet camp. Russia would buy the sugar the United States had banned.

The CIA organized an army of several hundred right-wing Cuban exiles and sent them to invade Cuba. They landed at the Bay of Pigs in April 1961. The CIA was expecting a walkover, as in Guatemala. But the Cubans were solid behind Castro and the exiles were cut down on the beaches, then surrendered. The United States had been humiliated. That gave joy to young nationalists and socialists all over Latin America who began to study the Cuban example of rural guerrilla warfare. Che Guevara, the most radical of the Cuban leaders, would later call for "One, Two, Three, Many Vietnams!"

The Bay of Pigs had given men like Lyndon Johnson pause. They could lose without local support. But it also meant they did not want to lose again, and not to a guerrilla army.

The third area concerning Washington was Indonesia. On one side there was the Indonesian Communist Party (PKI) with 3 million members, the largest Communist party outside the Communist bloc. On the other side was the Indonesian army with the support of the right-wing Muslim parties (the left-wing Muslims, who were even more numerous, were Communists). Indonesia's economy was in crisis. Unemployment was rising in the cities, and the price of rice had risen so far above wages that workers had trouble eating. But driving the crisis, above all, was land. The government had decreed limited land reform. In Java and Bali, both in the center of the country, the Communists on the ground were mobilizing the sharecroppers and tenants to drive down the rent on land. This was happening village by village, town by town, each demonstration a trial of strength.[27]

Everybody could see the crisis was heading towards a resolution. One side would win, one lose. Between the army and the Communists stood Indonesia's President Sukarno, the leader of the revolutionary war of independence against the Dutch. Sukarno played the Communists and the army against each other.

He and Jawaharlal Nehru, India's prime minister, were the leaders of the neutralist bloc in the Cold War. The Communist strategy was to support Sukarno as a progressive leader, praise him to the skies, and count on him to protect them from the army.

Indonesia was just south of Vietnam. Vietnam had no important natural resources and did not matter economically. This is important. American businesses were not making significant profits out of Vietnam. Indeed, South Vietnam was costing the American government money. Indonesia, however, was a far larger country. It was strategically important—the islands of Indonesia lie across the trade routes from Japan, China, and the Pacific to the Indian Ocean. Indonesia was the fifth most populous country in the world. Vietnam mattered to the American government for the example it set. Indonesia mattered for itself. Vietnam had rice. Indonesia had oil.

President Sukarno had nationalized the oil companies, and the American ruling class hoped to get that oil back. Even if they did not, that oil mattered to Japan. There were real profits to be made in Indonesia. So ever since Indonesia's revolution, American policy had been to arm and build the Indonesian army.

In September 1965 the crisis reached a head. A coup failed. The Communists may or may not have been involved, but it didn't really matter. The class struggle on the ground was throwing the army and the PKI against each other anyway. The army moved against the PKI, and the Communist leadership looked to Sukarno for protection. The only thing Sukarno could have done was to call on the millions of Communists, the landless, and the workers to rise. He was not about to do that. Sukarno let the Communists go. Their leaders, surprised and bewildered, did not organize an insurrection.

But because the Communists were a real mass movement on the edge of power, the army had to organize extensive massacres to break them. The army and the right-wing Muslim parties came for the Communists, town by town, village by village, in Java and Sumatra. The American ambassador, Marshall Green, reported "wholesale killings" to Dean Rusk in Washington, and said he had "made it clear that the Embassy and USG were generally sympathetic with and admiring of what the army is doing."[28] The army asked the embassy for weapons and got them. Ambassador Green kept giving the army lists of Communists to kill. He knew, of course, that the army had perfectly good lists of its own. He was just showing support. According to the historian Gabriel Kolko, "On December 4, as they were both clamoring for yet more killing, Green wrote to Rusk that over 100,000 but not more than 200,000 had been murdered in northern Sumatra and central and eastern Java alone."[29] Then the soldiers got in boats, went to Java, and started there. By the time it was all over, the CIA estimated that 250,000 to 500,000 Communists were dead. Some later estimates go up to 1 million, but the official Indonesian estimate a decade later was 450,000 to 500,000.[30]

It was one of the terrible massacres of the twentieth century. It destroyed the Indonesian left wing. The landlords and capitalists were safe, and for twenty years memory and fear ruled Indonesia. Indonesia was, and is, much more important to the American ruling class than Vietnam. But as Dwight Eisenhower said:

> What do you think caused the overthrow of President Sukarno in Indonesia? What do you suppose determined the new federation state of Malaysia to cling to its independence despite all the pressure from outside and from within? . . . Well, I could tell you one thing: the presence of 450,000 American troops in South Vietnam . . . had a hell of a lot to do with it.[31]

Or as Ambassador Green said in 1967:

> The United States military presence in Southeast Asia emboldened the army [in Indonesia], but it had no decisive effect on the outcome. . . . It is perhaps better to look at in negative terms. If we hadn't stood firm in Southeast Asia, if we hadn't maintained a military presence, then the outcome might have been different.[32]

In early 1965 the U.S. government faced a choice in Vietnam—get out and lose, or really go to war. If it had gotten out, then the Communists in Indonesia would have been massively encouraged. The Indonesian army would not have looked to America for support. It might well have made its compromises, and it might not have had a choice. One of the things the American government was doing in Vietnam was buying time for the army to smash Communism in Indonesia.

The fourth area of the world that really mattered to the American ruling class was the United States. One of the roots of anti-Communism had been an attack on the left wing in the American working class. That had worked. But, from 1960 on, there was the civil rights movement in the South and then riots and urban uprisings in the black ghettoes in the North. Martin Luther King had led a mass demonstration in Washington. Anti-Communism was beginning to sound old-fashioned. Lyndon Johnson's great worry about Vietnam in 1965 was that it would be so costly economically and politically that it would destroy his "Great Society" plan for civil rights and a war on poverty. That plan was a reaction to the black movement, North and South.

It turned out Johnson was right. Vietnam did wreck his program. More than that, America lost the war. This is now often taken to mean that U.S. involvement in Vietnam was a catastrophically stupid mistake. However, one side always loses a war, and in retrospect their politicians and generals always look stupid. But neither side ever goes to war without a reason to fight and some hope of winning. The U.S. government had both those in Vietnam.

The U.S. government also managed to persuade the governments of Australia, New Zealand, South Korea, and the Philippines to send small numbers of troops to fight alongside their own troops in Vietnam. The other Western governments, including the British Labour Party, backed the United States in Vietnam. The only exceptions were France, in part, and Sweden and Canada, which provided refuge for American deserters.

3

FIREPOWER

Let's pause for a moment and summarize the argument so far. In Vietnam there was a three-cornered struggle. In one corner were the landlords and businesspeople allied first to French colonialism and then to the United States. In another corner were the poor and landless peasants in the South. Many of them were members of the Communist Party or joined the guerrillas.

In the third corner were the leaders of the Communist Party. They had led the peasants against French colonialism. After 1954, partly under pressure from China and Russia, they had, in effect, decided to let the South go, and concentrate on building their own state in the North. But the class struggle in the South would not go away. The new government in the South had its base among the landlords. They felt they had to fight to regain control of the land, and that meant they had to eliminate the Communists who remained in the South. Those Communists were peasants. Faced with the choice between death and fighting back, the Communists eventually forced the leadership of the party in the North to back them in an insurrection.

By 1965 this insurrection had won the support of the majority of the people in the countryside. It was not, for them, fundamentally a conflict with American imperialism. It was a war over land ownership.

But the United States intervened massively in 1965 for several reasons. It had already sent 18,000 troops and was publicly committed. A defeat in Vietnam would weaken anti-Communism in America, and help to open a space for the new Left in the unions and the growing, radicalizing civil rights movement. A defeat in Vietnam would weaken the position of ruling classes and American-backed regimes in many other countries. A defeat would also be a defeat in the Cold War, where the rulers of America and Russia competed for political and economic power in the world.

In other words, both the Pentagon and the Vietnamese Communist Party found their policies shaped by class struggles they could not avoid. This chapter is about what the war was like for the people who fought it, particularly the GIs. It argues that the cruelty of that war was a response to the class struggle in Vietnam. Once committed, the Pentagon had to be cruel, because it was intervening on the side of a ruling minority, and the subject majority was organized and confident.

This chapter also looks at the experience of American troops in terms of class. At a basic level, being sent to Vietnam was an event in the class struggle in America. The children of the rich did not go. But once the GIs arrived, their experience was shaped by the cruelty they were ordered to carry out and the fact that they could see they were defending the rich against the poor in Vietnam. These two things made them desperate. That desperation was a result of class struggle in both Vietnam and America. To see how all this worked, we begin with the air war.

THE AIR WAR

The United States bombed South Vietnam, North Vietnam, Laos, and Cambodia. The planes dropped over 8 million tons of explosives. This was roughly three times the weight of bombs dropped by all sides in World War Two, and the explosive force was equal to 640 of the atom bombs used on Hiroshima.[1]

Just over 58,000 Americans died in Vietnam, and 250,000 soldiers in the South Vietnamese army. There are no precise counts of the number of dead Viet Cong and civilians. The best estimate is between 1.5 and 2 million, though the Vietnamese estimates are higher. Hundreds of thousands more people died in both Laos and Cambodia. That puts the total dead at roughly 3 million, most of them from the air war.

This seems extraordinary, but it made sense. The Pentagon understood more or less clearly that the Viet Cong had the support of the villagers. As Defense Secretary Robert McNamara put it in a memo to President Lyndon Johnson in 1966:

> By and large, the people in the rural areas believe that the GVN [Government of South Vietnam] when it comes to it will not stay but the VC [Communists] will; that cooperation with the GVN will be punished by the VC; that the GVN is really indifferent to the people's welfare; that the low-level GVN are tools of the local rich; and that the GVN is ridden with corruption.[2]

The Viet Cong had roughly 250,000 to 300,000 guerrillas in the field. At the height of the war there were 500,000 U.S. troops in Vietnam. Only about one in six were combat troops, and the rest were support. On the ground, the Viet Cong outnumbered the American combat troops three or four to one[3] and had the support of most of the villagers.

The Pentagon and the White House decided to equalize with artillery and planes. They were not winning in South Vietnam, so they bombed North Vietnam for years. At first they said they were attacking military targets, industrial sites, and infrastructure. They dropped enough bombs to destroy all that, over and over, and still the North Vietnamese fought. The North Vietnamese distributed what industry they had all over the country, they dug shelters, and they got more aid from China to replace the trucks, oil, and weapons they lost. On that level, the bombing did not work.

But there was another reason for the bombing, a stronger one, less often stated. The bombs would inflict such "damage" or "punishment," by which they meant so many dead, that the people of North Vietnam would force their leaders to negotiate peace. And in the South, the bombing would reduce the number of Viet Cong and drive the villagers who supported it into the cities as refugees.

It was the logic of attrition. And it was a bombing war because America was a great industrial capitalist power. That was its strength. It was how the men in Washington thought. They had come out of World War Two the greatest power on earth, not because their soldiers were braver or their officers smarter, but because American industry had mobilized more might, more bangs and bucks, than any other country on earth. That was its strength. It was a corporate, industrial power, and it fought a corporate, industrial war.

In 1967 Malcolm Caldwell, a teacher at the School of Oriental and African Studies in London and a Maoist, visited North Vietnam to investigate the effects of the bombing:

We interviewed Dr. Oai, who witnessed the repeated bombing of the Quynh leprosarium. The first raid occurred at 8pm on 12 June 1965, the planes flying over and then returning to drop twenty-four bombs and five missiles. A night nurse was wounded. The following morning, all patients had been evacuated, but at 1:45 pm on 13 June 1965 when some of the patients had returned, large numbers of U.S. planes came over and bombed and strafed the hospital in turn. The center was demolished completely. In the following few days, the Americans returned again and again until the sanitarium had been completely destroyed. The raids of 12–21 June 1965 were reported to have killed 140 patients in all. Dr. Oai was moved to another hospital, while the remaining patients were dispersed to a variety of institutions. . . . Three other eye-witnesses . . . corroborated the testimony of Dr. Oai in important details—ie, the height of the planes, the fact that the bombs were followed up by strafing of the patients and staff as they sought shelter.[4]

It is a strange picture, the planes flying low, strafing the nurses and the lepers as they fled from a burning building. But this was standard operating procedure—first the reconnaissance flight, then the bombs, then the strafing.

Often the planes dropped anti-personnel cluster bombs the second time around instead of strafing. The South Vietnamese called them "mother bombs, [because] they exploded in midair and released from 350 to 600 baby bombs. When these hit the ground, each one exploded into thousands of metal pellets. (Later, fiberglass—invisible to X-rays and thus harder and more painful to remove—was used.)"[5] By the end of the war, one cluster bomb could hold 180,000 "fleshettes"—"little arrows" that cut flesh.[6]

In the North the bombing particularly concentrated on hospitals, schools, and churches. By 1967, 391 schools had been destroyed in the North, along with ninety-five health institutions, over eighty churches, and thirty Buddhist pagodas. The lepers Dr. Oai worked with were bombed thirty-six times. This seems monstrous. What was probably happening was that in most parts of North Vietnam, hospitals, schools, and churches were the only brick or cement buildings of two stories or higher. When the pilots flew over, looking for a target, those buildings were the only things they could imagine were barracks.[7]

Moreover, the U.S. planes had quite rapidly bombed all the "legitimate targets" in Vietnam. With the tonnage they were dropping, they had to bomb somewhere else. Back in Washington, President Lyndon Johnson was personally picking every target. But in the air, facing the flak and not fooled by the maps, the pilots dropped what they had where they could. If they had any bombs left, it was dangerous to land. So they dropped them in the South China Sea or in "free fire zones" in South Vietnam. After yet another target mix-up, Captain Richard Sexton of the United States Air Force confided to his diary what many airmen felt: "It doesn't matter if we lose the war as long as the paperwork is filled out and some boob keeps his empire."[8]

And the pilots knew the people below them were not simply

civilians. They were also a very concrete enemy. Wilfred Burchett, an Australian Communist journalist, reported from North Vietnam that it had "become a nationwide duty to study plane silhouettes, to memorize characteristics of speed and altitude; to recognize planes by their sounds; to know how many lengths ahead of a certain type one must aim if it is in level flight and at which point of the nose to fire if it is dive bombing."[9]

That made it dangerous to fly low. Colonel Jack Broughton, an F-105 fighter-bomber pilot, wrote in his book *Thud Ridge*:

> If he went down, he would have been faced with the intense small arms and automatic weapons fire that even extended down to handguns; and don't even think that a handgun can't knock down a big bird if it hits the right spot. When the bugle blows and thousands of people lie on their backs and fire small-caliber personal weapons straight up in the air, woe be unto him who is unfortunate enough to stray through that fire.[10]

Bombing North Vietnam was the most dangerous job an American could do in Vietnam. For every forty sorties (flights by a single bomber), one was shot down; the United States lost a total of 3,719 planes and 4,869 helicopters in Indochina during the Vietnam War.[11] The crew were often able to eject and parachute down. It is a sign of the strong discipline of the North Vietnamese government that so many of them were not killed by the people who captured them but were sent to Hanoi. The North Vietnamese government knew how important those prisoners of war could be in negotiations. The suffering of those airmen in the "Hanoi Hilton" prisoner of war camp, and they suffered a great deal, can partly be explained by the fact that North Vietnam was a dictatorship and its prisons were not nice places. But much of it can be explained by the fact that their jailers had relatives who lived under those bombs.

As the war went on, the U.S. government turned more and more to B-52s. They flew so high they could not be seen or heard before the bombs exploded, so they were safer for the pilots, and they did a lot of damage. Napalm, a jellied gasoline dropped from planes, was widely used. The gasoline burns and the jelly makes it stick to the person's body. An American pilot explained:

> We sure were pleased with those backroom boys at Dow [Chemical Company]. The original product wasn't so hot—if the gooks were quick they could scrape it off. So the boys started adding polystyrene—now it sticks like shit to a blanket. But then if the gooks jumped under water it stopped burning, so they started adding Willie Peter [white phosphorous] so's to make it burn better. It'll even burn under water now. And one drop is enough; it'll keep on burning right down to the bone so they die anyway from phosphorous poisoning.[12]

He was exaggerating. People often survived napalm. In 1966 the American reporter Martha Gellhorn visited napalmed children in a hospital in South Vietnam, and wrote in the *Ladies' Home Journal*:

> Before I went to Saigon, I had heard and read that napalm melts the flesh, and I thought that's nonsense, because I can put a roast in the oven and the fat will melt but the meat stays there. Well, I went and saw those children burned by napalm and it is absolutely true. The chemical reaction of this napalm does melt the flesh, and the flesh melts right down their faces onto their chests and it sits there and grows there. . . . These children can't turn their heads, they were so thick with flesh. . . . And when gangrene sets in, they cut off their hands or fingers or their feet; the only thing they cannot cut off is their head.[13]

The American flyers sang songs about their work, in bars and clubs and quarters, after flying. Major Joe Tuso, who flew sixty-nine combat missions in 1968–69, later collected these songs. Some are triumphant. Many are full of fear. A few, like "Chocolate Covered Napalm," are anti-war. "Strafe the Town and Kill the People" (sung to the tune of Jerry Livingston's 1955 "Wake the Town and Tell the People") is full of angry irony:

Strafe the town and kill the people,
Drop your napalm in the square;
Do it early Sunday morning,
Catch them while they're still at prayer.

Drop some candy to the orphans,
Watch them as they gather 'round:
Use your twenty millimeter,
Mow those little bastards down.

Strafe the town and kill the people,
Drop your high-drag on the school;
If you happen to see ground fire,
Don't forget the Golden Rule.

Run your CBU down main street,
Watch it rip off arms and hair;
See them scurry for the clinic,
Put a pod of rockets there.

Find a field of running Charlies,
Drop a daisy-cutter there;
Watch the chunks of bodies flying,
Arms and legs and blood and hair.

See the sweet old pregnant lady
Running cross the field in fear;
Run your twenty mike-mike through her,
Hope the film comes out real clear.[14]

The ranch hands sang "Spray the Town" to the same tune. They were the men of Operation Ranch Hand, which dropped Agent Orange and other herbicides on the South Vietnamese countryside to kill the trees and destroy the guerrillas' cover. Like much of the bombing in South Vietnam, it was also intended to drive peasants off the land and into the cities so the guerrillas would have nobody to support them. The ranch hands' song goes like this:

> Spray the town and kill the people,
> Spray them with your poison gas;
> Watch them throwing up their breakfast
> As you make your second pass.

> Get the spray pumps working double
> Slightly offset for the breeze;
> See the children in convulsions-
> And besides it kills the trees.

> See them line up for the market,
> Waiting for a pound of rice,
> Hungry, skinny, starving people—
> Isn't killing harvests nice.[15]

THE WAR ON THE GROUND

Now we turn to the ground war.

The politicians who ran the American War in Vietnam did not send their children to fight there. They sent the children of the American working class. About 80 percent of the American soldiers who saw combat came from blue-collar families. About 20 percent had fathers in white-collar jobs, but mostly routine ones.[16] These men were forced to go to Vietnam. The majority were drafted. Many more joined the military because they were about to be drafted. And some joined to get steady work, or because they were in trouble at home.

The government and the draft boards protected the sons of the rich. College students were not drafted until they finished their studies. And as the demand for men increased the army began taking people who had failed their intelligence tests.

People knew the draft was discriminatory. A firefighter who lost his son Ralph in Vietnam told an interviewer in 1970:

> I'm bitter. You bet your goddamn dollar I'm bitter. It's people like me who gave up our sons for the country. The business people, they run the country and they make money from it. The college types, the professors, they go to Washington and tell the government what to do. . . . But their sons, they don't end up in the swamps over there, in Vietnam. No sir. They're deferred, because they're in school. Or they get sent to safe places. Or they get out with all those letters they have from their doctors. Ralph told me. He told me what went on at his physical. He said most of the kids were from average homes; and the few rich kids there were, they all had big-deal letters [from their doctors] saying they weren't eligible. They looked eligible to Ralph. Let's face it: if you have a lot of money, or if you have the right connections, you don't end up on the firing line in the jungle over there, not unless you want to. Ralph had no choice. He didn't want to die. He wanted to live. They just took him. . . . It's the Ralphs of America who pay every time.[17]

In 1970 roughly half of young Americans had at least started college. A fifth of American troops in Vietnam had been to college, and only 7.2 percent had graduated. Almost all of them were officers. And even they were not from elite schools—the Harvard class of 1970 sent two men to Vietnam.[18]

Until late in the war these men did not know, could not know, what they were getting into. Basic training did not teach them. The American government could not explain to its people that a large majority of the villagers in Vietnam opposed their presence, so the sergeants at boot camp could not explain it either. And without that elementary fact you could not understand the war.

In previous wars American soldiers had served unlimited tours of duty. In Vietnam they did one-year tours. This was a political decision to reduce opposition to the war at home. Officers served six-month tours of duty, so every career officer could get a chance to "punch his ticket" in a real war.

But the short tours made for military disaster. Units were not replaced—men were replaced into units. This made it harder for them to rebel. They counted the days 'til they left, and by the time they understood the war they were gone. But it also made it harder for them to fight, and an awful lot of time had to be spent teaching new recruits what the war was really like.

The recruits flew out to Vietnam in chartered commercial planes, air-conditioned, with seat trays and meals and pretty civilian cabin crew. Gerald Kolb, an enlisted man in the 25th Infantry, flew in that way in 1967. As they approached Vietnam:

> A hush came over the cabin of the plane. All of the joking, singing and cajoling stopped. You could have heard a pin drop. The stewardess was crying, and some of the men were, too. When the door of the plane opened, we were hit with a musty, rank, urine-like odor. It was very hot. We passed a bunch of guys whooping and hollering. They were going home.[19]

Richard Deegan got off the plane in Danang in 1966:

> We were walking by and this crowd of marines waiting to get on the plane to go back to "The World" [the United States] started telling us all this shit: "You guys ain't gonna make it home"; "They'll kill every fucking one of you"; "The gooks are better than you guys." Yeah! They were really fucking with your mind. They even said, "Hope you die, you bastards."[20]

It was their first shock, the first understanding of the scale of death they were walking into. As one veteran, John Hendricks, said in 1985:

> That's what I can't get out of my head—the bodies . . . all those bodies. Back then we didn't give a shit about the dead Vietnamese. It was like: "Hey, they're just gooks, don't mean nothin'." You got so cold you didn't even blink. You could even joke about it, mess around with the bodies like they were rag dolls. And after a while we could even stack up our own KIAs [killed in action] without feeling much of anything. It's not like that now. You can't just put it out of your mind. Now I carry those bodies around every fucking day. It's a heavy load, man, a heavy fucking load.[21]

The logic was the same as with the air war. American soldiers and marines faced a population who mainly supported the guerrillas, and the guerrillas outnumbered the American forces. The American government, the CIA, and the senior generals understood all this. But once they had thrown their support behind the South Vietnamese government, they felt compelled not to lose. There was much at stake and they had few strategic alternatives. They decided to use what General William Westmoreland, the American commander in Vietnam, called a "war of attrition." But every dead Vietnamese, civilian or guerrilla, was counted as a dead enemy. In effect, the American plan was to kill the Vietnamese until they gave up.

The pressure for this was relentless. The Pentagon demanded statistics. In some rear units the officers chalked the cumulative kills on a board. Officers knew their careers would depend on their numbers. And although the officers seldom said, "Kill all the civilians you can," they seldom criticized anybody for doing that, and often praised them.

This put the soldiers in a horrific position. They arrived in Vietnam as individuals and were assigned to companies. They had no training for what they faced, because the army and Marine Corps could not admit what kind of war they were fighting. So the slightly more experienced soldiers had to train the new men, and fast. One marine remembered his training at Khe Sanh:

That first patrol we went to where some Marines had ambushed a bunch of Viet Cong. They had me moving dead bodies, VC and NVA [North Vietnamese army]. Push this body over here out of the way. Flip a body over. See people's guts and heads half blown off. I was throwing up all over the place.

"Keep going. Drag this body over there."

"For what?"

"You're going to get used to death before you get in a firefight and get us all killed. You're a [machine-gunner] and gunners can't panic on us."

That first time everything was just coming up. Scared to begin with, then all of a sudden I'm looking at this shit. I moved some more bodies and after a while I stopped throwing up. But I wasn't too happy about the whole situation.

They noticed that I wasn't throwing up no more and they gave me about a ten minute rest. They're laughing and joking.

Next, I had to kick one dead body in the side of the head until part of his brain started coming out the other side. I said, "I just moved a dead body. What are y'all telling me?" The logic, I didn't see it then, I understood it later. At the time I thought, "These fuckers been up here too long. They are all insane." I'm going through my changes and the rest of these guys are laughing.

"Kick it," they said. "You are starting to feel what it is like to kill. That man is dead, but in your mind you're killing him again. Man, it ain't no big thing. Look-a-here." And they threw some bodies off the cliff and shit.

"Go ahead. Pick one up and throw it off. But when you can kick his brains out, you'll know what it is when they say to kick out somebody's brains. So . . . Kick." They meant it. The chant started, "Kick . . . Kick . . . Kick." . . .

I'm kicking now. I'm kicking and I'm kicking and all of a sudden, the brains start coming out the other side.[22]

Later he understood:

They were serious men, dedicated to what they were doing. [They were] teaching me . . . not to fall apart. I saw it happen. I saw guys get themselves killed and almost get an entire platoon wiped out, because they panicked or because they gave up or because they got wounded and couldn't deal with their own blood. They had this thing about teaching a boot [a new man] exactly what he's got to deal with and how to accept the fact of what he really is.[23]

What he really was at Khe Sanh was bait. The population either supported the guerrillas or were too scared to betray them. So the American generals could only fight the guerrillas by sending the American soldiers and marines out on patrol. If and when the guerrillas chose to attack, the Americans on the ground would then call in artillery and bombers to blast them.

This terrified the GIs—they were always waiting to get hit. Their enemy almost always chose the time and place of battle. And between 15 and 20 percent of Americans killed in Vietnam died from "friendly fire"—the artillery and bombs they called in.

Another 20 to 25 percent died when they stepped on mines. The ones who didn't die thought about those mines every step they took. Michael Call was in the 25th Infantry division:

We begin to walk with our eyes fixed on the ground, looking for some telltale sign we should avoid. I ask myself: "Is that little thing ahead the three prongs of a Bouncing Betty [a mine that springs up to waist height and then goes off] or just three blades of grass?" As my right foot moves in front of my left foot, I carry on a debate in my mind on whether I should place it down on that rock just ahead or behind it. Or in front of it. Or on that side of it. But now I face another dilemma. If I choose to step to the side of the rock, which side do I choose? These gooks are very clever. They must figure out I still want to place my foot on hard ground. So, maybe they put the mine under a rock. Maybe I should move over to the left a little or to the right. Then again, why not place my foot in the step of the guy ahead of me. But he is already too far ahead. And if you walk too close to him, he will get pissed off because if I trip a mine he'll get blown away too. What do I do with my right foot? I say, "I can't stand on my left foot forever." I finally put my right foot down and nothing happens. My next decision is what to do with my left foot, which, in the act of walking, comes up when the right foot goes down.[24]

Every step, hour after hour, counting off 365 days.

Del Plonka was an officer, a platoon leader in the 25th Division:

There were these things called stick mines. It's nothing more than taking a dead piece of wood attached to a mine with a trigger device—to knock the stick over and it goes. Usually, they use land mines, and land mines are designed to blow up tanks. Needless to say, when this young man tripped the stick mine and it went off, he lost both legs immediately. He was more or less split open from the groin area to his neck. The best I could do was put him in a poncho. It was a very sickening sight, seeing all that blood and seeing that poor young man with that face just looking at you with those bewildered eyes, and, well, it stays in your mind.[25]

When a mine went off, the GIs could not see the man or woman who set it. But every villager they had passed in the last hour knew where the mine was. The guerrillas told them or left warning marks. Sometimes, often, the soldiers snapped and beat or killed the next Vietnamese they saw.

They were fighting an enemy they could not see. They were constantly afraid, and helpless, and they knew they were losing.

The officers were pushing them to report dead Vietnamese. Washington wanted a body count.

Robert McNamara, the Secretary of Defense, had been brilliant at systems, numbers, and accounting control at Ford. Now he shone the same brilliance on Vietnam. The reporter David Halberstam writes of McNamara at a military briefing:

> Sitting . . . for eight hours watching hundreds and hundreds of slides flashing across the screen showing what was in the pipe line to Vietnam and what was already there, he finally said, after seven hours, "Stop the projector. This slide, number 869, contradicts slide 11." Slide 11 was flashed back and he was right, they did contradict each other. Everyone was impressed, and a little frightened.[26]

McNamara was in charge of the war, first under Kennedy and then under Johnson. He ran the war like the Ford Motor Company. You had the capital, you had the hardware, and you had the men—they were just labor. Halberstam again:

> One particular visit seemed to sum it all up: McNamara looking for the war to fit his criteria, his definitions. He went to Danang in 1965 to check out the marine progress there. A marine colonel in 1 Corps had a sand table showing the terrain and patiently gave the briefing: friendly situation, enemy situation, main problem. McNamara watched it, not really taking it in, his hands folded, frowning a little, finally interrupting. "Now, let me see," McNamara said, "if I have it right, this is your situation," and then he spouted his own version, all in numbers and statistics. The colonel, who was very bright, read him immediately like a man breaking a code, and without changing stride, went on with his briefing, simply switching his terms, quantifying everything, giving everything in numbers and percentages, percentages up, percentages down, so blatant a performance it was like a satire. Jack Raymond

of the *New York Times* began to laugh and had to leave the tent. Later that day Raymond went up to McNamara and commented on how tough the situation was up in Danang, but McNamara wasn't interested in the Vietcong, he wanted to talk about the colonel, he liked him, the colonel had caught his eye. "That colonel is one of the finest officers I've ever met," he said.[27]

In all those numbers, the bottom line was the body count. Because the Communists had the support of most of the villagers, the only way to defeat them was to kill so many that the few who were left could bear it no longer. And if you could not find the guerrillas, and usually you couldn't, you killed the people until they told the Communists to stop. The body count was not a trick or a bureaucratic obsession—it was the strategy.

The pressure from Washington reached all the way down. Every general and colonel who passed the pressure down, who made the men kill, was making his career: "Infantry officers knew their opportunities for advancement were largely dependent on the size of the body counts they reported."[28]

Michael Clodfelter was an infantryman with the 101st Airborne in 1965:

We arrived in country expecting to encounter uniformed communist hordes, but found instead this strange small people wearing peasant garb and those inscrutable smiles. We . . . found it hard to believe that these weak, undernourished-looking peasants could really present a threat and a danger to all our battalions of big, husky, heavily armed GIs. It seemed a laughable country and a laughable war—until we started running into explosive evidence of the enemy's existence, until we started becoming a part of the red results of their cunning and courage. And then, slowly, as fear mounted frustration and rode down a crippled confidence, as callousness started taking over from condescension in our attitude to the Vietnamese, our vision blurred, clouded over, and refocused. Where before we had found it difficult to see the enemy anywhere, now we saw him everywhere. It was simple now; the Vietnamese were the Viet Cong, the Viet Cong were the Vietnamese. The killing became so much easier now.

As the value of Vietnamese life went down in your estimation, so too did the realizations start to sink in that your body and your life was really of very little importance to the men and the machines who ran the war. . . .The machine would not care that a man had died, only that another part of its inventory had been lost and would require replacement, like the destroyed tank. And like the totaled tank, the Army would simply put in another order at another factory—a boot camp, where your replacement was being tooled and trained on a different kind of assembly line. It was just exactly as hard and heartless as that and it was a heavy thing to accept—though accept it we inevitably did.[29]

Clodfelter was in McNamara's army, part of what the GIs called the "Green Machine." He was in the "Hard Core" squad of the First Platoon of Charlie Company. One man in the platoon, Atticus Tate,

wasn't like the rest of us, we said, not even like those of us who, under the burdens and blows we had to take, sometimes gave in to the temptation to cruelty. He enjoyed the killing. . . . He was the company crazy, the regulation madman; the one kill-happy psychotic that every unit seemed plagued with, as if required by some demonic T.O.&E. (Table of Organization and Equipment) chart. . . .

We hated him because what he had done we could do. . . . Maybe one more month in Nam, one more buddy blown apart by a booby trap, maybe the Tate would come out in all of us.[30]

In October of 1966, the Hard Core squad were patrolling the mud and paddies of Phu Yen province. They had killed nobody, and the officers were pushing them. The zero body count "was making life miserable for all the corpse counters all the way up to the battalion C.O." Then Tate and some of the other men in the First Squad killed an "unarmed straggler." Tate "taunted us so unmercifully on our lack of scalps that several members of the Second Squad, their 'Hard Core' honor at stake, resolved to count coup [to strike the enemy; to scalp]."[31]

The next day they passed an old man in a village. Frightened, he just kept repeating, "No VC here," in English, over and over. A little further on they found three guerrillas lounging in front of a house. There was a stunned moment, and the guerrillas grabbed their guns and were gone.

The squad had lost the body count. They went back for the old man. The sergeant and two men pulled him out of his house. Clodfelter and the rest "took up defensive positions in a vegetable garden," surrounding the house to protect the execution. Clodfelter tried to look away from the old man and the sergeant behind him, but his eyes were drawn back, wanting to be a part of it. Yet he kept telling himself it wasn't really going to happen:

> One of the paratroopers pointed his M-79 grenade launcher at the doomed peasant. . . . Hesitation locked the trooper in a sweating embrace, filled the garden with a strangling tension, seemed to stop the very rotation of the earth and the passage of time. . . . I arose from my morass of sweat and dread to scream out words of protest . . . words that I should have loosened at the first moments of this horror. A shot reared, drowning out my frantic shout. . . .
>
> I would, in effect, still be shouting those unheeded words of protest in dozens of anti-war marches for years after I left Nam. I am still screaming them out today . . . too late, far too late.[32]

The old man didn't die immediately. He lay there twitching. The soldiers urged each other to kill him, each one reluctant. Finally one rifleman let loose a volley from his automatic. Still the old man did not die. The rifleman put his gun next to the old man's head and finished him.

They had a body count. They turned away, in shame. And then

one man reminded the others they had promised to show Tate the ears. A soldier sliced them off with his bayonet. "Upon reaching the platoon position, the grenadier proudly displayed his trophies, still dripping blood, to a much impressed Tate. We had joined his ranks."[33]

It is important to remember that the officers were pushing the body count. That body count was being totaled at battalion headquarters, again in Saigon, and again in Washington. Marine Lieutenant Philip Caputo landed at Danang in 1965:

General Westmoreland's strategy of attrition also had an effect on our behavior. Our mission was not to win terrain or seize positions, but simply to kill: to kill Communists and to kill as many of them as possible. Stack 'em like cordwood. Victory was a high body-count, defeat a low kill-ratio, war a matter of arithmetic. The pressure on unit commanders to produce enemy corpses was intense, and they in turn communicated it to their troops. This led to such practices as counting civilians as Viet Cong. "If it's dead and it's Vietnamese, it's VC," was the rule of thumb in the bush. It is not surprising, therefore, that some men acquired a contempt for human life and a predilection for taking it.[34]

Some units held competitions to see which platoon could get the highest "box score," like in baseball. A few units gave rest and recreation leave in the rear to men who did particularly well.[35] Of course, with time everybody learned to pad the result. They counted civilians and children. If they found somebody blown to bits, they counted each bit. They counted blood traces, each drop, as a separate kill. They counted the water buffaloes they shot, and the monkeys. Pretty soon they learned to invent dead bodies. In reaction, the more gung-ho officers insisted on "confirmed kills"—ears.

This meant that men like Tate, the exceptions who enjoyed killing, were almost never punished. In the units where the commanding officer insisted on ears for every body count, nobody said anything—nobody was punished or reprimanded. The Tates delivered for the McNamaras.

THE WRONG SIDE

The GIs were under pressure to kill, and they knew they were on the wrong side. Again and again, returning veterans in the 1960s said the other side were the only people in the country who knew what they were fighting for.

Jeri Luici, an infantryman at Cu Chi near Saigon, remembered coming back to the camp after a firefight:

> We humped in just before dawn, and fighting was still going on. There were over a hundred bodies. Later that day, we found more surface graves. . . . To give you an idea of how steadfast the people we were fighting were, I found a dead VC medic who had tied himself to a bamboo clump, with a morphine syringe stuck in his arm, as he was bleeding to death. He had an RPG [rocket-propelled grenade] at the ready with the safety off. Another guy was clutching one of our claymores [a mine]: he was going to try to detonate himself on our perimeter. Amazing.[36]

Thomas Giltner was platoon leader at Cu Chi:

> We faced mostly local VC, peasants armed with World War II rifles and no heavy weapons. They were taking on the best army in the world. They received their training from the local cadres. We respected them from day one. . . . They did an awful lot with awful little. . . .
>
> They were tremendously inventive. We used to capture home-made rifles created out of metal pipes and bits of fence post. We never put out antipersonnel mines: we knew they would be dug up and used against us. Claymores were strictly accounted for, but they were still stolen. We always worried about Charlie getting

sophisticated weapons. Once our whole battalion was roused out at night and sent looking for a starlight scope which was lost. We found it. We really worried about him getting a field piece. . . . The Vietnamese were just so ingenious. We all knew they were poor, not stupid.[37]

The GIs could often see that they were workers oppressing other poor people. In the later stages of the war American soldiers simply refused to fight. But in the early stages they felt the only choice was to fight or die. So the knowledge of what they were doing only made them angrier and more desperate. One soldier, like many, returned home to America from Vietnam to be met by his parents at the airport:

They drove home in silence and sat together in the kitchen, and his mother, in passing, apologized for there being "nothing in the house to eat." That did it; he broke. Raging, he went from cupboard to cupboard, shelf to shelf, flinging doors open, pulling down cans and boxes and bags, piling them higher and higher on the table until they spilled over onto the floor and everything edible in the house was spread out in front of them.

"I couldn't believe it," he said, shaking his head as he told me. "I'd been over there . . . killing those poor bastards who were living in their tunnels like rats and had nothing to eat but mud and a few goddamn moldy grains of rice, and who watched their kids starve to death or go up in smoke, and she said nothing to eat, and I ended up in the kitchen shouting: Nothing to eat, nothing to eat."[38]

Those children—the American soldiers expected to be greeted by friendly children. Their fathers and uncles had told them about the children overseas in World War Two. You gave them candy and they loved you. The American soldiers all met children begging for food as soon as they came to Vietnam. If they did not feed the children, the kids screamed abuse at them. If they did, the children fell on them, tearing at their clothes, going through their pockets, making clear their need and their hatred.

The old soldiers told the new soldiers the truth: those children hate us. They know where the mines are. They want us to die.

But still the GIs saw themselves in those children. Most had grown up working-class, often very poor. Many of them knew what it was like to go hungry or be laughed at in high school because they didn't have the right clothes. And now, suddenly, they were unimaginably rich compared to those children. But they would still be poor when they went home.

So they hated it when the children begged. And because they hated the feeling, they sometimes hated the children. Soldiers in different parts of Vietnam remember throwing full cans of combat rations at children from trucks: throwing them as hard as they could. An army combat engineer said:

> We threw full C-ration cans at kids on the side of the road. They'd be yelling out, "Chop, chop; chop, chop," and they wanted food. They knew we carried C-rations. Well, just for a joke, these guys would take a full can . . . and throw it as hard as they could at a kid's head. I saw several kids' heads split wide open, knocked off the road, knocked into the tires of the vehicle behind.[39]

A marine said:

> When they originally get in country [Americans] feel very friendly toward the Vietnamese and they like to toss candy at the kids. But as they become hardened to it and kind of embittered against the war, as you drive through the village you take the cans of C-rats and the cases and you peg 'em at the kids; you try to belt them over the head. And one of the fun games that always went was you dropped the C-rats cans or the candy off the back of your truck so that the kid will have time to dash out, grab the candy and get run over by the next truck.[40]

And a peasant woman in Beautiful Waters remembered the marines:

> I was walking along the road with my son, who was wearing a
> hat. There was a string to hold the hat to his chin. One of the
> American soldiers grabbed the hat, and pulled my son up and
> under the wheels of the truck. The truck stopped, but it was too
> late. [The boy was crushed]. . . . He was my only son, and my
> sadness is so deep that it will never end.[41]

The historian Christian Appy says that these stories are "not easy
to understand, and veterans who are plagued with guilt for incidents like this do not themselves fully understand what led them
to behave so cruelly or how they might have found in it a 'joke'
or a 'fun game'."[42] But the soldiers saw the children's hatred and
need, and they could not bear it.

4

GUERRILLAS

We turn now to what the war was like for the guerrillas and North Vietnamese soldiers.

The tunnels of Cu Chi, more than anything else, give some idea of the courage of the Vietnamese resistance.[1] Cu Chi was in Hau Nghia province, just north of Saigon. The tunnels were originally dug in the 1940s, when the Communist-led Viet Minh were fighting French colonialism, as hiding places for the guerrillas and bomb shelters for the villagers. When the war in South Vietnam began in the 1960s, the Viet Cong dug more tunnels and began to link them together, from one village to another. Cu Chi was an ideal place for tunneling. In the Mekong Delta to the south, the water table was too close to the surface. In the hills to the north, the ground was too hard. But the red clay of Cu Chi was easy to dig, and then it hardened into tunnel walls that seemed to have the strength of concrete.

No one person or officer decided to build a tunnel network. But by the time the American 25th Infantry built a base at Cu Chi in 1966, there were hundreds of miles of underground passages, many of them below the massive American base. They even had street signs down in the tunnels so guerrillas from other places could find their way.

The Viet Cong lived in the tunnels. At night they could come out, pick off Americans, and dive back into the tunnels, the trap doors hidden by leaves. Some snipers even surfaced inside the barbed wire of the American base.

The tunnels were deep and narrow. They tried to make the

passages about five feet in diameter, but in places they were much narrower. If the Americans found the entrance, they had to crawl, knowing there was somebody waiting for them in the dark with a knife, trying to breathe without making a sound. Very few American soldiers went down those tunnels. Those who did, the "tunnel rats," found it terrifying. If they saw what they thought was an enemy, they had only one chance to fire. In the compressed, narrow tunnels, the sound of a gunshot would send the man firing temporarily deaf and stunned.

Off the passages, the guerrillas built larger rooms for sleeping, cooking, meetings, and storage. They dug every day. Tom Mangold and John Pennycate, the British historians of Cu Chi, interviewed many survivors of the tunnel warfare on both sides. Nguyen Than Linh, a Viet Cong officer, remembered, "Old men made baskets for carrying the earth, old women did the cooking, young men and women used their strength to dig the earth. Even the children did their share by gathering leaves to cover the trap doors."[2]

They lived down there for years. Ventilation was a constant problem, according to Le Van Nong, a farmer turned guerrilla:

> The tunnels we were in stank and we stank. The tunnels were usually very hot, and we were always sweating. . . . At night [we] tried to cook the rice for eating the next day. If there was no time to prepare the rice, we went without food for the whole day until the next night, and we tried to come up to cook. It really wasn't possible for us to cook underground, the smoke was always asphyxiating, you just could not breathe, there was no air down there anyway. Sometimes we were driven to attack the Americans and make them go away, just so we could come up and cook at night, cook in the open. You cannot imagine what pleasure it gave us.[3]

As the war went on, however, the guerrillas found that the American troops on patrol left a lot of food lying around—combat rations, canned meat, and chocolate. The good thing was that these could be eaten cold, without cooking.

They also depended on the American troops for weapons. Captain Linh said, "We hardly received any . . . weapons from the North. We received only mine detonators and delay fuses. We needed explosives and fortunately soon found them lying all around us on the ground."[4]

In 1966 one battalion of American troops at Cu Chi fired 180,000 artillery shells in one month. "In one month, throughout South Vietnam, the Americans fired about a trillion bullets, 10 million mortar round, and 4.8 million rockets. And this was just the beginning of the war."[5] A proportion of those shells did not explode. The guerrillas took them down into the tunnels. With painstaking care, they sawed gently through the shell casings and used the explosive to make new mines. They used the Coke cans the Americans threw away to make grenades.

Vien Phong was a poet who worked in the tunnels, writing and printing leaflets for distribution by the underground in nearby Saigon. He slept in a hole three feet high dug out of the side of a tunnel:

> I had not dug the shelter too deep, for we learned from bitter experience that the deeper the shelter, the greater the chance of being buried alive after a bombing attack, so I built a moderately strong shelter that could deal with the bomb fragments. When the enemy carried out their anti-guerrilla operations above, I went into my sleeping shelter, lit a candle, and read books or poems until the air was so foul I had to extinguish the candle and lie in the complete blackness of eternal night, listening to the tanks and guns above me. I did not know, and nor did my comrades, whether we had judged the depth of our tunnels correctly. One lay there, wondering if a tank would crash through the ceiling of your sleeping chamber and crush you to death, or worse, not quite to death.[6]

Vien Phong hated the gas too. The American soldiers often pumped poison gas into the tunnels. Mangold and Pennycate write:

> Whether the gas was acetylene or the anti-personnel CS riot gas, which burned the skin and tortured the eyes and nose, the effects were horrendous.
>
> Vien Phuong [sic] remembered having to lie prone during gas attacks, staying alive only by breathing very slowly, sucking in the air remaining in a shallow layer on the floor underneath the creeping gas. Death, if it came, would be agonizingly slow asphyxiation, a dreadful wretching in the stinking blackness of one's own ready-made grave.[7]

Dang Thi Linh was originally from Saigon. Helicopter gunships had killed both her father and mother in separate incidents. She worked as a dancer in one of the traveling theatre groups the Viet Cong sent around to raise morale. They performed in the tunnels and were very popular. Peasants traveled from the surrounding villages and came down into the tunnels to watch. Air was always a problem. Above ground, the audience would have sung along with the performers. Below ground, the audience was usually silent, so as not to use up the air.

When Dang Thi Linh was pregnant, she found the tunnels unbearably hot. But she danced right up to the day before she gave birth. When the pains came, she had to crawl along to the hospital room. That was hard going, as with her bump the tunnel was too narrow. But she made it.

She was afraid of infection after the birth. There were no clean clothes, and the tunnels were filthy because there was no way to get rid of urine and feces. American doctors discovered that 100 percent of the tunnel guerrillas that U.S. troops captured had worms or other intestinal parasites, and half of them had malaria. But Dang Thi Linh's daughter lived. She took the child out of the tunnels, spent six months in a relatively safe area, and then left the baby with its grandfather and went back underground:

> I stayed in the tunnels until 1968 and then joined the Tet offensive in Go Vap. After that I returned to work in the tunnels until 1970, when I returned to Saigon city to work for the revolution. I was caught that July and sent to prison for three months. I was tortured by the ARVN soldiers and an American who was in the cell. They beat me up and passed electricity through my body. Eventually, on 19 May 1975, I was reunited with my daughter. She was nearly eight years. . . . Then I was reunited with my husband. He was very seriously wounded and has been unable to work since. We get a state pension; we live in one room.

The British interviewer asked her if she would do it again. "That's a very hard question to answer," she said.[8]

Pham Sang, originally a civil servant, went below ground to write for the theatre groups. He kept filling his plays with love songs that were a great hit with audiences. His superiors wanted him to write war songs. So he wrote, for instance, "Cu Chi, The Heroic Land":

> We are Cu Chi people who go forward to kill the enemy
> We go through danger, bullets and fire to fight for our native
>   land.
> Our country is a fortress standing against the Americans,
> Cu Chi is a heroic land.
>
> Let's grow manioc plant all over the bomb craters and make
>   them green.
> We kill the Americans with their own shells and bomb.
> We kill the enemy and increase our production,
> Those were our glorious victories.[9]

And then Pham Sang went back to the love songs. Buy Lap, his superior officer, told him even love songs should be political. Pham Sang found that when he tried, though, the result didn't seem to work. One song, for instance, began, "I love you, I miss you and wait for you, liberation fighter, let's fight the enemy together."[10]

The higher officers grew concerned that too many villagers were coming down into the tunnels to listen to Pham Sang's performers. They said the cultural troupe was there to entertain the fighters, and only them. So Pham Sang took his performers up top at night. They found that the bomb craters left by B-52 plane raids were big enough for natural theatres. They put a few planks in the bottom of the crater to make a clean dry stage. The audience sat in caves dug into the sides of the crater above the stage. Now everyone had enough air to sing. When the bombers and helicopters came over, the performers joined the audience in the shelter of the caves.

Vo Hoang Le was a guerrilla surgeon. Because the guerrillas could not take their wounded to hospital, Dr. Vo did what he could for wounds in the tunnel, which was mainly amputation. He operated with netting made from American parachutes hung above the patient to stop the dirt from the ceiling from falling into the wound. Usually he had no anesthetics, and about half the amputation cases died from shock and pain.

The women had no rags for menstruation. Vietnam, including Communist Vietnam, was a prudish society. The women were ashamed of the way their clothes smelled and would sneak out at night to wash. And some of the guerrillas, particularly the young, would go above ground some nights to sing together. They dug deep and repaired weapons in there, even grenade launchers. Once they hid an armored personnel carrier underground.

Vo Thi Mo was one of the women in the tunnels. She came from the village of Ben Suc, a Viet Cong stronghold. In 1967 American troops, led by an officer named Alexander Haig, came to Ben Suc. They killed a few people, rounded up the rest, and took them off to a camp surrounded by barbed wire. They took the animals too, burned all the houses, and bulldozed the village flat. Finally they put "ten thousand pounds of explosives and a thousand gallons of napalm in a crater in the center of the ruined village, covered them with earth," and blew the whole thing up. General Bernard Rogers reported to his superiors: "One of the major objectives of [Operation] Cedar Falls had been achieved. The village of Ben Suc existed no longer."[11]

Vo Thi Mo was already a guerrilla platoon leader when her village was destroyed. One day she was on guard at a tunnel entrance when three American soldiers sat down nearby. They could not see her and she had them in her sights. But she paused. She was curious.

The American soldiers shared cookies and candy with each other. They took out what seemed to be letters from home and read them. Vo Thi Mo was fascinated. They do what we do, she thought. The Americans read each other's letters and began to cry. This also the guerrillas did. She could not shoot them.

Her company messenger, crouched next to her, raised his gun to shoot the Americans. Silently, she knocked it away.

The guerrillas held an inquiry on Vo Thi Mo the next day, in effect a field court martial. She had not done her duty, but her platoon messenger testified passionately in her defense. He worshipped Vo Thi Mo. They had been through several battles together, she leading her platoon of twenty-four women, the boy messenger running back and forth through the bullets for orders from the higher officers. She had been in the army for four years, she was older than he, and he had only fought for a year. The court martial listened to him and let Vo Thi Mo off with a reprimand.

Vo Thi Mo was 17 years old. Her platoon messenger was 10.

THE TET OFFENSIVE

The Tet Offensive in 1968 changed everything for the tunnel fights. It was a shattering defeat for them, but also a terrible embarrassment for the American government at home.

In late December of 1967, the invitations to the New Year's Eve party at the American embassy in Saigon said, "Come see the light at the end of the tunnel."[12] It was a joke. For months, the generals had been telling Lyndon Johnson, and he had been telling the American people, there's light at the end of the tunnel. Things are dark now, we can't see clearly, but hang on a bit longer and we'll win.

That was American New Year in Saigon. Vietnamese New Year, the festival of Tet, was on 31 January 1968. U.S. Navy Lieutenant Dick Shea wrote a poem about Tet in 1965:

Tet
vietnamese new year
today tomorrow and the day after
the viet cong sent a message saying
they were not fighting during tet
all vietnamese went home
or disappeared somewhere
very few guards still on duty
interesting
how they call the war off
and put their toys away for three days
hard for an american military mind to comprehend.[13]

The American embassy was expecting the same thing for Tet in 1968. But the Front had been assembling its forces for weeks. The North Vietnamese Army had created a massive diversion at Khe Sanh, in the "Demilitarized Zone" (DMZ) along the border with North Vietnam. General Westmoreland had thrown everything he could into Khe Sanh. It was the kind of battle he understood—

artillery, air strikes, and American machine guns mowing down human waves of Orientals. A real battle, like Korea, like the movies. But while Westmoreland read body counts from the DMZ, the National Liberation Front moved into position to take the cities.

All Vietnamese over 35 at the time remembered where they were in August 1945, when Hanoi, Saigon, and every town of any size rose against the Japanese and the French. For all of them, those days defined a revolution. Now, in 1968, they were going for urban insurrection, finally. The Front had been fighting for a long time, with great courage. Its generals were not sure they could continue. One big push, they told their people. We march into the cities and the people will rise with us.

On Tet they struck, throwing in everybody they could. The tunnels of Cu Chi were the base for the assault on Saigon. Fighters flooded into the city. That morning, sappers from the tunnels assaulted the American embassy in the heart of Saigon and held part of it for hours. The world saw the television pictures and saw one of the sappers was a woman.

There was fighting in the streets of Saigon. In Hue, the Front took almost the whole city, and the guerrillas of Beautiful Waters joined the fight.

With great courage, they failed. On the streets of Saigon, the chief of police blew out the brains of a captured guerrilla, and a cameraman captured the moment for American TV. In Hue the guerrillas held the old imperial city and its beautiful buildings, fighting house to house with exhausted U.S. marines. The world saw the pictures of a guerrilla on a ruined wall, gun in hand, and the tired and desperate stare of a wounded marine. More than half of Hue had been destroyed by the time the marines retook it.

In the city of Ben Tre, in the Mekong Delta, the American army flattened every building. The American officer in charge told reporters, "It was necessary to destroy the city in order to save it," and newspapers around the world carried that quote.

What the world, and the American people, saw was that the White House had been lying to everybody. Two days into Tet, Lyndon Johnson gave a press conference. He said that the Tet Offensive was a failure, it was all over, and anyway he had known about it beforehand. These were lies and, what was worse, obvious lies. There was no more light at the end of the tunnel. The American people had been told that the Viet Cong were North Vietnamese soldiers who had invaded South Vietnam and terrorized the peasants, and that America was winning the war in the countryside. Now people in America could see what the GIs had seen—the courage of the Vietnamese resistance.

The American photographers, the TV cameramen, and the reporters in Saigon and in the newsrooms were already opposed to the war. Now they saw their chance. Enraged, exultant, and professional, they raced through the streets, filming, screaming down the phone home, making them run those pictures, hoping that the newsroom forced the editor to run the story, that the word got out, that people could see. What the world saw was that the greatest power on earth, with all those weapons, all those big white men, had been humbled by peasants.

The guerrillas, however, had expected Saigon and Hue to rise. It didn't happen.

The problem was that the Communists could not organize the working class. Six years later Tran Bach Dong, the man in charge of the Communist underground in Saigon, said during a conference underground in the jungle that the National Liberation Front's organization in Saigon was "wonderfully successful—the intellectuals, students, Buddhists, all of them"—except for the workers, where organization was "worse than bad."[14] He was removed from office and humiliated, not because the organization was worthless, but because he said so, and what he said was both true and embarrassing for the Communist Party.

The party, after all, claimed to be a Communist party, a Marxist party. The core idea of Karl Marx's Marxism was that workers can take over the world and liberate all humanity. Marx argued that the Industrial Revolution had produced a new class—the working class. These were people who owned nothing and had to sell their labor for wages in order to live. Before Marx's time, poor peasants had risen up again and again, in many countries. But the peasants were in the villages. They would storm the city, take it over, and then hand power to some educated class in the towns. They might even share out the land. But once they had done so, they would all want to become small farmers producing for a market. In time, the market would re-create classes of land-owners and poor peasants. The new working class, Marx said, was different. They worked in the cities, at the center of the system. They were far better educated. And the circumstances of their working lives threw them together. Peasants were always divided by arguments over fields and inheritance. The only way workers could take over from their masters was to take over the whole corporation and the whole economy. So, for the first time in history, there was an oppressed class that could take over the cities and the whole system.

When Marx published *Capital* in 1867, the great majority of this new working class were manual workers. Some of these were relatively unskilled. Some were machinists or carpenters and the like, who had done an apprenticeship and were proud of their skills and craft. Now a substantial proportion of the working class are white-collar workers, like teachers, social workers, and office workers. They, like the old skilled workers, however, have to sell their labor to live and do what the boss tells them. In most countries, they are also the group joining labor unions at the fastest rate.

Marx argued that people were part of this working class quite independently of whether they thought they were "middle-class" or anything else. The economy made them working-class. They had to work and do what they were told. The task of socialists, for Marx, was to argue with the workers around them that we are all stuck in this class, and our interests are opposed to those of the employers.

In North Vietnam, however, party bureaucrats, not workers,

ran the state. The party spoke of a working-class line and the leading role of the working class. But what they meant was the line they chose and the leading role of the party.

They had particular difficulties building any organization among workers in the South. The obvious way to do that was to organize unions, support strikes, sell a regular underground newspaper, and try to build underground committees in each workplace opposed to both the employer and the state. This was the classic Communist way of organizing. There were workers in the South, and strikes. By 1973 the bombing in the South had created so many refugees that 70 percent of people now lived in the cities. The peasants had become workers, or were at least scrabbling for a living in the city.

But the Vietnamese Communists were committed to building an alliance of classes in the National Liberation Front. Crucial to that alliance were the "progressive bourgeoisie." These people were the employers and managers of the workers. If the Communists tried to organize the workers over daily grievances on a daily basis, as they did try to organize the peasants, they would lose the support of the businessmen and managers. Faced with the choice, the Communists did better at organizing the managers. This was partly because party leaders felt a natural affinity with businessmen and managers. The same sort of people, with the same sort of education, ran both North and South. And most of them had relatives of the same class on the other side.

But there was a deeper problem. Because the party had pushed through land reform in the North, they were able to advocate it in the South and in that way respond to peasants' economic grievances. But because they did not allow workers in the North to have unions or strikes or independent workers' committees or meetings or newspapers, they could not advocate these practices in the South without raising the question of why this wasn't happening in the North. In other words, if the party had made strikes and workers' power central to its work in Saigon, it would have had to change in Hanoi.[15]

And that is why Saigon was weakest at Tet, Hue was stronger, and Ben Tre was strongest of all. In Saigon the rising had to have the workers. Hue was smaller, closer to the countryside. Ben Tre was a small city in a sea of peasants. But Saigon was the capital, the key.

There was one more problem. Workers' risings do not happen with a secret command. They take the form of mass strikes, then demonstrations, then more little strikes and protests and more mass demonstrations, building up to a moment of general strike and insurrection. The strength of such a rising is that in the end it pits a whole city against the police and the army, and the soldiers will not fire on the crowd because included in that crowd are their friends and family. The risings of 1945 had been like that. Such risings are protean, creative, democratic, and chaotic. Yet the whole tradition of the Vietnamese Communists to that point had been military. So by 1968 they could only conceive of an urban rising as a military event, happening by command, with the people supporting the army.

Had they concentrated on deepening and extending the sort of movement that was seen in the demonstrations of the Buddhist monks, they might have organized a march of all Saigon. By 1968 it would have been politically impossible for the American army to fire on a crowd of a million—and the GIs would probably have refused to do it. But the Communist leaders could not organize that crowd.

So after Tet the guerrillas had to retreat, carrying their wounded where they could, their cover blown. The guerrillas took a terrible beating in many areas. In Long An province, south of Saigon, one unit of 1,430 had only 640 survivors after Tet. Another of 2,018 had only 775 survivors. And then the B-52s came. By the end of the war, the guerrillas had lost 84,000 "combatants" in a province with a total population of 350,000 men, women, and children—one person in four.[16]

In Cu Chi district, the local guerrillas lost 883 killed and 3,670 wounded in the first six months of 1968. The 7th Battalion, with a normal complement of 320, lost 122 killed and 116 wounded during Tet. A captured guerrilla finance officer told his interrogators:

> We had lost many cadre during the 1968 offensive and its aftermath. . . . My own operations were becoming more and more difficult and dangerous. The taxation situation had deteriorated tremendously, because the people were disenchanted with us. We had promised to topple the puppet government with the [Tet] General Offensive and had collected extremely heavy taxes on the basis of this pledge. In 1969, when I attempted to tax again, the people were angry about this. This attitude combined with the decimation of our cadre and the enemy build-up, resulted in a great drop in taxes collected.[17]

Then came endless B-52 raids on Cu Chi. Truong Nhu Tang was not a Communist, but he was a high official in the National Liberation Front. For a time after the Tet Offensive, he lived in a camp not far north of Cu Chi, just across the border in Cambodia. He remembered B-52 raids as

> an experience of undiluted psychological terror, into which we were plunged, day in, day out, for years on end. From a kilometer away, the sonic roar of the B-52 explosions tore eardrums, leaving many of the jungle dwellers permanently deaf. From a kilometer, the shock waves knocked their victims senseless. Any hit within a half kilometer would collapse the walls of an unreinforced bunker, burying alive the people cowering inside. Seen up close, the bomb craters were gigantic—thirty feet across and nearly as deep.[18]

Truong was lucky. He was living in a high Viet Cong command post, and Russian intelligence trawlers often radioed warnings of B-52 strikes to his camp:

Often the warnings would give us time to grab some rice and escape by foot or bike. Hours later we would return to find, as happened on several occasions, that there was nothing left. It was as if an enormous scythe had swept through the jungle, felling the giant teak and go trees like grass in its way, shredding them into billions of scattered splinters. On these occasions . . . the complex would be utterly destroyed: food, clothes, supplies, documents, everything. It was not just that things were destroyed; in some awesome way they had ceased to exist. You would come back to where your lean-to and bunker had been, your home, and there would simply be nothing there, just an unrecognizable landscape gouged by immense craters.

Equally often, however, we . . . had time only to take cover as best we could. The first few times I experienced a B–52 attack it seemed, as I strained to press myself into the bunker floor, that I had been caught in the apocalypse. The terror was complete. One lost control of bodily functions as the mind screamed incomprehensible orders to get out. On one occasion a Soviet delegation was visiting our ministry when a particularly short-notice warning came through. When it was over, no one had been hurt, but the entire delegation had sustained considerable damage to its dignity— uncontrollable trembling and wet pants were the all-too-obvious outward signs of inner convulsions. The visitors could have spared themselves their feelings of embarrassment; each of their hosts was a veteran of the same symptoms.[19]

The bombing had a logic of its own. After 1968 the targets kept shifting, but the rate of bombing did not. When there were pauses in the bombing of North Vietnam, more bombs were dropped on South Vietnam, Laos, and Cambodia.

In Laos, the Geneva peace settlement of 1954 had arranged a neutralist government led by Prince Souvanna Phouma of the royal family, which included the leader of the Communist Pathet Lao guerrillas, Souvanna Phouma's cousin Prince Souvanna-phong. But the CIA built a secret army among the Hmong minority in the mountains, and eventually succeeded in organizing a right-wing military coup in the capital. In November 1968, President Johnson stopped the bombing of North Vietnam as part of an attempt at peace negotiations. In 1969 there were 300 sorties a day over Laos. George Chapelier, a United Nations official, saw what that did to the main Pathet Lao stronghold, the Plain of Jars:

> Prior to 1967, bombing was light and far from population centers. By 1968 the intensity of the bombings was such that no organized life was possible in the villages. The villagers moved to the outskirts and then deeper into the forest as the bombing climax reached its peak in 1969 when jet planes came daily and destroyed all stationary structures. Nothing was left standing. The villagers lived in trenches and holes or in caves. They only farmed at night. All of the interlocutors [I talked to], without any exception, had their villages completely destroyed. In the last phase, bombings were aimed at the systematic destruction of the material basis of the civilian society. Harvests burned down and rice became scarce.[20]

A quarter of the population of Laos became refugees. Fred Branfman talked to the people in the refugee camps through an interpreter. One man from the Plain of Jars said:

> One day a plane came bombing my ricefield as well as my village. I had gone very early to harrow my field. I thought: "I am only a village rice farmer, the airplane will not shoot me." But that day truly it did shoot me and wounded me together with my buffalo, which was the source of a hundred thousand loves and a hundred thousand worries for me.[21]

Branfman asked people to draw pictures of the bombing. One man drew a man and a boy and explained:

These two, father and son, don't have hands and feet on account of a bomb dropped by the airplanes that didn't explode right away. They thought it would never explode and went to pick it up to look at. It exploded. . . . Now they can't do anything. But [they] did not come away with us. The father said he would not go anywhere if he was killed for it, because he regretted the loss of his land, ricefield, cows and buffalo. Even though they couldn't work, they could still look. . . . Better to die in the village. That was the decision of these two.[22]

Bao Ninh was a junior officer in the Glorious 27th Youth Brigade of the North Vietnamese army. Five hundred soldiers went South with the brigade in 1969, the year after Tet. Bao was one of the ten survivors. His novel *The Sorrow of War* describes living under the B-52s in the jungle of the central highlands, month after month, year after year.[23] The hero of the novel is named Kien. In 1969 his Battalion 27, the "Unlucky Battalion," is bombed at the end of the dry season:

The enemy sent napalm spraying through the jungle and a sea of fire enveloped them, spreading like the fires of hell. Troops in the fragmented companies tried to regroup, only to be blown out of their shelters again as they went mad, became disoriented and threw themselves into nests of bullets, dying in the flaming inferno. Above them the helicopters flew at tree-top height and shot them almost one by one, the blood spreading out, spraying from their backs, flowing like red mud.

The diamond-shaped grass clearing was piled high with bodies killed by helicopter gunships. Broken bodies, bodies blown apart, bodies vaporized.

No jungle grew again in this clearing. No grass. No plants.

"Better to die than surrender my brothers! Better to die!" the Battalion Commander yelled insanely; waving his pistol in front of Kien he blew his own brains out through his ear. . . .

After that battle no one mentioned Battalion 27 any more,

though numerous souls of ghosts and devils were born in that deadly defeat. They were still loose, wandering in every corner and bush in the jungle, drifting along the stream, refusing to depart for the Other World.

From then on it was called the Jungle of Screaming Souls. Just hearing the name whispered was enough to send chills down the spine. Perhaps the screaming souls gathered together on special festival days as members of the Lost Battalion, lining up on the little diamond-shaped grass plot, checking their ranks and numbers. The sobbing whispers were heard deep in the jungle at night, the howls carried on the wind. . . .

Kien was told that passing this area at night one could hear birds crying like human beings. They never flew, they only cried among the branches. . . .

Here, when it is dark, trees and plants moan in awful harmony. When the ghostly music begins it unhinges the soul and the entire wood looks the same no matter where you are standing. . . .

Living here one could go mad or be frightened to death. Which was why in the rainy season of 1974, when the regiment was sent back to this area, Kien and his scout squad established an altar and prayed before it in secret, honoring and recalling the wandering souls from Battalion 27 still in the Jungle of Screaming Souls.

Sparkling incense sticks glowed night and day at the altar from that day forward.[24]

They made their altars in secret because the ritual they used was part of the traditional Vietnamese religion of ancestor worship. For the higher officers, and the Communist Party members among them, that was forbidden superstition.

The B-52s created craters deeper than the tunnelers of Cu Chi could dig. Many guerrillas were buried in the tunnels, and for those who remained the passages lay open to the sky. The guerrillas left the tunnels of Cu Chi.

The guerrillas were stronger in some areas of South Vietnam than others, but everywhere they were weaker than before. Now they faced the Phoenix program.[25] Phoenix was organized under William Colby, then the CIA station chief in Saigon and later the director of the whole CIA. The staff were CIA agents, South Vietnamese soldiers, and South Vietnamese police. Their aim was to target the "Viet Cong Infrastructure" (the people in the resistance) and assassinate them. The difficulty was in knowing who they were. So under Phoenix anybody could inform on anybody else anonymously for a cash reward. That way, many Communist and Front leaders were eliminated—but so were a lot of other people. It was an extortionist's paradise, and President Thieu also used it to kill many of the supporters of a rival general, "Big" Minh. Tens of thousands died. The CIA insisted on some proof—not proof of guilt, but proof that a person had died, a body. One agent complained that the local police were bringing in every body they came across. But Phoenix was also an opportunity for the landlords hiding in the cities, who did know who their enemies in the villages were, to get their revenge.

Phoenix agents also worked with American military sweeps. The GIs would go through a village and round everybody up. The Phoenix people took away anybody who looked suspicious and anybody on their lists of minor Viet Cong supporters. Some of these people were killed, but the majority were sent to local and provincial torture centers and then released after a few days or weeks. If they went home or to another village, they were picked up again pretty soon in another sweep and sent to the torture center again. This happened over and over. The Phoenix people were not making a mistake—they had quotas.

After Tet, the 101st Airborne came to the village of Beautiful Waters. Michael Clodfelter, who screamed in protest as his platoon cut off the old man's ear, served with the 101 in 1965. Now the "Screaming Eagles" built a base, Camp Eagle, on the land of Beautiful Waters.

The villagers told Trullinger they found the Americans cruel and nervous like the French. Sometimes the 101 just went crazy and fired for minutes into the night. That was especially hard for the villagers with fields near the base. The 101 seemed to like shooting water buffaloes too, and children had to stop sitting on their buffaloes. There were endless searches of the village, beatings, and some rapes.

Before Camp Eagle came, the guerrillas had been strong in Beautiful Waters. As one peasant said, the villagers had spoken of the men who oppressed them, and finally had the courage to say their names aloud. But in 1968 the guerrillas had to leave the village, only returning sometimes at night. Trullinger estimates that support for the Viet Minh and then the National Liberation Front had always been 70 to 80 percent of the village. But after 1968, solid support was down to about 50 percent. Government support, usually 5 to 10 percent, had climbed to 15 percent. The other 35 percent of villagers were exhausted, and waiting.

The Front told the villagers not to take jobs at Camp Eagle, and most of the civilian workers on the base came from other villages. The villagers found the Americans almost unimaginably rich, these men who had grown up the hard way in their own country. All of their food was imported, everything they needed was imported, and a lot of it was wasted, dumped on the garbage dump outside the base. Poor villagers, particularly old people and children, picked through that garbage dump regularly and found things they could use or sell. The dump trucks kept coming as they searched, and the bulldozers would level the dump regularly. Occasionally children from Beautiful Waters died when they didn't see the bulldozer coming and it buried them.

In one sense the strategy of attrition was working. The bombs, the guns, and Phoenix were killing an awful lot of civilians, but they were wiping out the guerrillas in the process. After 1968 the Viet Cong had almost no organization left in Saigon. When the Communists finally won in 1975, there were many villages that could no longer produce a Communist committee.

THE EXPERIENCE OF WOMEN

The American armed forces were winning the war in the villages, and at the same time the war was hollowing out the society of South Vietnam. Vietnam had long had prostitution. Prostitution by the poor for the rich had always been an important family value. But there was an explosion with the Americans and the new wealth in the cities. Women, men, and children did it to live.

Frank Snepp was a CIA analyst and interrogator in Saigon. In 1973 the last American troops had left, but the South Vietnamese government still held power in the cities. Snepp went to Mimi's Flamboyant Bar for a beer:

> I heard for the millionth time a bar girl drone on about her long-lost American GI. He's gone. She's a mother. But now, unlike 1969 or '70, she who tells the tale is no more than thirteen or fourteen, only beginning to discover what so many others before her are trying to forget. "I'm no animal," she says, "but the Americans make love to me as if I was." And she pounds her fist in her hand to demonstrate. But then one of her favorite customers comes in and she is all smiles and sweetness. Soon she is gone for the night.[26]

Snepp had a Vietnamese lover, "Tu Hua" (a pseudonym). In 1975 the Communists were closing in and a pilot in the South Vietnamese Air Force bombed the presidential palace in Saigon. Snepp, at work in the embassy, got a call from Tu Hua. He asked if she was all right:

> "Okay," she said, "but scared. When the big bang went off I was. . . ."
>
> "Yes," I coaxed, trying to sound calm and unconcerned.
>
> "I was taking a shower."
>
> "Well, you were lucky," I said, unable to keep from laughing. "That bathroom's a safe place. Well away from the windows."

"No, it was terrible," she insisted. "I don't want to die with no clothes on."

I laughed again and reassured her all was well. But as I hung up the phone I couldn't help wondering at how curious her reaction was. Tu Hua, after all, had spent much of her childhood dodging shrapnel in the streets of her native village in the delta, and a good many of her teenage years working in the bars of Tu Do. And now, as if she were still an innocent in the world, she was worrying about dying in the buff![27]

For Snepp, it's a joke. He does not understand why a prostitute would be afraid of dying naked.

When the GIs went to those prostitutes some were angry and hurt, and they used the woman to hurt back. Some were looking for love, and trying to give it, or just wanted someone to hold them. Some were looking for sex because they were in a world full of death. Some built relationships of love with Vietnamese women. But the war and the inequality degraded both the prostitutes and the GIs.

It was not only prostitutes whose deepest fear was dying naked. Le Minh Khue, later a writer, joined the North Vietnamese Army when she was 15, in 1965, and served for the next ten years of the war. She worked mostly at keeping open the Ho Chi Minh Trail, the dirt road through the mountains of Laos that the North Vietnamese used to take supplies down to the South. These supplies were crucial, so the American planes constantly bombed the trail. Le Minh Khue remembered her teenage years:

Men bury the dead in peacetime. During the war, women had to do it. In the morning, they would get up to prepare the white cloth to bury the day's dead, make the coffins, and dig the burial trenches. Getting ready for what was to come. Sometimes, the burial trenches were bombed and they had to take the bodies out to rebury them. Some bodies were in pieces, some had exploded like bombs from the pressure. . . .

One night I went to bathe in a stream. It was dark, and something bumped into me. It was a dead body, floating there. What I feared the most was dying naked, while bathing, or having my clothes blown off by the bomb pressure. It happened to a lot of the girls. It was terrible, but we were young and we made jokes.[28]

And there were hundreds of thousands of rapes. Duong Thu Huong went south as an officer in a North Vietnamese Communist Youth Brigade when she was 21. In 1990, after she was expelled from the Communist Party for dissent, she wrote a novel about the war. She writes of a patrol:

We moved towards the corner of the forest from which the horrible odor seemed to emanate. We found six naked corpses. Women, their breasts and genitals had been cut off and strewn on the grass round them. They were northern girls: We could tell by their scarves made out of parachute cloth and the lotus-shaped collars of their blouses. They must have belonged to a group of volunteers or a mobile unit that lost its way. Perhaps, like us, they had come here to search for bamboo shoots or vegetables. The soldiers had raped them before killing them. The corpses were bruised violet . . . girlish bodies rotted, decomposing into swollen old corpses, puffy as dead toads. Maggots swarmed in their wounds, their eyes and mouths. Fat white larvae. They crawled over the corpses in waves, plunging in and out of them. . . .

"Let's bury the girls," I said.

Vultures circled and shrieked overhead. . . . Sweat beaded and glistened on our faces. The odor of rotting flesh hung in the air. We gathered the corpses, fighting with vultures and the maggots for each shred of flesh. We buried them. The girls' pockets were empty; not a single slip of paper, just a few pieces of red and blue yarn, a few betel nuts. The yarn to tie their hair, the betel nuts to clean their teeth. They must have believed they would see their men.

The earth was shallow here, so we had to bury the corpses in a small circular pit. By the time we finished, the maggots had formed a dense mass. Lanh threw a handful of dead leaves over them in a pile and set fire to it. You could hear the maggots crackle.[29]

This is a novel, so perhaps Duong saw that and perhaps she did not. But that is what women soldiers like Duong feared all the time. There are descriptions of the rapes from the American side, too. In 1968 Leonard Gonzalez was on almost constant patrol with a "Charlie Company" under Captain Ernest Medina of the 11th Infantry in Quang Ngai province along the coast. Some of the men raped on every patrol. Gonzalez remembered:

Take one squad say, it's a small village, one squad would go from the back, one goes from the front, and the other is going through. Now the one that is going through is having their fun. . . .

One squad got one girl—one lady. Then they told me, "Go in there," and I said, "No, I won't." So what I did is I went inside and she looked real bad. The only thing I can do for the lady is, like, I got the canteen and wiped her. She was awful perspiring. I wiped her forehead. I tried to hold her up. She got scared of me, I was part of them. I tried to tell her I don't have nothing to do with it. I helped her up to her feet. I took her to the well, got some water from the well. . . .

Then another squad heard about the thirteen guys who did their thing with this woman, and were going to try her out and I told them to leave her alone, and then at that time I just walked off. I said: "Forget it." I don't want to kill my own men. I tried to tell her: "Get out of here—go," She was going to run . . . but, like after thirteen guys got to her it's hard to walk.[30]

The rapes were part of an integrated policy of terror. Armies do not rape systematically unless the practice is permitted, and effectively encouraged, from the top. During the 1980s, for instance, the Soviet Union invaded Afghanistan and fought guerrillas there for seven years. It was, many people inside and outside Russia said, Russia's Vietnam. It was fought in much the same way, with free fire zones, bombing, napalm, and helicopter gunships. Between half a million and a million Afghans were killed. But there was almost no rape by Russian soldiers or by Afghan guerrillas. This was not because it was foreign to anybody's culture. The Russian army raped their way across Germany in 1945. Afghans had often used rape before as a way of humiliating political enemies. It has been common across South Asia and has been used by Pushtuns in Pakistan, by both sides during the ethnic cleansing that accompanied the partition of Pakistan and India in 1948, and by the Pakistani army in the war in Bangladesh in 1971. Tens of thousands of Kashmiri women were raped by Indian soldiers as they put down the rising in Kashmir in the 1990s. But in Afghanistan in the 1980s, the commanders on both sides were clear that rape would be a political disaster, losing them enormous support.

Rape does not happen because men are like that and cannot stop themselves. It happens when commanders encourage it. The rapes Gonzalez was witnessing were part of a policy that prepared Charlie Company for something worse. After repeated patrols, Captain Medina called the company together one evening in March 1968 and told them that the next day they would be taking a village that was a Viet Cong stronghold. He ordered them to kill everybody in the village, My Lai.

Varnado Simpson was a rifleman in Charlie Company. He was 19 when he entered the village the next day. He shot a woman. Years later, he remembered:

> I went to turn her over and there was a little baby with her that I had also killed. The baby's face was half gone. My mind just went. The training came to me and I just started killing. Old men, women, children, water buffaloes, everything. We were told to leave nothing standing. We did what we were told, regardless of

whether they were civilians. They was the enemy. Period. Kill. If you don't follow a direct order you can be shot yourself. Now what am I supposed to do? You're damned if you do and you're damned if you don't. You didn't have to look for people to kill, they were just there. I cut their throats, cut off their hands, cut out their tongue, their hair, scalped them. I did it. A lot of people were doing it and I just followed. I just lost all sense of direction.

Simpson personally killed about twenty-five people. Lieutenant "Rusty" Calley, the officer in charge on the day, shot over one hundred. Rape and killing went together, both part of a larger terror. Simpson said later:

Do you realize what it was like killing five hundred people in a matter of hours? It's just like the gas chambers—what Hitler did. You line up fifty people, women, old men, children, and just mow 'em down. And that's the way it was—from twenty-five to fifty to one hundred. Just killed. We just rounded them up, me and a couple of guys, just put the M-16 on automatic, and just mowed 'em down.[31]

That day Leonard Gonzalez was with another platoon 500 meters away. He saw the sergeant take a girl of about 16 into a house. When she came out, she had no pants. Gonzalez had watched two hours of killing, not knowing what to do. Now he begged the girl's mother, in English, to get her some pants. But other men moved in on the girl. According to the historians of the massacre, Michael Bilton and Kevin Sim:

Several men saw three GIs with the girl. One had penetrated her, one was having oral sex with her. . . .
   In a pile outside a hootch [Gonzalez] saw seven naked women aged between 18 and 35—their corpses dotted all over with tiny dark holes. The sight really sickened him. . . . Roschevitz was ex-

plaining how they came to be naked to a group of men standing nearby. He forced the women to undress with the intention of having sex with all of them. If they didn't strip, he told them, he was going to shoot them. He singled out one woman, telling her to "boom, boom" him. She became hysterical and the other women panicked, yelling, screaming, and begging for mercy. Roschevitz decided to let them have it. He fired several rounds [of buckshot] and killed them all.

Later, as they were leaving . . . Gonzalez saw the young girl who had been raped. Once more she was without her pants, walking alongside some of the men. Gonzalez thought the girl figured that if she stuck close to them, they probably wouldn't kill her.[32]

The My Lai massacre was ordered by the officers and covered up by them later, all the way to the generals. When it was finally exposed in the United States a year later, only one man, Lieutenant Calley, was convicted of any offense. He served four and a half months of his sentence before he was paroled.

The guerrillas tried to be different from the American army. Sometimes their artillery hit village houses and killed people. Then the local commander would visit the bereaved family, stand before their eyes and their rage, and say he was sorry.

The National Liberation Front said, in all its talks and leaflets, that in a free Vietnam men and women would be equal. Men and women are not equal in Vietnam today. But what the guerrillas meant, what women like Vo Thi Mo understood when they went into the tunnels, was that it would not be a carnival of rape and prostitution.

The landless peasants had gone to war for land. Now they were fighting for decency too. They had begun fighting for themselves. Now they were fighting for a vision of humanity.

In 1967, a 19-year-old woman guerrilla was captured and tortured. Then researchers from the American RAND Corporation talked to her. She told them that the leader of the Village Liberation Women's Committee had recruited her to the Front "against her family's wishes." She had joined because the Front members she met were "living embodiments of heroes of our legends; they are the men who stand up to fight the evil in order to protect the people."[33] And if she was released, she was going right back to join them.

5

PROTESTERS

Three weeks before the Marines arrived in Vietnam and the massive build-up of troops began, the American student movement against the war began too.

In March 1965, thirty teachers at the University of Michigan met. They had mostly supported Johnson against Goldwater, and they felt they were campaigning for peace and against war. Now Johnson was giving them war. They decided to stop normal classes for one day and make the university "a massive classroom against the war."[1] They got the support of fifty teachers on a petition, and the university administration became threatening. The teachers got cold feet and met again. One of them, a young anthropology instructor named Marshall Sahlins, suggested a compromise tactic—something called a teach-in. The teachers would meet with interested students in the evening after class.

Three thousand students showed up and debated the war until 8 A.M. the next day.

There were teach-ins at over one hundred universities that spring. At the University of California in Berkeley, another radical stronghold, the teach-in lasted thirty-six hours. Thirty thousand students attended in all, with up to 12,000 there at any one time.[2]

The Students for a Democratic Society called a national demonstration in Washington on 17 April 1965. SDS was by far the largest organization of the Left, with 100,000 members on college campuses. Many of them were beginning to think of themselves as revolutionaries. But everybody was astonished by the size of the protest in Washington—25,000 people.

That doesn't seem like a lot now. But then it was amazing. Doug Dowd was a professor at Cornell University and had been a radical right through the 1950s:

> I was teaching at Berkeley during the Korean War. Jesus Christ, you couldn't get anybody to say anything against the Korean War. . . . Everybody was scared shitless to identify themselves with being against that war because it meant, quite obviously that you must be a ranking member of the Communist Party. . . . [In 1965] it was as though spring had arrived after a very, very long fucking winter.[3]

On the weekend of 15 and 16 October, 25,000 people demonstrated in New York City, 15,000 in San Francisco, and a total of 100,000 across the country. In November, 30,000 demonstrated in New York City, and in March 1969 there were 50,000 in New York City.

What had changed America since the Korean War was the civil rights movement. It had legitimated dissent. Many people, white and black, had been in the movement. Most of the whites and some of the blacks had started out as liberal middle-class students. They expected America to deliver equality. In the South, they expected the federal government to protect them from the sheriffs and the Klan. What they found out was that the FBI followed them, but did not follow the Klan. Blacks were terrorized out of the vote in Mississippi, and civil rights activists organized a Mississippi Freedom Democratic Party delegation to the Democratic Party convention in 1964. The Democrats seated the old white racist Mississippi party instead.

Many former liberals had learned that American society was systematically racist and unfair, that the government and the Democratic Party lied to you, and that the only way to change society was to organize, sit in, and demonstrate.

When the Vietnam War came along, it was not that hard to see it was a racist war. Stokeley Carmichael of the Student Nonviolent Coordinating Committee (SNCC), the main radical civil rights organization, said in 1967 that the draft was "white people sending black people to make war on yellow people in order to defend the land they stole from red people."[4]

Muhammad Ali was the world heavyweight champion boxer, a black man, and a Muslim. He refused to be drafted, saying he had no quarrel with the Viet Cong (and implying he had a quarrel with somebody else). He was threatened with prison, stripped of his title, and banned from working at his trade. He stuck to his principles.[5]

Greg Payton was a marine in Vietnam in 1968:

> The first sergeant was telling me one day about gooks [Vietnamese] . . . gooks this, gooks that. That was the first time I [realized] . . . "A gook's the same as a nigger," I remember telling him; then he said, "You're a smart nigger." He said that to me, just me and him.[6]

Martin Luther King Jr. was privately opposed to the war. He was a pacifist, after all. But his whole political project was to unite the liberals, the labor leaders, and the civil rights leaders in a bloc that could change the Democratic Party. And his funding came from those same liberals and labor leaders. They told him again and again throughout 1966 that if he spoke out on Vietnam publicly, it would damage the civil rights cause and the real powers in Washington would never take him seriously. King was at first quiet. But he was haunted by a picture of napalmed children he had seen in *Ramparts* magazine. The black struggle was moving from the South to the North, and the ghetto uprisings there had not been nonviolent. Young black workers respected Dr. King— they cried when they listened to his speeches—but they were moving beyond him politically, beyond nonviolence and the Democratic Party. Under pressure from them and his conscience, King gave a speech at Riverside Church in New York on 4 April 1967:

As I have walked among the desperate, rejected and angry young men I have told them that Molotov cocktails and rifles would not solve problems. . . . They asked me if our own nation wasn't using massive doses of violence to solve its problems, to bring about the changes it wanted. Their questions hit home, and I knew that I couldn't ever again raise my voice against the violence of the oppressed in the ghettos without having first spoken clearly to the greatest purveyor of violence in the world today—my own government. . . .

[Blacks are dying] in extraordinarily high proportions relative to the rest of the population . . . to guarantee liberties in Southeast Asia which they had not found in Southwest Georgia and East Harlem.[7]

The White House liberals said King's speech made no difference. But it had a shattering effect on the generals. They did not say anything in public. But in 1965 almost a quarter of combat deaths were black. In 1966 it was 16 percent. In 1968, after King's speech, it was 13 percent, in 1970 down to 9 percent, and by 1972 only 7.6 percent. Year by year, the generals were pulling black men out of combat. Overall blacks accounted for 12.6 percent of combat deaths in Vietnam, roughly equivalent to their share of the population.[8]

White radicals too could see the war was racist. They believed that if the Vietnamese were white, they would not have suffered cruelty and killing on the same scale (in this, they may have been wrong).

Moreover, from 1964 the black movement was becoming nationalist and separatist. The black radical students were constantly told by King and the Southern Christian Leadership Conference that they couldn't go too far because the white people wouldn't like it. By this, they meant the white people in Washington and those leading the UAW. But the black radicals turned away from all white people. The Communist Party had been a serious organization among the working class, with black leaders and black activists on the ground. After the 1950s, that was gone. The radical tradition that did survive in the ghettoes was the black nationalism of Marcus Garvey and the Nation of Islam. The major movement people saw in the world in the 1950s and 1960s was the movement for colonial freedom. So when Stokeley Carmichael stuck his fist in the air on a march in Mississippi and said "Black Power," it made sense.

That left a lot of white radical students from the civil rights movement with nothing to do, and a feeling they ought to organize white people like themselves. Enter the war. And it was natural to organize teach-ins after civil rights sit-ins, natural to meet and demonstrate, and to march on Washington.

These radicals found a ready audience. The students they were talking to were patriotic liberals. But there was a contradiction in their heads. Many people now say that the media brainwashes everybody with constant lies. That is partly true—the media does lie, on a grand scale. But the reason it has to lie is that people are not brainwashed. Most of us have fundamentally different values from the values of the ruling class. The people in the White House knew that South Vietnam was a dictatorship and that mass murder was happening there—they had organized the coups and were counting the bodies. But the government and the media had to say that America was defending democracy and not committing mass murder, because most Americans were against dictatorship and mass murder. And the radicals could show pretty easily that South Vietnam was a dictatorship and the war was cruel.

In 1965, 15-year-old Craig McNamara had an argument with other boys at his prep school about the war. He phoned his father, the secretary for defense, and asked for more information so he could show those boys they were wrong. His father sent him more and more information, but it didn't make sense to Craig. By the time he got to Stanford University, Craig McNamara was marching against the war.[9]

Anti-war feeling was higher among workers than among the middle class. This is in part because people with more money tend to be more interested in preserving the status quo. They are also likely to have more education, which might lead one to presume they would be more anti-war—everyone is taught that the education system makes people more liberal and tolerant. This widely held view is not, however, supported by opinion polls in Europe and North America.

The historian Marilyn Young writes that

> from the start, opposition to the war was strongest among poorer and less educated Americans, those who would have to fight and die. In 1966, according to a survey conducted by the University of Michigan, only 27 percent of those with college educations favored withdrawal from Vietnam as opposed to 41 percent of those with an eighth grade education.[10]

In a referendum in 1966, 41 percent of people in Dearborn, a white working-class suburb of Detroit, voted for American withdrawal: "later research found [the vote] was inversely associated with citizens' socioeconomic level, with blue-collar workers more disapproving of the war than professionals and managers."[11]

Educated left-wing people often find this point difficult to grasp. As the historian Mike Marqusee says:

> Until 1970 blacks, low-income families and the over-sixties were the only sections of the population in which greater numbers favored withdrawal rather than escalation. Yet the notion that anti-war sentiment was largely a white middle-class student phenomenon remains widespread, among both critics and some (white, middle-class) veterans of the movement.[12]

The historian James Loewen, in his useful book on teaching American history, *Lies My Teacher Told Me*, reports an experiment he ran with students in courses at the University of Vermont. He asked them to guess the percentages of college graduates, high school graduates, and high school dropouts who supported American intervention in Vietnam in a poll late in the war. They quite consistently assumed that the more educated were more against the war.[13] So did students at Dartmouth College when my friend Nancy Lindisfarne ran the same experiment. The reason, in both cases, was that they "knew" middle-class professionals were more liberal than working-class rednecks.

The children of the working class were coming back from Vietnam. They told their friends and relatives that the only people worth respecting over there were the enemy. Those people came back to working-class neighborhoods and jobs long before the television turned against the war. Many of the middle-class people who changed their minds thought it was television that moved people. Those who were close to somebody who went felt differently.

And even if, in the end, middle-class young men did not have to go to Vietnam, they thought they would have to. They were afraid, but, more importantly, they didn't want to be cruel. Most of them were headed for lives as teachers or social workers, or in minor office jobs. In America then and now, about half of young people start college and about a quarter finish. That quarter have an easier life, but they aren't the ruling class. They mostly still have to make a living.

On 15 April 1967, 300,000 people marched against the war in New York. Fred Halstead, a leader of the anti-war movement and an old socialist, exulted, "It was a hugey."[14]

On 20 October, the demonstrators started coming to Washington. They were going to march to the Pentagon. The Yippies, a loose network of young, white, hippie, dope-smoking anarchists, announced they were going to levitate the Pentagon.

The ruling class was scared. That night it filled the Pentagon with troops, "rifles, tear gas machines, helmets . . . trucks and jeeps of the First Army." At the White House, First Lady Lady Bird Johnson told her diary, there was "much talk of tomorrow" at dinner: "There is a ripple of grim excitement in the air, almost a feeling of being under siege."[15] The next day 150,000 demonstrators marched through Washington, with signs saying both "Negotiate" and "Where is Oswald when we need him?" They listened to speeches and marched on the Pentagon. There they met a wall of troops. A demonstrator went down the line of soldiers, putting a flower in each rifle barrel. There was pushing and hitting as the demonstrators tried to break through the nervous soldiers and arrests were made.

On the roof of the Pentagon, generals watched and "army sharpshooters crouched uneasily, weapons in hand." The ruling class watched from the windows. Richard Helms was the head of the CIA. He later told the historian Tom Wells, "I don't think there was any doubt that they took a look at that mob around the Pentagon and nobody liked the look of that at all. And I certainly least of all. I'd had experiences with mobs all over the world and I didn't like the look or sound of this one bit." Secretary of the Army Stanley Resor told Wells, "It was a very impressive thing, thirty-five thousand people right there under your nose." Paul Nitze was the official in charge of organizing the defense of the Pentagon that day. Three of his four children were in the crowd.[16]

Many of the warlords had at least one child who turned against the war. It hurt them. Dean Rusk's son Richard, "caught between love for my father and the growing horror of Vietnam," had a nervous breakdown. In October 1969, staffer William Watts was working in the White House on a speech for President Nixon "announcing a major escalation of the war." He took a break from work to walk on the White House lawn and went over to the gate to get a better look at the protesters outside, part of a nationwide moratorium. He saw his wife and children walk by, "each holding a candle." He felt like throwing up: "It was very painful to be on the other side of the fence."[17]

Demonstrations worked. It wasn't just the family pain. After all, almost all those men lived with the pain rather than hurt their careers. It was the experience of having a mass of people against you, and sudden vulnerability at home, in America. Richard Helms had certainly seen angrier mobs when he worked for the

CIA—the people outside the Pentagon were nonviolent. But it was far beyond anything Helms could have imagined happening in America.

In late 1966, Pentagon whiz kids explained to Lyndon Johnson that they could save lives by carpet-bombing Hanoi and the port of Haiphong, thus ending the war sooner than otherwise. They had fed numbers into their computers and proved that dropping the atom bombs on Hiroshima and Nagasaki in 1945 had saved 750,000 lives. Johnson said to them, "I have one more problem for your computer—will you feed into it how long it will take five hundred thousand angry Americans to climb the White House wall out there and lynch their President if he does something like that?"[18]

Massive demonstrations legitimated dissent about the war. Every big demonstration sends home people who argue for the cause of the demonstration and inclines people to listen to them. By November 1970, a majority in the opinion polls thought the Vietnam War was a mistake. Only 35 percent approved of the president's "handling of the war." And MacGeorge Bundy wrote in a memo to Johnson, "Public discontent with the war is now wide and deep."[19]

And then came the Tet Offensive, in January 1968. As we have seen, Tet was a terrible defeat for the Viet Cong. But in the United States, and across the world, what people saw on their televisions was that the guerrillas were far stronger, and had far more support in Vietnam, than they had been led to believe. While the guerrillas were dying after Tet, the American ruling class was deciding it had to wind down the war. McNamara, the secretary of defense, realized his side was losing the war in 1967. He said so, directly to President Johnson and indirectly to Congress, and was kicked upstairs to run the World Bank.

His replacement at the Department of Defense, Clark Clifford, was confronted with Tet and a request from General Westmoreland in Vietnam for 206,000 more troops, to bring the total to

700,000. Clifford was a longtime member of the ruling class. The way he put that to his colleagues in March 1968 was:

> I make it a practice to keep in touch with friends in business and law across the land. I ask them their views about various matters. Until a few months ago, they were generally supporting of the war. They were a little disturbed about the overheating of the economy and the flight of gold, but they assumed that these things would be brought under control, and in any event they thought it was important to stop the communists in Vietnam. Now all that has changed . . . the idea of getting deeper into the bog strikes them as mad. They want to see us get out of it. These are leaders of opinions in their Communities. . . . It would be very difficult— I believe it would be impossible—for the president to maintain public support without the support of those men.[20]

This is the authentic voice of the ruling class: the light touch, the total assurance.

The "overheating of the economy and the flight of gold" were real worries. The war was costing the government a lot, and that produced a boom in America—full production and full employment. But because the war was so unpopular, it was impossible for Congress to raise taxes to pay for it. Without such taxes, and with full employment, Americans were using their extra income to buy goods from abroad and the American government was in effect borrowing from abroad. Both of these things made the American balance of payments worse. The dollar was the world's basic currency—since World War Two, other countries had traded internationally in dollars—and the dollar was linked to the price of gold. By 1967, with America borrowing more money than it was lending and buying more goods than it was selling, banks and traders in other countries were trading their dollars in for American gold reserves. Those reserves were shrinking, and the U.S.

government was approaching the point where the dollar could no longer be tied to gold.

This was a problem, but only because the war was unpopular and taxes couldn't be raised. There were other major problems. American economic dominance was steadily eroded as other economies grew faster, and all major industrial economies found that the rate of profit was falling after about 1966. But neither of these problems was caused by the Vietnam War, nor were they solved by ending the war. And when the dollar did eventually come off the gold standard under President Nixon, it still remained the world's major reserve currency.

This is why the economy and the gold standard were important worries for American business in 1967, but not decisive ones. What was decisive was Tet.

But if Clark Clifford and the ruling class had turned against the war, Lyndon Johnson still wanted to win it.

In 1968, which was an election year, Senator Eugene McCarthy ran against Johnson as a peace candidate in the first Democratic primary in conservative rock-ribbed New Hampshire. Johnson won, but only by 230 votes. Bobby Kennedy, JFK's brother, was waiting in the wings. Bobby had worked for Senator Joe Mc-Carthy (of "McCarthyism"), had been an early supporter of the Vietnam War, and favored sending the troops in 1965. But unhappy with Johnson for many reasons, Bobby had turned against the war in 1967. After the New Hampshire primary, he saw Johnson could be beaten and threw himself into the race for president. He was likely to win the Democratic nomination.

Clark Clifford was, he said later, "more conscious each day of domestic unrest in our own country." Clifford called in the "Wise Men"—the State Department's senior advisory group.

The Wise Men spoke for the ruling class. They "included men with close links to the world of finance, corporate law and big business,"[21] a former chairman of the Joint Chiefs of Staff, and a former secretary of defense. Dean Acheson, the liberal architect of the Cold War as Truman's secretary of state, chaired the Wise Men. The Wise Men had met with Johnson back in 1965, when he was balking at sending troops to Vietnam. Then they told him he had to intervene for American power in the world. In 1967 they had met again and approved the war. Now they were unanimous for peace, and all had the same reason. As one said, "The divisiveness in the country was showing with such acuteness that it was threatening to tear the United States apart."[22]

Dean Acheson went to that meeting with an editorial from the *Winston-Salem Journal* in his pocket. It said that because of the war Americans had "lost sight of our national priorities, [and] the most crucial priority of all [is] of course, the home front."

"I could have written it myself," Acheson said.[23]

For the American ruling class, when push comes to shove, its central priority is control of America. And this was priority time.

Chicago

Lyndon Johnson gave in to the Wise Men. He refused General Westmoreland's request for 206,000 more troops in Vietnam, and announced on television that he would not run for a second term as president.

Four days later, Martin Luther King was murdered in Memphis, Tennessee. Most black people assumed that the assassin had been hired by white power in some form, by the FBI, white businessmen, or the Ku Klux Klan. They did not expect a proper investigation of this death (and there has never been one).

King had carried his people's hopes. After his death, one black radical said to me, "You know, I don't agree with Doctor King, you have to go further, but every time I listen to his speeches I cry." Many felt that way. His murder had proved that his politics of nonviolence and negotiation did not work. But his people honored him that weekend in the only way they could, in rage and sorrow, fire and riot. All over the country, the black inner cities went up in flames—there were riots in more than one hundred cities. Now the ruling class faced an anti-war movement and an enraged black movement.

But for the moment, most of the war protesters assumed peace would come quickly. America had stopped bombing North Vietnam. Washington was talking to Hanoi. Bobby Kennedy was the peace candidate, and he was winning in the primaries. Then in June, a Palestinian worker, a refugee in Los Angeles, shot Kennedy dead because Kennedy was a Cold Warrior who supported Israel. Now Eugene McCarthy was the anti-war candidate again, and the students and young liberals came back to him.

The nomination was to be decided at the Democratic Party convention in August in Chicago. The Yippies and some of the radicals in SDS called for a week of demonstrations outside the convention. Only a few thousand demonstrators showed up. This was partly because Mayor Richard J. Daley and his Chicago police force had made it clear that the demonstrators would be met with force, issuing heavy warnings and shooting dead a Native American demonstrator the day before the convention. The liberal wing of the peace movement had also discouraged people from going to Chicago, saying it would make the Democratic Party look bad. But the main reason there were so few demonstrators was that most peace protesters now assumed the war would end soon.

The people had voted for peace in the primaries. The convention nominated Hubert Humphrey, Johnson's vice president, a loyal supporter of the war. The few thousand demonstrators in Chicago broke through the police cordons and made it to Michigan Avenue, outside the convention and the delegates' hotel. The police gassed and beat them. The floor of the convention smelled of gas, and Senator Abraham Ribicoff of Connecticut told the convention on live television that the police were using "Gestapo tactics on the streets of Chicago."[24] Outside, the National Guard trucks patrolled the streets, guns ready. The demonstrators chanted, "The whole world is watching! The whole world is watching!" And it was.

1968 was becoming the "Year of '68." In America there were the riots for Martin Luther King and the Chicago demonstration. A mass student movement in Mexico was only broken when hundreds were gunned down in Mexico City. In May, student demonstrations in France led to the largest general strike in world history. In Czechoslovakia a reforming wing of the ruling Communists tried to introduce "socialism with a human face." In August, Russian tanks rolled into Prague, and students and workers crowded around the tanks, protesting. In Pakistan, student demonstrations and workers' strikes in Karachi brought down the military dictatorship. In Italy, the two red years of strikes began. In Germany, Poland, Argentina, Japan, Thailand, Sri Lanka, Afghanistan, Iran, Turkey, Yugoslavia, Bolivia, and Chile, students demonstrated, workers went on strike, and revolution was in the air.[25]

And it had all started with Tet, with a world seeing that America, the greatest power on earth, could be defeated.

The American ruling class faced a contradiction. It wanted out of Vietnam. But it did not want the consequences of losing, of public humiliation in the atmosphere of 1968. If Tet had begun all those struggles, TV pictures of the American troops leaving and the guerrillas marching joyously into Saigon would give heart to larger struggles inside America and all over the world.

So in 1968, the American government began peace negotiations in Paris with North Vietnam and the National Liberation Front. It stopped bombing North Vietnam. But it bombed South Vietnam, Laos, and Cambodia for seven more years, and American troops stayed in South Vietnam for five more years.

Richard Nixon, the Republican candidate for president, campaigned in 1968 by saying he had a secret plan to end the war. Hubert Humphrey, the Democratic candidate, knew he could win the election if he promised to end the war. Loyal to Johnson and the ruling class, Humphrey supported the war, and Nixon won the election. Voters preferred a man with a secret plan to end the war to one with a public plan to continue it. Once Nixon was elected, he faced the same problem as Johnson. Nixon had

been a lifelong anti-Communist. He explained his plan to his aide
Bob Haldeman:

> I call it the madman theory, Bob. . . . I want the North Vietnamese
> to believe I've reached the point where I might do anything to
> stop the war. We'll just slip the word to them that, "for God's
> sake, you know Nixon is obsessed about Communists. We can't
> restrain him when he's angry—and he has his hand on the nuclear
> button,"—and Ho Chi Minh himself will be in Paris in two days
> begging for peace.[26]

Nixon was trying to end the war without losing it. The White
House began planning Operation Duck Hook—saturation bomb-
ing of Cambodia and North Vietnam, invasions of Cambodia and
Laos, and nuclear bombing of North Vietnam if necessary.

Duck Hook was meant to be secret from the American people
but a clear threat to the North Vietnamese leadership. In 1969
most Americans waited for Nixon to make peace. When they
realized he would not, and that the Paris peace talks were hopelessly stuck in arguments about the shape of the negotiating table,
the protesters returned.

In November 1969, 500,000 people demonstrated in Washington. It was bigger than Martin Luther King's civil rights March
on Washington in 1963, and was the biggest demonstration in
American history. For thirty hours, a single file of people marched
from the Arlington National Cemetery, each one carrying a sign
with the name of a destroyed Vietnamese village or an American
who had died in Vietnam. Empty buses ringed the White House,
bumper to bumper, with armed troops behind them as half a
million demonstrators passed. The radicals demonstrated outside
the Justice Department and the police in gas masks waded in,
beating people, filling the air with gas. I was among the protesters,
and the gas made me heave so hard I projectile vomited. Attorney
General John Mitchell watched from the window and felt it was

like the Russian Revolution.[27] It wasn't. But it was more than
Mitchell or I had ever seen.

Nixon wanted to quiet the protesters but not lose the war. On
20 April 1969 he announced he would withdraw 150,000 troops
from Vietnam in the coming year. But at the same time Duck
Hook continued. Ten days later Nixon invaded Cambodia. The
Vietnam War had already engulfed all of Indochina. In both Cambodia and Laos, Communist guerrillas fought the governments,
and American planes supported the governments by bombing the
people. The Viet Cong used areas of Cambodia near the Vietnamese border as a refuge, and North Vietnamese troops and supplies came down a dirt road, the Ho Chi Minh Trail, in Laos.
The king of Cambodia, Sihanouk, had tried to keep his country
out of the war, but quietly allowed secret American bombing of
the Viet Cong and Khmer Rouge (Red Cambodians) on his land.
This was not enough for the American government, which sponsored a coup by Sihanouk's defense minister, Lon Nol. The coup
was not popular with Cambodians. The Khmer Rouge recruited
and American bombing in Cambodia increased. Nixon's invasion
of Cambodia was a message to Hanoi, but it was also an attempt
to shore up Lon Nol.

Nixon, announcing the invasion of Cambodia on television,
said, "If, when the chips are down, the world's most powerful nation, the United States of America, acts like a pitiful helpless giant,
the forces of totalitarian anarchy will threaten free nations and free
institutions throughout the world."[28] These words have been
treated as a joke. But Nixon meant them, and they expressed what
half the ruling class were feeling. If they lost in Vietnam, free
enterprise would be threatened by Communism and "anarchy"—
by which Nixon meant democracy from below.

Former Ambassador to Indonesia Marshall Green came home
from work after Nixon's speech on Cambodia. Green was in
charge of the Far Eastern desk at the State Department, and by
now a dove on Vietnam:

I came back to my house, and my son came into the room where I was talking to my wife. He denounced the position that the President had taken, and he said, "I don't want to see you again." And he left. And we didn't see him again for weeks. . . . You were driven to brink of suicide, you really were.[29]

Student strikes and occupations swept the colleges. I was living in Knoxville and was one of about fifty white radicals, hippies, and dopers who had been holding a small anti-war movement together at the University of Tennessee. When Nixon announced the invasion, we called a demonstration for the next evening, expecting a few hundred. The university plaza filled and overfilled, and there were thousands and thousands there. The men all seemed to have short hair, the women perms. The fraternities and sororities were there. Nixon had told us the "silent majority" supported him. But he had promised peace and made war, and now the silent majority were with us.

Kent State University in Ohio was in a conservative area too. Two days after Nixon announced the invasion of Cambodia, on Saturday night, a crowd of 2,000 set fire to the Reserve Officers Training Corps building on campus. The governor sent in the National Guard. On Monday at noon, there was a rally of 1,000 on campus. A few students threw rocks at the National Guard. The historian Kenneth Heineman takes up the story:

The soldiers assembled, conferred among themselves, and marched away from the students and towards Blanket Hill. Arriving at the top of the hill near the pagoda, they turned and fired into the crowd. In thirteen seconds the Guardsmen expended sixty-one rounds. A few hundred feet away in the parking lot, Alison Krause fell mortally wounded. Danfora took a bullet in the wrist and Grace, shot in the foot, writhed in agony. Loaded onto an ambulance, Grace watched as medical attendants pulled a blanket over Sandy Scheuer's head. . . . A young female runaway knelt beside Miller and, arms outstretched, wept.

Stunned silence. Then hysterical crying. Marilyn Hammond frantically searched for her husband and, finding him unharmed, fainted. An antiwar student and Vietnam veteran, with blood all about him, stared into the distance. The students spontaneously sat down on the ground. When the Guard commander ordered them to move or be fired on again, freshman Mim Jackson stoically awaited death.[30]

Glenn Frank, a conservative geology professor and World War Two veteran, had tried to defend the ROTC building from the students on Friday night. Now he saw the students shot, and about to be shot again:

Glenn Frank pleaded with the officer to desist, but was curtly dismissed. With tears welling in his eyes and voice cracking, he urged students to leave the Commons: "They're going to shoot us again. We're going to be slaughtered. They've got guns and the guns are at our throats." Slowly, the students arose and dispersed. A colleague then helped the trembling professor home.[31]

In those few minutes Professor Frank had joined the protesters in his heart, saying "they" and "we." Alison Krause, 19, Jeffrey Miller, 20, Susan Scheur, 20, and William Schroeder, 19, were dead. Schroeder was attending college on a Reserve Officers Training Corps scholarship.[32]

It was nothing, really, four people dead, compared to what was happening to the Vietnamese. Nothing even compared to what was happening to the American troops over there. Hardly anything compared to the blacks killed by police in the riots in Los Angeles and Detroit. But it was new. Nixon and the ruling class were raising the stakes. And at Kent State they had been protesting Cambodia, Vietnam, all that killing. Sometimes political killings are just atrocities, but sometimes they happen at moments when mass feelings are ready to change history. Roughly 4,350,000[33] students marched and protested at 1,350 colleges, and 536 colleges went on all-out strike. In California the state governor, Ronald Reagan, closed the whole state university system. The American Federation of State, County and Municipal Employees came out against the war.

On a week's notice, 150,000 people demonstrated in Washington. "Those few days after Kent State were among the darkest of my presidency," Richard Nixon wrote later. Henry Kissinger was effectively in charge of foreign policy. He wrote of those days:

> It was a time of extraordinary stress. Washington took on the character of a besieged city. . . . The very fabric of government was falling apart. The Executive Branch was shell-shocked. . . . Exhaustion was the hallmark of us all. I had to move from my apartment ringed by protesters into the basement of the White House to get some sleep. . . . [Nixon], deeply wounded by the hatred of the protesters . . . reached a point of exhaustion that caused his advisers deep concern . . . [and he seemed to be] on the edge of a nervous breakdown.[34]

Duck Hook was finished. Nixon announced that all American troops would be out of Cambodia by the end of June. The protests had worked.

But all the way through the war, many of the demonstrators did not think that their protests worked. Most of these were liberals who expected the system to work. They had been raised in the belief that America was a democracy where the government responded to the wishes of the people.

Instead, the ruling class looked out the windows of the White House at the protests, and it judged what it could get away with and when it would have to bow to the popular will. Even when it gave ground to the protesters and began to negotiate, it insisted that it was not influenced by the protesters.

The liberal protesters had expected some satisfaction, some truth, not an endless class struggle. Yet the war was still going on, with all the killing. So many of them switched from feeling that you could reform a basically decent system to feeling that you couldn't change anything at all.

They saw two alternatives—either the system was responsive to people or it was against them. They had no understanding of class struggle—that the people who run the system are always opposed to the majority of the people, but can be forced into doing things if that majority pushes them hard enough. Many of them felt you could not change the majority of Americans. This came from a contempt for the working class. Abbie Hoffman, the Yippie leader, later put it this way, talking of Archie Bunker, a right-wing working-class character on TV:

> We deliberately chose to go for the children of the Bunkers because we could not get the Bunkers. It was kind of hard to appeal to . . . that class of Americans because many of them were beating us up and sending us to jail. . . . Most Americans don't give a shit, period. . . . I am convinced . . . that the dumping of tea in the Boston harbor alienated the majority of Americans at the time.[35]

At a small student rally in Knoxville in 1969, a refugee from the Hungarian workers' uprising in 1956 got up to speak. He suggested we go out to the factories at Oak Ridge and leaflet the workers against the war. We looked at him as if he were mad. The idea of leafleting scared us. We were sure, quite wrongly, that workers supported the war. When he suggested that we shop with small shopkeepers to support the little man, that was more on our wavelength.

But of course many students did not have contempt for workers. Many came from working-class homes, many were working their way through college, and there were always individual workers on the demonstrations. The problem was political. Anti-Communism had broken socialism in the unionized working class. Millions of people were moving towards revolution in their heads, thinking, "I am a revolutionary." But they did not think that meant activity in the unions, or that American workers could change the world. This was true of workers too.

For instance, in the days after Kent State, I was a teacher at Knoxville College, a black college across town from the mostly white University of Tennessee. The students at Knoxville College came from working-class homes—the black upper middle class did not send their children to places like Knoxville College. Many of our students worked in the car plants in Detroit in the summer to pay their tuition. If they were lucky and they graduated, they hoped for jobs as local organizers for the Girl Scouts, parole officers in Georgia, or cabin crew for an airline. They were workers.

After the shootings at Kent State, they held back for a few days, saying, "It's a white people's thing—we don't want to get involved," but feeling inside they wanted to act. Finally there was a meeting in the gym. Out of about 810 students at the college, 800 came to the meeting. The student body president from the mostly white University of Tennessee came to speak. He was a black Vietnam veteran, which says something about how Tennessee was changing. He urged the Knoxville College students to strike over Kent State. They voted 800 to zero to strike.

Next morning, 800 were on picket lines blocking every road into the college. They let the teachers cross on condition that we go to a meeting of our professional association, the American Association of University Professors, and vote on joining the strike. We voted two to one to strike. The governing board of the college met, twelve white Methodist ministers, and voted twelve to zero to join the strike.

They did so because everybody knew the students had guns in the dormitories. If the police or the National Guard were called onto campus, they would use those guns, and then the police or the Guard would slaughter us. (A week later, the police opened fire on an unarmed crowd at Jackson, a black college in Mississippi, killing Philip Gibbs, 21, and James Earl Green, 17, a student at Jim Hill High School.[36] Even after Kent State, they could do that to black people.)

Our strike was far more militant and far more united than that of the white students across town, because the students at Knoxville College were working-class, black, far more oppressed, and far more angry about everything. But there was one weakness. The same picket lines that stopped the teachers allowed the catering workers through so they could cook and serve the students' meals. The legacy of the anti-Communist crusade was that working-class black students on strike did not even think of mobilizing the working class (nor did I).

In an earlier chapter, I quoted a firefighter whose son Ralph died in Vietnam. His wife, Ralph's mother, spoke to an interviewer in 1970:

> I think my husband and I can't help but thinking that our son gave his life for nothing, nothing at all. . . . I told him I thought [the protesters] want the war to end, so no more Ralphs will die, but he says no, they never stop and think about Ralph and his kind of people, and I'm inclined to agree. They say they do, but I listen to them, I watch them; since Ralph died I listen and watch as carefully as I can. Their hearts are with other people, not their own American people, the ordinary kind of person in this country. I know when someone is worrying about me and my children, and when he says he is, but he's really elsewhere with his sympathy. Those people, a lot of them are rich women from the suburbs, the rich suburbs. Those kids, they are in college. . . . They don't come out here and try to talk to us. . . . I'm against this war too— the way a mother is, whose sons are in the army, who has lost a son fighting in it. The world hears those demonstrators making a noise. The world doesn't hear me, and it doesn't hear a single person I know.[37]

She was wrong in one way. There were many like her in the antiwar movement. But she was basically right: the voices of people like her were not heard.

But without the protesters, without all their class contempt or class confusion, without all their impatience and craziness and ego-tripping leaders and bullshit and faction fights—without all that mess and all that energy, she would have known that her son died for nothing and been unable to say it out loud.

The student revolt did not stop the war. But it limited the killing. Very few of us tried to organize workers. That was the legacy of anti-Communism. But we did make possible a working-class revolt against the war in the armed services. That is the subject of the next chapter.

6

THE GIs' REVOLT

Ron Kovic's father was a checker at an A&P supermarket on Long Island in New York state. He worked hard, long hours to take care of his family. The spring before Kovic graduated from high school, his father made him take his first job, stacking shelves in a supermarket. But:

> I didn't want to be like my Dad, coming home from the A&P every night. He was a strong man, a good man, but it made him so tired, it took all the energy out of him. I didn't want to be like that, working in the stinking A&P, six days a week, twelve hours a day. I wanted to be somebody.[1]

Ron Kovic joined the Marines out of high school and went to Vietnam. He made sergeant. American soldiers served one-year tours in Vietnam, counting the days, and very few volunteered for a second year. Kovic was one of the few. He was wounded the second time and was paralyzed from the waist down. Back in America he did physical therapy, tried hard, and learned to live in a wheelchair. Later he wrote a book about it—*Born on the Fourth of July.*

In the book, Kovic tells how he heard about a place for paralyzed American veterans in Guadalajara, Mexico, called the Village in the Sun. He went there and it was wonderful. Everybody else was in a wheelchair too. He didn't have to apologize for other people's discomfort there. He could go to prostitutes who were mostly polite and didn't show pity. He felt very lonely when one of them told him she had a child and was only doing this for the money. But it was good to play with another person's body, and good to have a woman hold him.

One night he went out with another Vietnam veteran named Charlie. They drank a lot and smoked some weed:

> In the last whorehouse [we] went to Charlie got in a wild fight with one of the whores. He punched her in the face because she laughed at him when he pulled down his pants and told her he couldn't feel his penis anymore. He was crazy drunk and kept yelling and screaming, swinging his arms and his fists at the crowd. . . . "That goddamn fucking slut! I'm going to kill that whore for ever laughing at me. That bitch thinks it's funny I can't move my dick. Fuck you. Fuck all of you goddamn motherfuckers! They made me kill babies! They made me kill babies!" Charlie screamed over and over again.[2]

The owner of the brothel was furious, threatening Kovic and Charlie. Kovic was scared. But he couldn't move, because all he could think was that Charlie was saying things he'd been feeling for a long time.

Kovic thought a lot about one particular night in Vietnam. His unit had been sent out on patrol. They were afraid, and they thought they saw something, maybe the enemy, in a hut. Somebody opened fire, and then they were all firing madly. They stopped firing, and there was screaming from the hut. Sergeant Kovic and five men went to see what was in the hut.

Writing about it, Kovic referred to himself as "he":

> Molina turned the beam of his flashlight into the hut. "Oh, God," he said. "Oh Jesus Christ." He started to cry. "We just shot up a bunch of kids."
>
> The floor of the small hut was covered with them, screaming and thrashing their arms back and forth, lying in pools of blood,

crying wildly, screaming again and again. They were shot in the face, in the chest, in the legs, moaning and crying.

He could hear the lieutenant shouting at them, wanting to know how many they had killed. . . . A small boy . . . was still alive, although he had been shot many times. He was crying softly, lying in a large pool of blood. His small foot had been shot almost completely off and seemed to be hanging by a thread. . . . He heard a small girl moaning now. She was shot through the stomach and bleeding out of the rear end. . . .

The marines stared, stunned, and then Kovic took out his medical kit and started trying to bandage the spurting wounds. The other men helped him or stood around:

The lieutenant had just come up with the others. "Help me," he [Kovic] screamed, "Somebody help!" "Well, goddamn it sergeant! What's the matter? How many did we kill?" "They're children," he screamed at the lieutenant. . . .

"Forgive us for what we've done!" he heard Molina cry.

"Get up," screamed the lieutenant. "What do you think this is? I'm ordering you all to get up."

Some of the men began slowly crawling over the bodies, grabbing for the bandages that were still left. By now some of the villagers had gathered outside the hut. He could hear them shouting angrily. . . .

The marines made the lieutenant call an evacuation helicopter to take the children to hospital:

The men in the hut were just sitting there crying. They could not move, and they could not listen to the lieutenant's orders. . . .

"You men! You men have got to start listening to me. You gotta stop crying like babies and start acting like marines!" The lieutenant . . . was shoving the men, pleading with them to move.

"You're men, not babies. Don't you people understand—they got in the goddamn way!"

When the medical chopper came, he picked up the little boy. . . . His foot came off and [Kovic] grabbed it quickly and bandaged it against the bottom stump of the boy's leg. He held him looking into his frightened eyes and carried him up to the open door of the helicopter.[3]

Looking back on that night, and other days, Kovic began to realize he had been used.

What made that clear was that he was still being used. He'd been born on the Fourth of July (Independence Day), and the American Legion put him up on the platform for the local Fourth of July parade, a disabled veteran in his wheelchair, a symbol. Then they wouldn't let him speak from the platform.

He started college, did his exercises, and while he was doing them he heard his leg break (he couldn't feel it). He went back to the Veterans Administration Hospital in the Bronx. He complained about the conditions there—there weren't enough staff and they didn't care. They couldn't afford to care, given the scale of suffering they were seeing. The American army in Vietnam had an emergency medical evacuation program that worked as none ever had before. In any previous war 200,000 men would have died, not 58,000. But that medicine meant that many men were permanently wounded, and many of them were in the Veterans Hospital in the Bronx.

The American government doesn't spend enough money on its Veterans Hospitals. Doctors know it's not the elite end of medicine. Kovic kept screaming at the staff to clean up the vomit on the floor. He screamed for a bath: "I asked to be treated like a human being." They put him in an isolation room.

His broken leg swelled up and the doctor suggested cutting it off. Kovic refused, so they operated instead. Afterwards they hooked tubes up to him in intensive care, pumping fluid into the wound and waste out of it, keeping the wound healthy. He wasn't going to lose his leg.

The pump stopped. The aide couldn't make it work. He got a doctor who explained that the pump was old and that they probably couldn't make it work. Kovic told them to get another pump. The doctor said the hospital didn't have another pump. Kovic couldn't believe it—a giant hospital in the Bronx with one pump. The doctor explained it was because of the war—all the money was going on the war, not the hospital. He was sorry, it wasn't fair, but it looked like Kovic was going to lose his leg.

A little more than an hour later, the pump started working again, all by itself, for no reason anybody could see. Kovic didn't lose his leg. When he got out of the hospital, he went back to college. Then Nixon invaded Cambodia and four students were shot at Kent State. There was a demonstration at Kovic's college. Back in Vietnam, Kovic had always hated hippie protesters. Now he joined the protest. He was shy, maybe because of the politics, maybe because of his wheelchair, probably both. He sat in his car on the edge of the protest all day and didn't get out, but he honked his horn in support.

Three things got Kovic to that protest. The first was the war, what he'd seen and done in Vietnam. The second was the anti-war movement. The third thing was class. He went into the Marines because of what his family was, what his father did, and the future he faced. Class was there in Vietnam too. It was why the lieutenant was the one trying to make them stop crying in the hut, telling them it didn't matter, trying to get them moving. That was class struggle, the lieutenant's struggle for his class and its orders. And the marines making the lieutenant call a medical helicopter for the children, that was their class struggle. Then, when Kovic came home, class was still there. It's why the hospital was the way it was. In America, people like him didn't matter. He was there in his car honking his horn because he had put the war and class together in his mind.

After that, he went down to the mass protest in Washington. Later he joined the Vietnam Veterans Against the War.[4] They were an organization of men like him, part of the peace movement. They went on the demonstrations with the rest, but they marched together and they held their own protests. From 1970 they were a growing part of the movement. In April 1971, a few days before the national demonstration in Washington, they set up a peace camp on the Mall. They wore fatigues and ran it like an army camp. The government told them they had to leave or they would be forcibly evicted. A delegation from the troops who would have to evict them visited the camp and promised the veterans they would refuse to do any such thing. The veterans refused to move. The government was bluffing. It knew the political cost of television pictures of clearing the veterans' camp, the screaming and the scuffling and some of the veterans disabled. At the last minute, it let the veterans stay.

Roughly 1,200 veterans marched to the capital, dressed in old uniforms and combat fatigues, to return their medals to their congressmen. They found a fence had been put up in front of the steps of Congress to stop them. The police guarded the fence. One by one, the veterans stepped forward and threw their medals over the fence at the Congress. Each man was supposed to say something as he stepped up:

"My name is Peter Branagan. I got a purple heart and I hope I get another one fighting these mother-fuckers."

"I hope that time will forgive me and my brothers for what we did."

"Second Battalion, First Marines—power to the people."

Ron Ferizzi from Philadelphia: "My wife is divorcing me for returning these medals. She wants me to keep them so my little sons can be proud of me. But three of my best friends died so I could get that medal."

Another man, pointing at the steps of Congress: "We're not going to fight anymore, but if we have to fight again it will be to take those steps."[5]

It went on for three hours. Some men had a lot of medals to throw because their friends who couldn't make it had given them theirs to return too.

The next month, May 1971, the Vietnam Veterans Against the War in Massachusetts had a weekend protest to mark Memorial Day. They planned to march from Concord to Boston in honor of Paul Revere, who rode from Boston to Concord on the night of 18 April 1775 to warn the dissident American colonists that the British troops were coming to take away their arms. On the first night of the protest, 500 veterans camped by the Old North Bridge in Concord, where the revolution had started when the colonists opened fire on the British the morning after Revere's ride. The officials of the town of Concord refused permission for the camp and threatened to clear it. Phone calls and a local radio station mobilized supporters. There were 1,000 veterans and supporters when the police came late that night, and they arrested 485 people. Many of the 485 gave the police only their name, Social Security number, and date of birth—19 April 1775.[6]

THE MOVEMENT IN THE ARMED FORCES

The Vietnam Veterans Against the War were important for far more than their numbers. They gave the rest of the peace movement a feeling of legitimacy, that they weren't against "our boys in Vietnam" but *for* them. But the VVAW was much smaller than the far bigger movement inside the armed forces.

That movement largely began with a few radicals who understood the importance of organizing in the army. A small group of Trotskyists, for instance, were important to *Vietnam GI*, a paper produced in Chicago with a print run of 15,000 and a mailing list of 3,000 in Vietnam.[7] The largest Trotskyist organization, the Socialist Workers Party, did systematic work around the bases from 1966 on. They also had a policy of not refusing the draft. They based this policy on the experience of the Russian Bolsheviks in World War One. Because the Bolsheviks were part of the working class, they had organized inside the army against the war, over-turned the officers, and taken their country out of the war. The SWP understood that was what had to be done in Vietnam too.

The SWP was a small organization, and the army began refus-ing to draft its members or keep them in the forces. But many went in and did good work. Joe Miles, for instance, was drafted to Fort Jackson in 1969 and started the movement there by "in-viting fellow black soldiers to listen to taped speeches by Malcolm X and discuss the need for GI organization." Miles was transferred to Fort Bragg, North Carolina, at three hours' notice, but the men he left behind founded GIs United Against the War. They got more than 300 signatures on a petition asking the base com-mander to allow them to hold a meeting on the base to discuss the war. He refused, so they got a lawyer and eight of them sued the army for denying their freedom of speech.

Meanwhile, at Fort Bragg, Miles had just recruited a second chapter of GIs United Against the War, most of them Vietnam veterans. They put out a newspaper, *Bragg Briefs*. This time the army transferred Miles to Fort Richardson, Alaska, where he formed a third chapter of GIs United, and they put out another paper, *Anchorage Troop*.[8]

But the organized socialist Left was simply not that big. Most of the early organizing was started by radicals not in any party, who simply set up coffeehouses in small cities near army bases. They provided coffee, a quiet and dignified atmosphere, and anti-war talk. A lot of GIs came and talked, and then the coffeehouse people and the GIs started to organize and put out an anti-war newspaper for the local base.

Once the coffeehouses had set the example and the movement got going, servicemen and women on a lot of other bases founded organizations of their own and put out their own papers. There were about 300 such newspapers in the armed services over the course of the war.

Frank Cortright was part of that movement, and he later com-piled a list of 245 papers. Most of them only came out for one

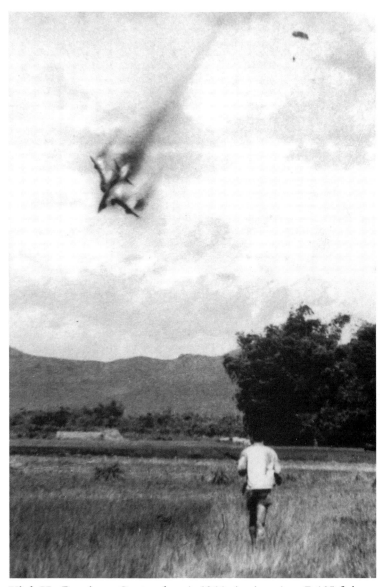

Vinh Hu Province, September 4, 1966. An American F-105 fighter-bomber falls to Earth after being shot down in the Red River Delta region. The pilot drifts beneath his parachute at upper right. This photograph became a classic image in the North, and was reproduced as a greeting card. (Mai Nam)

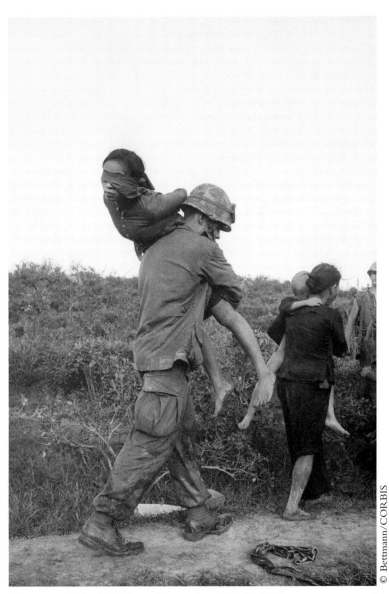

Danang, 1966. A U.S. marine carries a blindfolded woman suspected of Vietcong activities over his shoulder. She and other prisoners were rounded up during the joint Vietnamese–U.S. Operation Mallard. (Nguyen Tanh Tai)

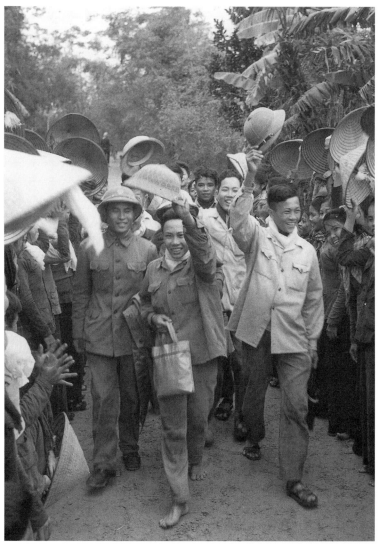

Nam Ha Province, 1966. Villagers in the Thanh Liem district in this northern coastal province say good-bye to soldiers going to the front. Some of the young recruits were too poor to afford shoes, but acceptance into the army was an honor, recalls the photographer, "and morale was high." (Mai Nam)

Huang Oai District, 1965. A mobile class in the war in Binh Da village, Ha Tay Province. (Mai Nam)

Vinh Linh, Quay Tri Province, 1968. Vinh Linh farmers fill a bomb crater with water, creating a trough for pigs and for growing water hyacinth. (Mai Nam)

March 30, 1966. Army medic with wounded comrade. (Steve Northrup)

Hai Duong, 1967. Militia women guard the Lai Vu Bridge between Hanoi and the port of Haiphong. Militia units, consisting mostly of men and women unfit for army duty, captured nearly all of the downed U.S. pilots. (Mai Nam)

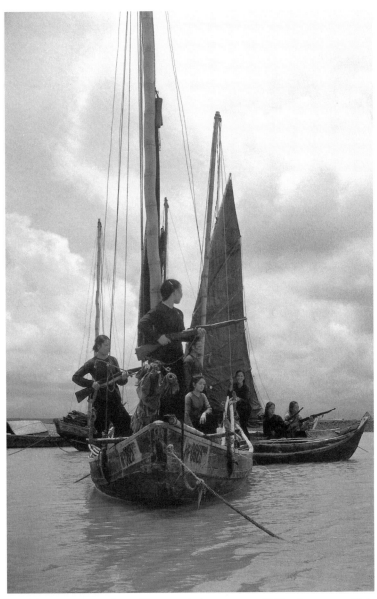

Haiphong, 1966. Guerrillas patrol the waters off Do Son, near Haiphong. Both Hanoi and Haiphong were bombed heavily in 1967. By war's end, the United States had dropped 8 million tons of explosives, roughly three times the weight of bombs dropped by all sides in World War II. (Mai Nam)

New York, April 15, 1967. Demonstrators applaud as a man burns his draft card during a Vietnam War protest in Central Park. 300,000 marched against the war that day in New York. (Photographer unknown)

Nam Ha Province, 1968. A woman rations out fish sauce to villagers in the North's central coastal region. Rationing was common, but this photo did not appear during the war because it didn't fit the propaganda mold. (Mai Nam)

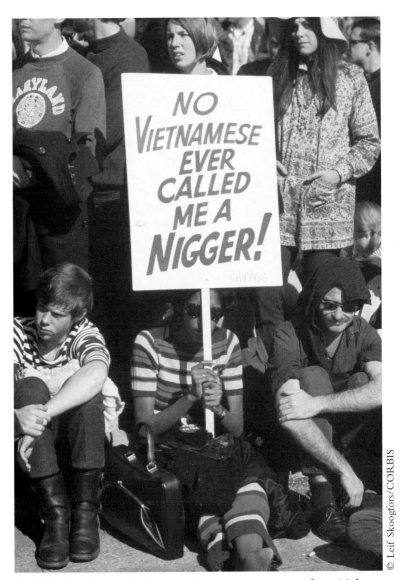

Washington, D.C., 1967. An antiwar protester quotes from Muhammad Ali. Until 1970, African Americans, low-income families, and the elderly were the only sections of the population in which greater numbers favored withdrawal from Vietnam. (Leif Skoogfors)

or a few issues. The people who put them out were investigated and transferred, sent to Vietnam, court-martialed and given long sentences, or dishonorably discharged and framed on other charges. But still the papers kept coming.

In the army and Marines, there was the *Fatigue Press* at Fort Hood, Texas; the *FTA (Fuck the Army)* at Fort Knox, Kentucky; the *Last Harass* at Fort Gordon, Georgia; the *Pawn's Pawn* at Fort Leonard Wood, Missouri; the *Ultimate Weapon* at Fort Dix, New Jersey; the *Attitude Check* at Camp Pendleton, California; the *Green Machine* at Fort Greely, Alaska; the *Napalm* at Fort Campbell, Tennessee; the *Arctic Arsenal* at Fort Greely; the *Black Voice* at Fort McClellan, Alabama; the *Fragging Action* at Fort Dix; the *Fort Polk Puke* at Fort Polk, Louisiana; *Custard's Last Stand* at Fort Riley, Kansas; *Whack!* produced by women at the Women's Army Corps School; and *Where Are We?* at Fort Huachuca, Arizona.

At bases overseas there were papers in, among other places, Paris, Kaiserlauthen, Baumholder, and Stuttgart. There were several papers in Heidelberg, including *FTA with Pride*; several in Frankfurt, including the *Voice of the Lumpen*, "affiliated with the Black Panther Party"; and several in Berlin including, at McNair Barracks, *Can You Bear McNair?* There was *Seasick* at Subic Bay and other papers in the Philippines, and *The Man Can't Win if You Grin* and other papers in Okinawa. There was the *Korea Free Press*, and there were many papers in Japan, including *Semper Fi*, produced jointly by marines and Japanese peace activists from the Hobbit Coffee House, and *Kill For Peace* at Camp Drake, Japan. In England there was the *Stars and Bars* and *Separated from Life*, which "evolved out of the haircut defiance case of Sgt. Dan Pruitt."

There were at least eighty-four papers in the Air Force and navy in the United States, including *Duck Power* in San Diego, California; *Harass the Brass* at Canute AFB, Illinois; *All Hands Abandon Ship* in Newport, Rhode Island; *Now Hear This* in Long Beach, California; the *Potemkin* on the U.S.S. *Forrestal*; the *Star Spangled Bummer* at Wright-Patterson AFB in Ohio; *Fat Albert's Death*

Ship in Charlestown, Massachusetts; the *Pig Boat Blues* on the U.S.S. *Agerholm*; and three papers at Kirtland Air Force Base in New Mexico: *Special Weapons*, *I Will Fear No Evil*, and *Blows Against the Empire*.

The anti-war movement was everywhere, on almost every base of any size. In El Paso, Texas, for instance, GIs for Peace was founded in August 1969 at a meeting of several hundred soldiers, many of them from the Defense Language Institute at Fort Bliss. Their purpose was to "promote peace, secure constitutional rights for servicemen, combat racism, improve enlisted living conditions, and provide aid to the local Chicano community." Ten of the men involved were transferred in the next five months, and the editor of their newspaper, *Gigline*, was sent to Vietnam. But others took their places. In November 1969 many of the soldiers at Fort Bliss were forced to march in the Veterans Day Parade in El Paso. A hundred GIs stood facing the reviewing stand, on the other side of the road, under a big banner saying "GIs for Peace." As the troops from Fort Bliss marched by, instead of saluting the reviewing stand, they saluted the protesters with peace signs and clenched fists.

Specialist Paul Fuchs, section leader of his Vietnamese class at the Defense Language Institute, was told to spy on GIs for Peace. He did that, became an organizer for GIs for Peace, sent false reports to army intelligence, and diverted their money to GIs for Peace. He and his friend Dennis Olney, locally referred to as the Fabulous Furry Freak Brothers,

> exhorted fellow classmates, all Army security trainees with top-level secret clearances, to resist orders to Vietnam. By the time Fuchs was removed as class leader (the Army finally realized something was wrong when he filed for conscientious objector status), twelve of the twenty-one original members of the class had deserted, obtained discharges, or filed for conscientious objector status.[9]

Fuchs was discharged from the army by court order and Olney received a medical discharge after he told them, "Someone injected LSD into my brain."[10]

The army canceled reveille at Fort Bliss. Less than half the soldiers on base were turning up for the 6 A.M. parade. In January 1970, some eighty GIs picketed a talk in El Paso by General Westmoreland, the army chief of staff and former commander in Vietnam, and "to avoid an embarrassing public confrontation, the general was forced to sneak in the back entrance of his hotel."[11]

And on 15 March, "approximately two thousand people, including more than eight hundred servicemen, came together for a festival of political speeches and rock music."[12]

These meetings, organizations, and newspapers were part of a much larger movement, a massive change in feeling. In Oakland, California, student demonstrators had tried to block the local center for induction into the armed services in 1967. They sat in the streets and they ran through the streets, and were gassed, clubbed, and arrested. They failed to block the center. But awareness had been raised. From October 1969 to March 1970, 50 percent of the draftees ordered to report to the Oakland Induction Center failed to turn up, and 11 percent of those who did show up only did so to state they were refusing to be drafted.

During the whole war, 206,000 people were reported to the federal Justice Department for refusing the draft.[13] I suspect that many of these people were middle-class and upper-class students. But between 1968 and 1975, over 93,000 people deserted (took absences without leave for thirty days or more) from the American army alone. They were less educated than the average soldier. In one government survey, 41 percent had less than nine years of education. They were working-class people who didn't have a chance to refuse the draft.

Roger Williams did a survey of deserters in exile in Canada during 1969 and 1970. He found a few were political activists, often educated and opposed to or ambivalent about the war before they went into the services. But the majority were "all-American boys" who "knew that the war in Vietnam was wrong" and had deserted rather than work for the war. Another 30 percent were confused because "the army which they had been taught was the noble defender of goodness and freedom turned out to be ugly, brutal and evil." Less than 5 percent had deserted because of personal reasons, family circumstances, or criminal trouble.[14]

Of course, American soldiers have always deserted. But the desertion rate tripled during the course of the Vietnam War, and at its height it was three times the rate of desertion at any point during the Korean War.[15]

In 1971, desertions ran seventy-three per 1,000 in the army and fifty-six per 1,000 in the marines. That means 7 percent of soldiers and almost 6 percent of marines deserted. And it wasn't just that. That year, 250,000 servicemen and women wrote to complain to their congressman or woman. In fiscal year 1971, for every one hundred people in the army, seven deserted, seventeen went absent without leave, twelve complained to Congress, two received disciplinary discharges, and eighteen were punished without a court-martial. (The figures are a bit inflated because some people must have done several of those things that year—you could be punished, go AWOL, come back, complain to Congress, and then desert.)[16]

At the beginning of the war, basic training was what it had always been—boot camp, hell, the place men learned to obey insane orders. By the last years of the war, boot camp was getting easier and easier and the drill sergeants were learning to negotiate with the men, because the army was scared they would just walk away.

The unrest was part of the wider movement in America. The newspapers and organizations on the bases would not have happened without the civilian peace movement. That movement had won the argument against the war. By 1970 a solid majority of Americans were opposed to the war, and that majority was larger among working-class Americans, the people who went into the armed services.

The unrest took on the cultural forms of the wider movement. The movement in the States was full of dope, long hair, hippies, and anarchism. In Vietnam the GIs painted peace signs on their helmets and wrote "FTA" (Fuck the Army) there and everywhere else. They smoked hash, opium, and heroin, partly to escape. Many men counted the days and obliterated each day. But the drugs were a form of cultural rebellion too. Just smoking pot openly was a rebellion in itself. In one of the few open demonstrations by GIs in Vietnam, over 1,000 people came to Chu Lai beach to protest the war on 4 July 1971. They didn't know what to do when they got there, so they had the largest pot party in the history of the war.[17]

Music was another way of expressing rebellion. In Vietnam and on bases in Germany, people chose their music to express their attitude to the war. The white rebels, the majority, were called the "juicers" and were into rock and roll. The blacks were into soul. The juicers and the blacks called the white career sergeants "lifers," and the lifers liked country and western. Nobody fought over music in combat. They had to stick together there. And blacks never fought with white rock and roll fans. But in the rear in Vietnam, and especially in Germany, many felt that "if blacks can account for up to twenty-two per cent of the dying they should have at least twenty-two per cent of the jukebox."[18] There were arguments, bitter looks, and sometimes fights.

Many of the black soldiers came from the big cities that had rioted in the 1960s. They had seen it as teenagers. When Martin Luther King was murdered in 1968, the inner cities of America went up in flames. The historian James Westheider interviewed two black veterans who were in Vietnam when King died:

"Some of the younger guys were just angry and just wanted to hurt someone," related Allen Thomas Jr, "and there were some fights between whites and blacks, but most of the men were simply in shock. Several hundred men just sat down in a field, drank, smoked pot, but mostly just talked." Serious violence was avoided because the black NCOs convinced the officers to "back off" for a few days and let the men work through their anger and frustration. "The unit was in stand-down anyway, and the last thing you wanted to do was set them off, you know, seasoned veterans with guns," Thomas said. James Hawkins agreed that "Dr. King's death changed things, it . . . made a lot of people angry—angry people with weapons."[19]

The black people in the army came from the inner cities. They brought black nationalism into the army. Westheider again:

> In Vietnam many blacks began to make and display black-power flags. Black marines in Da Nang designed one that would become a model for others. The flag had a red background to symbolize blood shed by African Americans in the war. A black foreground represented black culture. At the center were two spears crossed over a shield and surrounded by a wreath, meaning "violence if necessary" but "peace if possible." Across the flag was a legend in Swahili proclaiming, "My Fear is for You." Variations of the flag appeared in South Korea and Germany as well as elsewhere in Vietnam.[20]

In 1966 an average of two-thirds of black soldiers signed up again when their enlistment came to an end. It was a good job for a black worker compared to what was available in civilian life. By 1970 less than 13 percent of black soldiers were reenlisting.[21] In 1970 there were black political or cultural groups on almost every base in Germany, like the Black Action Group at the Panzer Barracks in Stuttgart, the Black Dissent Group at Smiley Barracks in Karlsruhe, and the Unsatisfied Black Soldiers around Heidelberg. They had a central defense committee, and on 4 July 1970, nearly 1,000 U.S. servicemen from all over Germany, mostly black but some white, attended a meeting in Heidelberg. That meeting demanded, among other things, equal promotions and family housing for black GIs, a committee of enlisted men who could veto sending any GI to the stockade, college preparatory classes for all GIs, and immediate withdrawal of all American forces from southeast Asia and all U.S. interests from Africa.[22]

After that, black and white GIs together began organizing at Nelligen Army Base in Germany. A strict new commanding officer was trying to knock the base into shape. There was harassment, many disciplinary charges, and unjust jailings. The soldiers replied with Molotov cocktails—firebombings on 21 July and on 10 and 14 August. They phoned in bomb threats and they let down the officers' tires, again and again. On 21 September, "following a weekend of growing friction and frustrated attempts to negotiate with officers, black and white GIs threatened to blow up the entire base." Two more firebombs had gone off that morning, and the army declared a 6:30 P.M. curfew and brought in truckloads of armed military police. But at 9 P.M. about one hundred GIs marched through the camp, despite the military police, shouting, "Revolution" and, "Join Us": "Several hours later they returned to barracks, but only after a pledge by provost marshal Lieutenant Colonel R McCarthy that no action would be taken against them." Nobody was punished for that march either, although general harassment of activists continued. And the march had been black and white. One black soldier told *Overseas Weekly*, "There is no racial problem between E-5s and below . . . that's one thing our demonstration has proved."[23]

From 1970 on, the fight against the war was moving from the campus to the barracks. The campus had to come first. A campus is an easy place to organize. Students are allowed to get away with a lot precisely because they are middle-class.

Workplaces are harder. Workers, particularly manual workers, are constantly driven by their managers. The armed forces are the hardest of all. The ruling class needs the army to defend it from insurrection at home. It needs them to follow inhuman orders and risk their lives in war abroad. People won't die without asking questions unless they are very scared. Any unrest in the armed services looks like mutiny, and mutiny threatens the whole rule of the rich over society.

This is not abstract. Industrial might and the ability to make war were the foundations of American power in the world. For big strikes, protests, and riots they call out the National Guard. In Berkeley, California, the students brought the National Guard over to their side three times during the Vietnam War. They knew those men were in the Guard to avoid the draft, and they talked to them.

Behind the National Guard is the army. In 1967, army units fighting to put down a democratic rising in the Dominican Republic were abruptly called back and sent onto the streets of Detroit to end the black uprising there. Many of those soldiers were black. At the same time, in Camp Pendleton, California, William Harvey and George Daniels organized a meeting among their fellow marines to discuss "why black men should fight a white man's war in Vietnam." Harvey was sentenced to six years and Daniels got ten.

At Fort Hood, in Killeen, Texas, the Oleo Strut anti-war coffeehouse held a love-in on 5 July 1968 that attracted 200 mostly white soldiers. In late August, the troops of the 1st Armored Cavalry learned that they were about to be sent to control the anti-war demonstration at the Democratic Convention in Chicago. More than one hundred black soldiers from the 1st Armored met all night to discuss "army racism and the use of troops against civilians." Their commander, General Powell, attended the meeting at one point, and the next morning forty-three men were arrested for "refusal to follow orders." The Oleo Strut coffeehouse and the white and black soldiers organized a massive defense campaign for the Fort Hood 43, and most of them got off with short sentences. But Private First Class Bruce Henderson, a white man and the first editor of the Fort Hood *Fatigue Press*, was tried for possessing tiny traces of marijuana in the lint of his trouser pockets and got eight years of hard labor (it was finally reduced to two years of hard labor on appeal).[24]

These rebellions were important. When the army goes over to the crowd in any great national confrontation, it is a revolution. That is what happened in Russia in 1917, in Germany in 1918, in Iran in 1981, and in the Philippines in 1985. It could happen in America. That, and the necessity to make people die for bad causes, is why discipline in all armed services is so tight. And that is one reason why the revolt in the army came after the revolt on the campuses.

The second reason is that labor unions were alive in the working class in the 1960s but political organization was dead. Most of the radicals and revolutionaries were in the student and civil rights movements, and they did not understand the importance of building alliances in the armed forces. But the unrest in the army was not simply a reflection of civilian unrest. It was also driven all the time by the men coming back from Vietnam. It was what they said, the fact that so many of them joined the movement, and that everything about them told the other soldiers the war was wrong.

But the most important part of the soldiers' revolt was in Vietnam.

FRAGGING

The GIs in Vietnam were working-class people ordered to smash a revolt of poor peasants. They knew this. They were sent to fight a cruel war, and encouraged to kill and count bodies. The contradictions they were caught in, the pain and confusion of being on the wrong side, drove many of them into cruelty. But those same forces, at the same time, could and did drive men to revolt against the war. It is not a matter of some good, kind soldiers who loved peace, and some brutal monsters who loved war. Men in the same situation, in the same units, often the same men on different days, did terrible things and also refused to do them.

In 1968, Tim O'Brien was a GI in the 46th Infantry on the coast of central Vietnam, near Hue. He wrote a good book about it afterwards, *If I Die in a Combat Zone, Box Me Up and Ship Me Home.*[25] His unit patrolled a village called "Pinkville" by the Americans. The year before, one of the hamlets in Pinkville had been the site of the My Lai massacre described in the last chapter.

A year later, Tim O'Brien and Alpha Company were still patrolling Pinkville, walking through My Lai. O'Brien, too, was terrified of mines all the time, watching every step, trying to outsmart the man who laid the mine, exhausted from fear. His unit did not talk about the fear much, but they all felt it all the time:

> Along the way we encountered the citizens of Pinkville; the non-participants in war. Children under ten years, women, old folks who planted their eyes in the dirt and were silent. "Where are the VCP" Captain Johansen would ask, nicely enough. "Where are all the men? Where is Poppa-san?" No answers, not from the villagers. Not until we ducked poppa's bullet or stepped on his land mine. . . .
>
> In the next days it took little provocation for us to flick the flint of our Zippo lighters. Thatched roofs took the flame quickly, and on bad days the hamlets of Pinkville burned, taking our revenge in fire. It was good to walk from Pinkville and to see fire behind Alpha Company. It was good, just as pure hate is good.
>
> We walked to other villages, and the phantom Forty-eighth Viet Cong Battalion walked with us. When a booby-trapped artillery round blew two popular soldiers into a hedgerow, men put their fists into the faces of the nearest Vietnamese, two frightened women living in the guilty hamlet, and when the troops were through with them, they hacked off chunks of thick black hair. The men were crying, doing this. An officer used his pistol, hammering it against a prisoner's skull.[26]

And yet these same men were beginning to refuse the war. The first week O'Brien was with Alpha Company, they came under a mortar attack one night. O'Brien grabbed his rifle, his helmets, and his boots and scrambled out of the barracks ready to fight:

> No one else came out of the barracks. I waited, and finally one man came out, holding a beer. Then another man, holding a beer.
>
> They sat on the sandbags in their underwear, drinking beer and laughing, pointing out at the paddies and watching our mortar rounds land.
>
> Later two or three more men straggled out. No helmets, no weapons. They laughed and joked and drank. The first sergeant started shouting. [He wanted them to fight.] But the men just giggled and sat on the sandbags in their underwear. . . .
>
> A lieutenant came by. He told the men to get their gear together, but no one moved, and he walked away. . . .
>
> The lieutenant hurried back. He argued with a platoon sergeant, but this time the lieutenant was firm. He ordered us to double-time out to the perimeter. Muttering about the company needed a rest and this had turned into one hell of a rest and they'd rather be in the boonies, the men put on helmets and took up their rifles and followed the lieutenant past the mess hall and out to the perimeter.
>
> Three of the men refused and went into the barracks and went to sleep.[27]

And nothing happened to them. The officers no longer dared to order men. They had to negotiate.

The first sergeant in Alpha Company was white. One of his jobs was to choose the men who would be transferred to support work, out of combat. The combat soldiers made fun of those men, called them "Rear Echelon Mother Fuckers," but they dearly wanted those transfers. The first sergeant would not transfer black soldiers. Four men were killed in combat in one day, and the first sergeant came out on patrol to fill in. He was killed; it looked like a mine hit him:

That evening we dug foxholes and cooked C rations over heat tabs. The night was hot, so instead of sleeping right away, I sat with a black friend and helped him pull his watch. He told me that one of the black guys had taken care of the first sergeant. It was an M-79 round, off a grenade launcher. Although the shot was meant only to scare the top sergeant, the blacks weren't crying, he said. He put his arm around me and said that's how to treat whitey when it comes down to it.

In two weeks, a black first sergeant came to Alpha.[28]

Somebody up top had got the message.

Fragging was beginning. The word "fragging" meant taking a fragmentation bomb and throwing it into the tent of a gung-ho officer or sergeant who kept leading you out on dangerous patrols. It was a way of disciplining the officers.

Officers were usually warned. Lamont Steptoe was an officer with the 25th Infantry in Cu Chi in 1969 and 1970:

Generally there was a pattern. If you were fucking with the men, they would generally warn you. When you came back to your bunk there would be a tear gas canister. . . . The next time there would be a booby trap, which when you tripped it would let you know it could have been real. The third time would be the real thing. It's not like you weren't warned.[29]

Other officers were warned just by leaving a grenade pin on their bunk, or throwing a smoke grenade into their tent. The point was not to kill. It was to stop killing.

In *If I Die in a Combat Zone*, there is a description of the GIs' reaction to what appears to be a fragging. Alpha Company got a new colonel, Colonel Daud, who was gung-ho. He liked combat assaults, flying out in helicopters, landing scrambling out terrified, patrolling the villages:

More Combat Assaults came in the next few days. We learned to hate Colonel Daud and his force of helicopters. When he was killed by sappers in a midnight raid, the news came over the radio. A lieutenant led us in song, a catchy, happy, celebrating song: Ding-dong, the wicked witch is dead. We sang in good harmony. It sounded like a choir.[30]

This was 1968. Already the officers had to negotiate with the men, and fragging was just beginning. Year by year it grew. According to one set of official figures, there were between 800 and 1,000 attempted fraggings in the armed services in Vietnam. According to the army there were 563 fraggings from 1969 to 1970, and from 1970 to 1972 there were 363 court-martials for fraggings. The great majority of these fraggings, 80 percent according to one set of figures, were directed at officers and NCOs. Most of them resulted in injury, not death. But the official figures miss most of the killings. They include only attempts with explosive devices, not with guns, which were easier to get. And in many cases nobody was prosecuted. The point had been made. To prosecute somebody was to keep up the struggle and possibly have more fraggings. A smart commander let it go. And if he didn't let it go, how was he to find out who did it?

Moreover, the usual way of killing officers in armies is to shoot them on patrol. This is doubtless what happened in Vietnam. It's what happened to the first sergeant in Alpha Company and it went on elsewhere. Miguel Lemus was in the 25th Infantry. Once his unit came back from a hard mission, scared and tired, and ninety of them smoked weed together:

It was party time . . . and this officer tried to be a hero—bust ninety guys. . . . We were along the trenches and they shot him. They threw him over a trench and shot him with a machine gun. No one said anything. Someone called on the radio and told them the captain had been shot by the gooks. . . . Who saw it? Nobody saw it.[31]

The best guess is that over 1,000 officers and NCOs were killed by their own men. David Addlestone, an army lawyer, said that other army lawyers with the 173rd Airborne "told of periods during 1970 and 1971 when violent attacks [on officers] were an almost daily occurrence."[32] Lieutenant Colonel Herbert of the 173rd Airborne told *Playboy* that in his battalion in 1969:

> There had been two attempts on the previous commander's life. There had been quite a few fraggings in that battalion, of both officers and senior enlisted men. One man had both his legs blown off; seven people had been wounded by a grenade, and a Claymore mine had been thrown right at the tactical operations center—a mine to kill the staff, for Christ's sake.[33]

A lot of fragging was directed against the sergeants, the "lifers" who were loyal to the corps and could get you killed. John Lindquist was in the 3rd Marines in 1969:

> One time they tried to frag the lifer's hootch, it didn't work because the grenade didn't go off. The lifers sat up there all night with a rifle waiting for somebody to try it again so they could blow them away. . . .
>
> They tried to get this CID [Criminal Investigation Division] guy, but the grenade got a gunney [gunnery sergeant] who had nothing to do with it and he lost a leg. . . . That rubbed me the wrong way.
>
> When I was down in Quang Tri they had three fraggings of first sergeants in 3rd Division. . . . It got so bad that each battalion was concertinaed off from one another [i.e., separated by concertina, or barbed, wire] so they wouldn't fight. . . .
>
> [We were] listening to Deep Purple and through the top of our hootch comes about five rounds of M16. They could have been lower. . . . Somebody could be dead or wounded because somebody's fighting next door with other marines. The ground war was no longer really working.[34]

Another marine, in an anonymous account:

> We started having war calls, which is like at midnight everybody in the outfit starts screaming, "Gooks in the wire". . . . And then you try to kill any of the lifers you didn't like.
>
> So we tried to get the CO a couple of times with a machine gun. One time his rack took nine holes. His cot, nine bullet holes. . . .
>
> So one night this guy named H booby-trapped his tent. And in the morning when he woke up it wasn't the CO that got it. It was the executive officer Captain J. . . . Captain K was the one we wanted to get. But J, it was good to get J 'cause he sucked too. They threatened to press charges against the whole outfit for mutiny. They were trying to figure out a way they could keep it hush-hush. Nobody wants to know the Marine Corps mutinied.[35]

Mark Jury was an army photographer in Vietnam in 1969 and 1970. He traveled all over the country:

> Fragging is an institution in Vietnam. If the lifers make life unbearable, the kids will warn him with a CS (tear gas) grenade. If he persists, they'll "frag" him with a real (fragmentation) grenade. . . .
>
> In the field there're no problems. If and when a lifer is assigned to a combat company, he's put in shape quickly; the kids have the option to simply kill him during a fire fight. One unit's new first sergeant arrived when they were pulling "palace guard"—security for headquarters. Usually it's a time for relaxation, but this guy was playing lifer, threatening punishment over "unmilitary appearance" and dope smoking. The first day back in the field, one of the kids, a 6 foot 3 inch giant with long hair and peace symbols, said, "Watch this."
>
> He walked over to where the lifer was carrying an AK-47 (the NVA automatic rifle) and said loudly, "Yeah, I'm gonna take my old AK with me tomorrow 'cause I think we are going to make

contact." Then he spun around and looked down at the sergeant, straight in the eyes, and slowly brought the barrel of the AK up and said, "Sarge, if we make contact tomorrow, you better be real careful, 'cause the new guys are the ones that get scared and do stupid things and get themselves killed. And, Sarge, those AKs do one helluva job on you."

The next time out with the unit, I learned that the sergeant had become a helluva good guy until he couldn't take it any more and was shipped back to the States.[36]

GIs sometimes collected money to put on the head of a particularly dangerous officer. The man in charge at Hamburger Hill, so called because the GIs assaulting it were chewed into hamburger, had $10,000 on his head. He got out of Vietnam alive. Not everybody else did. Barry Romo commanded a platoon of the 196th Light Infantry Brigade. He remembered:

My company commander had five hundred dollars on his head. And the reason was he was a coward. . . . The North Vietnamese started an ambush on us. My company commander di–died [ran] out of the area—took the other two platoons behind me and ran down the hill and left us there. We had to fight our way back down. . . . And after that my men collected five hundred dollars.[37]

There was another side to fragging. Ed Sowders was a medic at Cu Chi base hospital, on top of the tunnels, in 1968, and was organizing against the war:

We've all heard of fragging. We know what it is, so I want to be honest about this. Fragging is a two-way street. It's not always the GIs in popular rebellion against their NCOs and officers. It's also a very convenient way to get rid of any troublesome lower ranking GI. I was afraid of that. Military intelligence is already on my ass. They already developed a file on me. They're already spying on me.[38]

Fragging spread from the combat troops to the rear. In one case:

> We banded together, blacks and white, we banded together and
> said, "He's got to go, this sergeant's got to go. . . . We can't let
> them continue to run this platoon."
> We basically mutinied. At first we thought that murder was the
> answer. . . . It was going to be draw straws and frag the mother-
> fucker, right. Somehow that didn't happen. The next move was
> we'll go to the IG [inspector general] as a unit we'll lay out all
> these things we disagree with . . . making us stand formation, shine
> our shoes, and shit like that. Since we were NCOs, I was a ser-
> geant, number of other sergeants, we'd present our case. That's
> exactly what we did. They sent in new people. It was a question
> of dealing with him one way or the more violent way.[39]

Fragging, and threats of fragging, were not acts of mindless revenge. They were ways of disciplining the officers, forcing them
to negotiate. As Captain Barry Steinberg, an army judge, said,
"Once an officer is intimidated by the threat of fragging he is
useless to the military because he can no longer carry out orders."[40]

Yet fragging was not an attack on all officers. The senior officers, the brass, may have been intimidated by fragging but stayed
loyal to corps and career. The lieutenants and the sergeants split.
Many of the junior officers had been in ROTC in college to
avoid the war. Any great working-class movement splits the middle class. Remember O'Brien's lieutenant, leading the men in
singing "the Wicked Witch is dead." The Concerned Officers
Movement was founded in Washington, D.C., in 1970. It was
especially strong among naval officers, but by 1971 it had 3,000
members in twenty chapters. The chapter at Keflavik Air Force
Base in Iceland had its own anti-war paper, the *Stuffed Puffin*.[41]
The pressure of fragging widened the split between the officers
and NCOs. More and more simply cooperated in sandbagging.

O'Brien's unit was already doing that in 1968. They simply

went down the road a bit when ordered out on patrol, camped out, and made regular false radio reports.

The National Liberation Front had stated publicly at the peace negotiations in Paris that they would not fire on units who did not fire on them. They didn't always keep that promise. But many soldiers wore red armbands as a signal to the Viet Cong they didn't want to fight. And they simply refused to patrol, again and again and again, hundreds and thousands of times, all over Vietnam: "During his year of legal defense work in Saigon, David Addlestone heard of literally dozens of combat refusals, with nearly every case ending not in punishment but in negotiations between commanders and GIs."[42]

At Cu Chi, for instance, in November 1969, a twenty-one-man platoon on patrol simply refused Captain Frank Smith's order to advance. They told a reporter they were all on short time, near the end of their year in Vietnam. They wanted to live. In April 1970, men of the 7th Cavalry refused Captain Al Rice's order to advance down a dangerous path. There was a TV camera along on the patrol, and American viewers got to see Captain Rice and the men negotiating, "working it out," live. In December 1970, Lieutenant Fred Pitts of the 501st Infantry, his sergeant, and his whole platoon all refused an order to advance.[43]

There were many other incidents. In the 1st Cavalry there were thirty-five combat refusals in 1970. Across the army and the Marines, there were thousands during the war. In 1971 and 1972, troops were being withdrawn from Vietnam, but now there were more fraggings in an army of 200,000 than there had been in an army of 500,000. Nobody wanted to be the last American to die in Vietnam.

In 1971 an aerial photograph of a giant peace symbol carved into the Vietnamese countryside was reproduced in many GI anti-war newspapers. It looked as if it had been made by a bulldozer. It had been carved in the fields of the village of Beautiful Waters, just south of Hue, by the men of the 101st Airborne.[44] By January 1972 the 101 were gone, part of the soldiers' revolt.

THE FALL OF SAIGON

The fragging and the combat refusals went together. Military discipline is fierce, and pacifism is not an option for soldiers in combat. If they don't fight, they face the threat of being shot or
court-martialed. Soldiers who want to stop a war and stay alive
have to be prepared to shoot their officers, because their officers
are prepared to shoot them. That is what the GIs did.

Nixon, Kissinger, and the Pentagon were still trying to hold on
in Vietnam. Main force units of the North Vietnamese Army
remained in the jungles and mountains in strength. They were
tired, thinned out, and increasingly desperate, but they were still
a fighting force. The southern guerrillas were not, although they
still had the political support of the majority of the villagers. If
the Americans had stayed in some force, and if the American
troops had been willing to fight, then the United States could
probably have won at the cost of 2 or 3 million more dead.

But from 1970 the GIs stopped fighting and the Pentagon grew
desperate to get the troops out. In the *Armed Forces Journal* of June
1971, Colonel Robert Heinl, a Marine Corps historian, said what
the officers were thinking:

> The morale, discipline and battle-worthiness of the U.S. Armed
> Forces are, with a few salient exceptions, lower and worse than at
> any time in this century and possibly in the history of the United
> States.
>
> By every conceivable indicator, our Army that now remains in
> Vietnam is in a state approaching collapse, with individual units
> avoiding or having refused combat, murdering their officers and
> non-commissioned officers, drug-ridden and dispirited where not
> near mutinous.
>
> Elsewhere than Vietnam the situation is nearly as serious. . . .
>
> All the foregoing facts—and many more indicators of the worst
> kind of military trouble—point to widespread conditions among
> American forces in Vietnam that have only been exceeded in this

century by the French Army's Nivelle Mutinies and the collapse
of the Tsarist armies in 1916 and 1917.[45]

The revolt of the Tsarist troops in 1917 started the Russian
Revolution—Colonel Heinl was sounding a warning of revolution. Note that he said that the situation in the armed forces
outside Vietnam was almost as bad. The veterans were spreading
the rot. And note that he was saying this in the official *Armed
Forces Journal*. This was not a crank. This was the officer class
making a public statement of what it felt.

Stewart Alsop, a right-wing journalist close to the Pentagon,
wrote an editorial in December 1970. He described a "growing
feeling among the Administration's policymakers that it might be
a good idea to accelerate the rate of withdrawal . . . [because] discipline and morale in the American army in Vietnam are deteri-
orating very seriously." *Time*, writing on "GI dissent" early in
1971, said, "Officers from Chief of Staff William C. Westmoreland on down are known to be arguing that [the troops in Viet-
nam] are not being pulled out fast enough."[46]

There was, then, no point in keeping the troops in Vietnam if
they would not fight, but there was much danger. The last marines were pulled out in 1971. Negotiations dragged on between
Hanoi and Washington. In March and April 1972, the North
Vietnamese made main force attacks in strength in the north of
South Vietnam—conventional warfare. The intention was to
show Nixon what they could do and force him to negotiate seriously. The Viet Cong guerrillas were not part of this offensive,
which was a sign of how weak they had become in the villages.
The American government replied with massive bombing, to
show what it could do. It was a sign of its weakness that they did
not use American troops.

On 1 January 1972 there were 156,800 American troops in
Vietnam. By 30 June there were 47,000. In those six months, the
Americans lost 178 dead and 809 wounded, and the South Viet-
namese government forces lost 19,595 dead and 50,325 wounded.

These relatively low figures show that the American army was no longer fighting.

That left two cards in Nixon's hand—bombing and China. Nixon and Kissinger went to China in 1972 and made an informal agreement with the Chinese leaders. America would end its anti-Communist enmity to China and become China's ally against the Soviet Union. In return, the Chinese government allowed the Americans to understand it had no objection to increased bombing of North Vietnam, and promised to lean on Hanoi to make peace with the Americans.

The other card was bombing. If the army and Marines would not fight, the planes could still bomb. But those bombs were delivered by human beings too. The peace movement spread to the big aircraft carriers. The U.S.S. *Constellation*, based in San Diego, was due to sail to bomb Vietnam in October 1971. The anti-war movement in San Diego organized its own referendum on whether the *Constellation* should go or not. Forty-seven thousand civilians voted, and 82 percent were against the sailing. Six thousand nine hundred servicemen and women voted, and 73 percent were against the sailing. Nine sailors took refuge in a church and refused to go.[47]

The U.S.S. *Coral Sea* was to sail at the same time. Twelve sailors circulated a petition:

TO THE CONGRESS OF THE UNITED STATES FROM THE BROTHERS OF THE *CORAL SEA*

In our opinion there is a silent majority aboard ship which does not believe in the present conflict in Vietnam. It is also the opinion of many that there is nothing we can do about putting an end to the Vietnam conflict. That because we are in the military we no longer have a right to voice our individual opinions concerning the Vietnam war. This is where we feel that the majority of the *Coral Sea* has been fooled by military propaganda. As Americans we all have the moral obligation to voice our opinions. We, the people, must guide the government and not allow the government to guide us. In our opinion this action is even more justified for the military man because he is the one who is taking personal involvement in the war. The *Coral Sea* is scheduled for Vietnam in November. This does not have to be a fact. The ship can be prevented from taking an active part in the conflict if we, the majority, voice our opinion that we do not believe in the Vietnam war. If you feel that the *Coral Sea* should not go to Vietnam, voice your opinion by signing this petition.[48]

Over 1,000 signed the petition, about a quarter of the crew. When the *Coral Sea* sailed from California, 1,500 civilians demonstrated and thirty-five sailors stayed behind. Once the ship reached Hawaii, several hundred crew members attended the anti-war entertainment put on by Jane Fonda and her FTA (Fuck the Army) Show. When the ship left Hawaii, fifty-three sailors stayed behind. The radicals who were left on board began publishing a newspaper on the ship, *We Are Everywhere*.[49]

Then the bombing escalated in 1972 and there was unrest on all the aircraft carriers involved. As the U.S.S. *America* left Norfolk, Virginia, anti-war civilians in thirteen kayaks and canoes sailed in front of the great ship to block its passage. The Coast Guard was sent to remove them, and hundreds of sailors stood along the rail of the *America*, throwing garbage at the Coast Guard. As the *Oriskany* left California, twenty-five sailors deserted. A week later, ten of them surrendered to the navy with a public statement saying, "The only way to end the genocide being perpetrated now in South East Asia is for us, the actual pawns in the political game, to quit playing."[50]

On a munitions ship in New Jersey, activists on board ship asked the local Vietnam Veterans Against the War to organize a similar flotilla. As the Coast Guard fought the kayaks, seven men jumped from the *Nitro* into the sea. One of them, William Monks, said:

I jumped from my ship because of my beliefs against the war and the killing in Vietnam. . . . I also jumped for the many oppressed people in the military that think like myself, but because of the way the military functions, no one ever listens to these people. . . . I see no reason why I should have to fight in Vietnam. I didn't start this war. I have nothing against the Vietnamese people; they never hurt me or my family.[51]

The sailors were also discovering how vulnerable high-tech ships, especially aircraft carriers, were to sabotage. In fiscal year 1971, the navy reported to Congress that there were "488 investigations on damage or attempted damage . . . including 191 for sabotage [and] 135 for arson." In July 1972, a fire on the aircraft carrier *Forrestal* did $7 million damage and stopped the ship from sailing for two months. That same month, somebody put a paint scraper and two twelve-inch bolts into the gears on one engine and put the *Ranger* out of operation for three months.

Then, in October 1972, the carrier *Kitty Hawk* arrived in Subic Bay in the Philippines on the way home from bombing duty (the anti-war paper on the *Kitty Hawk* was called the *Kitty Litter*). Because sabotage had stopped the *Ranger* and *Forrestal* sailing, the *Kitty Hawk* was ordered to turn around and go back to bomb. On shore, black and white sailors got into a fight. Back at sea, only black sailors were questioned about the fighting. A hundred black sailors met to protest, the Marines were sent in to break them up, and fighting between black sailors and marines "with fists, chains, wrenches and pipes" lasted most of the night.

The same month, after a sit-in by black and white sailors on the *Constellation* supporting the demands of the ship's Black Front, 130 sailors were first given shore duty and then went on strike when ordered back onto the ship. None of them were punished and all were allowed to stay on shore.[52]

Throughout 1972 there were demonstrations on most U.S. air bases in Japan, Germany, and the United States. In Thailand and Guam, where people were flying directly to bomb, it was harder to organize. But from Guam one man wrote to Congress, "Ground crews no longer care whether or not their planes are safe and operational. Flights of crews do not wish to fly wasted missions and consequently abort when given the opportunity." Another wrote, "I for one, sir, do not wish to die as a mercenary for a foreign dictator."[53]

In May 1973 the Air Force had to announce a 40 percent cut in bombing Cambodia. The *Washington Post* said it was because

> the Air Force is facing a deepening morale crisis among pilots, and especially among crews of the B-52s. . . . High-ranking Defense Department sources say the morale situation at Guam has been poor for some time. . . . The morale problem at U Tapao Air Base in Thailand is also growing worse daily.[54]

In December 1972 Washington began the around-the-clock, twenty-four-hour "Christmas bombing" of Hanoi and Haiphong by 200 B-52s. The Chinese had assured the United States there would be no retaliation. But in Thailand on 18 December, Phantom fighter pilot Captain Dwight Evans refused to fly over North Vietnam. Captain Michael Heck refused to fly his B-52 on 26 December. He had flown over 200 combat missions, but he felt "a man has to answer to himself first."

The Vietnamese claimed they shot down thirty-four B-52s over Christmas. The Pentagon admitted to fifteen in public and more in private. The Air Force could not stand the losses.[55] Finally Washington folded and signed a peace deal in Paris in January 1973 agreeing to withdraw the last American soldiers from Vietnam. Although the U.S. government refused to have a coalition government in South Vietnam, there would be a cease-fire. Both the southern government and the guerrillas would hold what land they now controlled. North Vietnamese units would remain in the South, but the North Vietnamese government would hold back and not overthrow the southern government. In return, the Americans would give the North Vietnamese massive aid—$5 billion. American advisors and spies, but not soldiers, could remain in the South, and American aid to the southern regime would continue. The American government would stop bombing North Vietnam, but could continue bombing South Vietnam, Cambodia, and Laos.

The last American troops left in 1973. The peace held for a time, but few people expected it to hold forever. Everybody knew it was a victory for the Communists and a defeat for the American government. Almost everybody was surprised the southern government lasted for two years afterwards. It lasted because the North Vietnamese government tried to observe the treaty and hold back its people. Perhaps it feared American bombing and perhaps it expected American aid. North Vietnam was also under pressure from its Chinese allies, who wanted the peace deal to hold.

But President Thieu in South Vietnam knew he could not live with peace. He signed the peace agreement under American pressure, but the next day he announced that "if Communists come into your village, you should immediately shoot them in the head." And if anybody begins "talking in a Communist tone," he said, kill them "immediately."[56]

Hanoi urged the guerrillas in the South to observe the cease-fire. But their leaders remembered how Diem had slaughtered them after the 1954 peace deal in Geneva. They stood their ground and fought Thieu.

The Americans refused to pay North Vietnam the $5 billion they had promised. The leaders in Hanoi seem to have been surprised.

In Saigon the economy was collapsing, as American aid was cut, and as GIs and their dollars left. Unemployment rose and people grew increasingly desperate in the cities.

Hanoi had tried to observe the peace agreement. But the American ruling class simply wanted out and did not expect the deal to last. If they had, they would have supplied far more aid. Richard Nixon, the president, became increasingly isolated as the only important politician committed to President Thieu. Congress threatened to cut off all American aid to South Vietnam. Nixon was removed in the Watergate scandal, in part because of his continued support for Thieu. A new president, Gerald Ford, took his place.

In March 1975, the North Vietnamese army launched minor offensives north and west of Hue. President Thieu, his forces spread too thin, ordered them to pull back to Hue. As the retreat began, his army fell apart.

It was a conscript army. Seventeen percent of adult men in South Vietnam were in the army. They did not want to fight, and most of them had their families with them. As the retreat began, they left their units to look after their families. The army did not go over to the Communists. It collapsed and fled in fear, and suddenly the roads were clogged by an army of refugees.

In the end, there was no final battle for South Vietnam. The soldiers, the uncommitted people in the South, looked at the southern regime and said, "They cannot support us. They are morally bankrupt. We will not die for them."

Hue fell quickly, and the refugees, the landlords, the soldiers, and their families, the urban supporters of the regime, headed for Danang. The Americans were frantically evacuating the consular, AID, and CIA people the Paris peace deal had allowed them to keep in the country. An American on the last helicopter out of Nha Trang told a friend:

> As the pilot throttled the motors and prepared to pull off, an old Vietnamese man with a baby in his arms hobbled out of the crowd at the edge of the pad and lifted the child up toward the cabin, beseeching the Americans to take it aboard.... [An American] moved to the edge of the open hatch and smashed the old man full in the face with the heel of his boot. The baby dropped to the ground, and almost at the same instant the chopper . . . soared skyward.[57]

When Hue fell, there were 2 million refugees in Danang. There were 270 U.S. soldiers, two women, one child, and a few civilian

Americans on the last plane out of Danang. An American reporter on the planes said that "scores of people clung to the wings and the landing gear as the plane took off, and many were crushed under the wheels. Others fell off after it was airborne, and several bodies were later found mashed in the wheel wells themselves. The center aisle in the cabin glistened with blood."[58]

Commercial and naval boats tried to evacuate the refugees from Danang. One CIA man made it out to the *Pioneer Contender*. He found:

> [O]ver 1,500 South Vietnamese troops were sprawled, lounging, fighting among themselves on the main decks and the bridge, and practicing their aim at the hapless Vietnamese civilians in their midst. Less than thirty yards away an ARVN trooper was in the process of raping a Vietnamese woman while another soldier held her male companion at gunpoint.[59]

The CIA man helped escaping refugees clamber onto the ship. More than 1,000 people from different small boats fell into the sea and drowned as they attempted to come aboard. In smaller boats, refugees stood packed so tight that the living held the dead upright. One government soldier from Beautiful Waters was among them. He saw the other soldiers fight with guns and grenades in the surf to get to the boats ahead of each other, and the water ran red.

The soldiers were terrified of what would happen to them and their families. They expected the Communists would return the cruelty that had been done to them.

They did not. On 24 March 1975, as the southern army disintegrated and the northern tanks rolled on towards Saigon, the guerrillas walked openly on the paths of Beautiful Waters. They chatted with other villagers and told jokes, and they waved at the soldiers of the southern government as they retreated in trucks down Highway One. A handmade cardboard sign on the road said, "Victory without bloodshed." An old peasant, a former Viet

Minh, said in happiness, "We have fought for 20 years, and our fight will end in a few days."[60]

Three movements had defeated the American ruling class—the American peace movement, the GIs' revolt, and the peasant guerrillas. The greatest of these was the peasant revolt. Hundreds of thousands of Communists and guerrillas had given their lives, and millions of peasants had died because they would not or could not leave their homes. Tens of millions had grieved for them. The Vietnam War is a history of horror, of rape and atrocity. But it is also a story of unimaginable, endless courage, of what men and women and children were capable of when they fought for a fair share of the rice they grew—and a world run by decency.

7

VIETNAM AND CAMBODIA
AFTER THE WAR

In the spring of 1975, Communists took power in South Vietnam,
Cambodia, and Laos. All of Indochina, finally, was Communist.
The American War was over. For the moment South Vietnam
remained a formally separate state, but it was led by Communists,
and the leaders in Hanoi were the real power. Their mood that
summer was quietly ecstatic. At the foreign ministry, Indian journalist Nayan Chanda listened to a happy official recite a poem
written when Chinese invaders were defeated 200 years before:

> There are no more sharks in the sea,
> There are no more beasts on earth,
> The sky is serene,
> Time now to build peace for ten thousand years.[1]

It didn't work out that way. The problem was rice. Before the
war, North Vietnam had been developing along a state capitalist
model, following the example of Russia and China. But North
Vietnam was poor—in 1954, roughly four working adults in
1,000 were in industry. Development had to start from the control
of rice. In the late 1950s, the government in North Vietnam
persuaded most peasants into cooperatives. The state then took
part of the rice in taxes, and took more through compulsory state
purchases at very low prices. It is hard to find statistics for the
exact amount taken. But one study of a village in the North found
that during the American War roughly 30 percent of the crop
went to the state. By contrast, a 1988 law promised peasants that

the state would take no more than 60 percent of the crop. So we can assume a tax of 30 to 60 percent, but closer to 30 percent in the early years. In effect, the state had become the landlord.

In the cities, the North Vietnamese government squeezed the workers. State employees, including workers in modern industry, saw their real wages fall by 25 percent. At the same time, 25 percent of domestic product was being invested in industry, a very high rate, and the number of industrial workers grew to three people in one hundred. In other words, out of every one hundred bowls of rice the peasants produced, twenty-five went to buying machinery abroad, and to building factories and machines, while three went to industrial workers.

The peasants' rice and the workers' labor were building an industrial economy. The war with America threw that out of kilter. North Vietnamese industry was dispersed to the countryside, and half of it was destroyed in the bombing. Russian arms and Chinese rice kept the northern economy going during the war.

American money kept South Vietnam fed. But the war in the South forced the majority of southern peasants to flee the countryside. By 1975, 74 percent of people in the South were living in towns, cities, or refugee camps. Saigon had grown from 300,000 to 2 million people (the name was changed to Ho Chi Minh City in 1975, but most Vietnamese still call it Saigon).

With peace in 1975, the new government had to feed the cities of the North and South, and foreign aid was suddenly a problem. The North Vietnamese government was expecting massive aid from the United States. Two years before, Washington had promised to pay Hanoi $5 billion in reparations as part of the Paris peace agreements. But under Presidents Nixon, Ford, Carter, Reagan, Bush, and Clinton, they refused to pay it. Hanoi had been counting on that money, but the U.S. ruling class was not about to forgive its defeat. They punished Vietnam for twenty years, cutting off all aid and trade.

Where the American government led, the IMF and the World Bank followed. Where they led, most of the world's big banks followed. Vietnam attracted almost no Western or Japanese investment until 1990. During those years there was a boom in Southeast Asia, based on foreign investment and production for export, but Vietnam was shut out.

Chinese aid was suddenly a problem too. Since 1960 the Communists in Hanoi had been caught up in the larger rivalry between Russia and China.

The causes of this great power rivalry are complex. The Russian ruling class had treated China like another satellite economy to be exploited. Moreover, industrialization and class struggle were moving at different paces in the two countries. In Russia, the economy and military capability had partly caught up with the West in the breakneck exploitation of the Stalin years. From 1953 onwards, the rulers of Russia were trying to relax the brutal regime of prison camps. A more developed economy needed incentives, not slave labor. And they had seen most of the other bureaucrats of their generation packed off to those camps.

While the Russian leaders were trying to ease up on repression in the 1950s, the Chinese leaders were engaged in breakneck exploitation of their people. In China these were the years of forced industrialization in the "Great Leap Forward," which led to a famine that killed 20 million. Any attempt to relax repression in China would open the floodgates of anger from below. So the Chinese rulers could not follow the Russian lead. Moreover, the Russian leaders were talking about "peaceful coexistence" with the United States. The Chinese leaders could see that the United States government was still implacably opposed to them. So peaceful coexistence looked like a bloc between Russia and America directed at China.

In this context, China and Russia began to compete for leadership of the world Communist movement, and in the mid-1960s it seemed possible they would go to war along their long border. This was an enormous headache for the Vietnamese Communists. They needed the support of both Russia and China.

For much of the war they got it. Precisely because Russia and

China were competing for leadership of the world's Communist states and parties, they had to be seen as supporting the Vietnamese. After all, Vietnam was the place in the world where Communists were fighting American imperialism.

So the Vietnamese tried carefully to be neutral in the split between Russia and China. In this, they largely succeeded. Both Russia and China aided Vietnam despite repeated squabbles over delays and looting on trains carrying Russian arms to Vietnam.

In 1972 this began to change. The Chinese ruling class had weathered the upheavals of the Cultural Revolution in the 1960s, and was now more firmly in control. They were beginning a turn towards market capitalism when President Richard Nixon approached them for an alliance that would help him to get out of Vietnam. The Chinese ruling class saw the possibility of an alliance with America against Russia, and they took it.

After the Communist victory in Vietnam in 1975, the Chinese leadership no longer needed to be seen as supporting the Vietnamese. With the war over, Vietnam no longer made a difference in the international Communist movement. Neither Moscow nor Beijing any longer needed to be seen as Vietnam's big brother.

So the Chinese government insisted on Vietnam taking its side, and the Vietnamese government refused. From 1972 onwards the Chinese had been worrying about a strong Vietnam, allied to Russia, on their southern flank. To cement their alliance with the United States, and to keep Vietnam weak, they had urged the Vietnamese Communists to observe the Paris peace agreement and leave South Vietnam as a separate state. When Saigon fell in 1975, they were angry. The French diplomat François Missoffe reported from Beijing in early 1976, "It does not matter whether there are two or three Vietnams, the Chinese say, but that there should never be one."[2] When the Communists merged North and South Vietnam into one state in 1976, the Chinese leaders were furious.

China cut rice aid in 1976 and ended it completely in 1978. At the same time, Russian aid was cut from $350 million to $200 million. Most Russian aid had been gifts. Now it was loans.[3]

The Vietnamese government faced a rice crisis. It had to feed the cities. The obvious solution, in its terms, was to get the peasants in the Mekong Delta in the south into cooperatives like the peasants in the north. The Mekong Delta had 48 percent of the rice fields in Vietnam.[4] The land was good and the Mekong had always been the rice basket of Vietnam. However, there was a problem.

In 1975, Saigon fell to North Vietnamese tanks and regular army troops, not the Viet Cong. The southern resistance had been shattered after the Tet Offensive, so power now lay with Hanoi and the party leaders. But the southern villages were still full of people who had fought on their own land for twenty years. Where they had not shared out the land before, they shared it out in 1975. According to one set of figures, 70 percent of the peasants now controlled 80 percent of the land. They knew about the taxes and cheap rice sales in the north. They did not want the cooperatives, and they would fight if they had to.

The government's first tactic was to try to win control of the rice trade by attacking the big Chinese capitalists in Cholon, Saigon's Chinatown. These big traders bought the rice from the smaller traders, who bought it from the peasants in the Mekong Delta. So in 1978 the government took over the big trading companies in Cholon. But the big traders had already signed over their trading networks on paper to relatives and small traders. The peasants continued to sell to any traders who came to the villages rather than to the government at low prices.

The peasants refused to form cooperatives despite the party's efforts. In Binh My village, near Saigon, the party cadres bullied people relentlessly. They went to some people's houses twenty times, one cadre said, so many times that the household dogs came to know them and stopped barking.[5]

There, around Saigon and Hue, the cadres had some success. But they found it much harder in the Mekong Delta. Ben Tre province is a good example. Way back in 1960, Ben Tre city had risen in a great unarmed insurrection against the southern government. During Tet in 1968, the Viet Cong was so strong there that American bombers flattened the city. A decade later, in 1979, the new Communist government opened a model cooperative in Ben Tre province to encourage the peasants to join up. The peasants burned it down.[6]

By 1984, nine years after the end of the war, only 25 percent of the villages in the delta were organized into cooperatives, and many of these were on paper only.[7] In 1987 the government admitted defeat. It announced that the drive for cooperatives was over because almost every village in the Mekong had joined up. Actually, they had joined what the Vietnamese called "ghost cooperatives."[8]

Nor did the state ever gain control of the trade in rice. Private traders continued to buy and sell almost all the rice in the delta and much of it in the rest of the country.[9]

The rice in the Mekong Delta was the central surplus in the Vietnamese economy. The government's failure to control that rice meant that state capitalism, the strategy of squeezing the workers and peasants to develop state industry, would not now work in Vietnam.

That failure was a victory for the peasants of the Mekong. They had defeated the French, the Americans, and the Saigon government. Now they had stopped their leaders.

The government's first reaction was to try to squeeze more out of the cooperatives in the north. But the Red River Delta had less than half the land of the Mekong, and it was more thickly settled and less fertile. The northern peasants had been willing to make sacrifices during the war, when their sons were fighting and their homes were being bombed. With peace, they expected to pay less, not more. They began to plant only enough to feed themselves, because the rest would all go to the government.

The peasants would not let the state have enough rice. Washington was shutting Vietnam out of world trade and China was refusing rice. The leaders in Hanoi felt they could not survive without more Russian aid. To obtain that, they signed a mutual defense treaty with Russia late in 1978, and that pushed them into war with Cambodia and China.

CAMBODIA

We have to double back now to what had been happening in Cambodia. The history of Vietnam after 1975 is very much bound up with that of Cambodia—the Cambodian tragedy was the last act and the worst consequence of the American War.

Everybody who writes about the killing fields in Cambodia between 1975 and 1978 speaks of madness. But just as with insane human beings, if you sit and listen to their story you can often understand them. So it is with the insanity of nations. Each insanity has its logic and its history. The leaders of Cambodian Communism may have been insane, or maybe not. But tens of thousands of Cambodians did their killing for them. Millions of Cambodian peasants supported their terror in the beginning. To understand why a whole society seems to go insane, you have to understand the logic and the history, for madness has its roots in suffering.

Until 1970 Cambodia had been ruled by King Sihanouk, who tried to balance his interests between North Vietnam and America. The Viet Cong had bases on the Cambodian side of the border. The Cambodian Communists were called the Khmer Rouge—the Red Cambodians ("Khmer" is the word Cambodians use for themselves). They had bases in the jungle, and some support. King Sihanouk quietly allowed the Americans to bomb Communist bases on his territory.

In 1970 General Lon Nol deposed Sihanouk in a U.S.-supported coup. Lon Nol took Cambodia into open alliance with the United States. Sihanouk went into exile in China and formed an alliance with the Khmer Rouge. Now both radicals and traditionalists in the countryside opposed Lon Nol's government. That is one reason why President Nixon sent American troops into Cambodia in 1970, but the protests at home forced Nixon to call the troops back. The only thing the American government could do to support Lon Nol was to step up the bombing of Cambodian villages that supported the Khmer Rouge.

Then came the Paris peace agreement in January 1973. This provided for an uneasy truce in both South Vietnam and Cambodia. The Khmer Rouge refused to abide by the truce. With the last American troops withdrawn from neighboring South Vietnam, they could see the writing on the wall. Lon Nol was weaker now. They had far more support in the countryside.

The North Vietnamese Communists told the Cambodian Communists not to fight. The fall of Phnom Penh, the Cambodian capital, would destabilize the whole Paris peace agreement. The Khmer Rouge ignored their Vietnamese comrades.

Now the only power that could stop the Khmer Rouge was American bombers. Lon Nol had an army that would not fight for him. In most places, his government did not even have spotters, so the Americans just bombed, in B-52 raid after B-52 raid. The ground shook and the sky burned. In six months in 1973, they dropped one and a half times the tonnage of all the bombs dropped on Japan in the whole of World War Two. Cambodia was a small country, with 4 or 5 million people. The bombing affected most rural areas, because most of the countryside supported the Khmer Rouge.

Several hundred thousand people died in those six months, perhaps a tenth of the population, perhaps more. No country before or since has been subjected to bombing of that scale and intensity. And the B-52 raids were terrifying.[10]

That suffering does not completely explain what happened afterward, but nothing of what happened afterward can be understood without knowledge of that suffering.

The bombing worked. The Khmer Rouge halted their advance. The bombing had been so fierce because Lon Nol and the Americans were so weak on the ground. Now it continued, not as fiercely but still on a larger scale than Vietnam had seen. And while the Vietnamese peasants had a way of understanding the bombing—it had grown out of years of their struggle, and it was a response by the oppressor to that struggle—for the Cambodians it was cataclysmic, senseless, the modern industrial world exploding onto them.

The bombing lasted until the end of the war in 1975. What the Cambodian peasants learned was that the Lon Nol regime and its middle-class supporters in the cities were prepared to support anything the Americans did to them—anything.

The leadership of the Khmer Rouge decided that cities and all the people in them were the problem. They also decided they had to stand alone. When the Vietnamese Communists had made peace with the French in 1954, they had agreed to a separate South Vietnam, and told the Khmer Communists and nationalists to stop fighting. Just as the South Vietnamese Communists had to go North in 1954, so did most of the Cambodian Communist leaders. In 1961 a new leadership in Cambodia had launched a guerrilla war against Sihanouk, like the Viet Cong rebellion in South Vietnam. That time the Vietnamese Communists had urged them not to overthrow Sihanouk, whose neutrality Hanoi valued. Now, in 1973, the leaders of the Khmer Rouge interpreted the American bombing as a punishment because this time they had disobeyed Hanoi's orders not to fight.[11]

The leadership and the peasants had learned that the problem was the cities. The leadership had learned to beware of Vietnamese betrayal.

Then, in 1975, President Nixon was removed from office in the Watergate scandal. The U.S. Congress was about to cut off all funds being used to fight in Southeast Asia. The army of the Saigon regime began to melt, and the Khmer Rouge saw their chance. They took Phnom Penh with almost no opposition.

The advancing Khmer Rouge fighters were now overwhelmingly peasants, mostly young people who had grown up under the bombs. When they took the city of Battambang, they went to the airfield and destroyed those bombers.

Lon Nol's police, army officers, and pilots were ordered to

report to staging areas. They did so and were killed immediately. The leadership of the Khmer Rouge gave orders to send all the other city people to villages in the countryside.

The people sent to the villages were 30 percent of Cambodians. They were now called the "new people" in the villages. The peasants who had supported the Khmer Rouge were the "old people." The new people were expected to settle in the villages and work under the tutelage of the old people.

Most of the old people supported this policy. Kem Hong Hav was deported to Kong Pisei in the southwest:

> [There] the real poor people liked the Khmer Rouge. They were not so intelligent, and happy to eat equally with the educated and rich people with whom they were angry. They liked the system and they really hated the Phnom Penh people, because we had not struggled for the revolution and equality alongside the Khmer Rouge.[12]

You can hear an educated man's contempt for the peasants in that quote. But Kem Hong Hav also made it clear to the historian who interviewed him that the Khmer Rouge had no troops in that village. The village chief and the old people "were the Khmer Rouge":

> Just as before, the base people [the old people] worked hard, in front of us, as models for the new people. They did not stop for wind or rain. They worked harder than us, on behalf of Angkar [the Communist Party]. For us, who were not yet tempered, it was hard. We were angry but dared not say so. . . . The [most] ignorant ones had abandoned all their property and worked for Angkar; they had really forgotten the past, and were enthusiastic.[13]

Srey Pich Chnay, a student of fine arts in Phnom Penh, was sent to a village in the southwest. The peasants there told him: "You used to be happy and prosperous. Now it's our turn."[14]

The peasant hatred of the bombers lay behind the new regime in the village. When the war ended in 1975, the Khmer Rouge had already brought the peasants in most villages into collectives. Work was done together, in small teams, and the rice harvest was shared. Taxation was light.

It did not remain light. The leaders of the Khmer Rouge wanted a state capitalist development of Cambodia. These were the politics they had learned from Stalin in Russia, from Mao and the Chinese Communists, and from the Vietnamese. At the heart of this state capitalist politics, I have argued above, was the squeezing of peasants and workers to build a strong economy quickly. This required a police state—only a dictatorship can make the peasants give up their crops, and can break workers' strikes.

But Cambodia was an underdeveloped country, with little industry even compared to Vietnam, much less Russia or China. The people were not hungry. The land was lightly populated, with lakes and rivers full of fish. But industrial development would be a long, hard road. And Cambodia had far fewer people than neighboring Thailand and Vietnam. Moreover, the Khmer Rouge, and particularly their leader Pol Pot, distrusted the cities. Any forced development would be rural, on the backs of the peasantry.

Pol Pot and the Khmer Rouge leadership were trying to build state capitalism in the hardest possible circumstances. That meant working the peasants hard and policing them hard. There were precedents for such forced development. One was Stalin's terror in the 1930s. Another was the Great Leap Forward in China in 1958. That leap was fueled by the peasants' rice and work. It led almost immediately to famine. Nobody knows how many people died, but it was millions. The Chinese government then backed off. Pol Pot and his people sometimes spoke of their project as another Great Leap Forward. It was to have similar results.

Pol Pot and the Khmer Rouge leaders could not leap into an industrialized future. Given what modern American airplanes had done to them, they no longer wanted to. Yet Pol Pot was a nationalist. His vision was of a great agricultural country, hearkening back to a fantasy of a once great medieval Khmer Empire at Angkor Wat. The peasants would live in collectives, sharing small and equal rations of rice. Many of the new people from the city would be sent to work camps to build the great irrigation works Pol Pot thought were the glory of the old Khmer Empire. Symbolically, the name of the country was changed to Kampuchea, the land of the Khmers.

And much of the rice would go to the capital. Phnom Penh was almost empty. There were 20,000 civilians, many of them peasant girls of 12 to 14 who replaced the former workers in the factories. There were 20,000 soldiers. And there were Pol Pot and the leadership of the party, because this was still a dictatorship of the city over the country. The rank and file of the Khmer Rouge were peasants. The leadership came from the educated middle classes and the fringes of the ruling class in the city.

An awful lot of rice went to the capital. In 1977 the central government plan, for instance, provided for more than half of the expected crop in the southwest to be sent to the center. The same plan allocated none of the expected harvest in the northwest to the people there. It is not clear what they were expected to eat— probably nothing. The northwest was full of new people and more rebellious than the southwest.

It is unlikely that the government managed to actually corner all the rice in this way. But from the beginning, there was hunger in most of the collectives. Where did the truckloads of rice that left the villages go?

Some of it probably went to China (the evidence is not conclusive).[15] The Chinese government was Pol Pot's one ally. It gave guns, planes, trucks, technicians, military advisors, and diplomatic support. In return, Cambodia was China's one ally in the region against Russia and Vietnam.

Wherever the rice went, the fact was it was gone, and yet the Khmer Rouge leadership kept squeezing the villages for more rice. This was what produced the horror. The process moved at different paces in different places. It had a lot to do with the local leadership—some were kind and tried to protect the people under them. Some villages and regions were already hungry in 1975, and some not until 1978. But everywhere the process went like this. There was not enough rice. In some places the new people, the city evacuees, got the same ration as the old people, in some places less. But with less and less rice, the old people were tempted to keep more for themselves. In three years about half of the new people died, in roughly equal numbers from starvation, disease, and executions. Disease was caused by malnutrition and by overwork, because sick people who did not work did not eat.

This was a manmade famine (like all famines). In most places the dead were buried, but when there were too many they were left in the fields or thrown in the rivers. Seng Horl, a teacher sent to the southwest, said that famine killed 400 of the 1,100 people in his village in November and December 1976: "There was not enough ground to bury people. Bodies piled up." In Chen Leng's new village in the northwest, rations fell to half a can of cooked rice a day in 1977, with "less for children, and sometimes nothing for three days. People ate lizards and geckoes. . . . Even some of the gravediggers died on the job." In that village, as in much of Cambodia, all the women stopped menstruating.[16]

The less rice there was, the harder people were forced to work. They worked into the night. In certain lucky places, there was one day off in ten for political education. Fishing and foraging were forbidden. Tam Eng, an ethnic Chinese tailor in Phnom Penh, took her children to her Cambodian ex-husband's village in the south. They were sent to live in a special new village for Chinese people:

We were not allowed to eat our own eggs. If my children were caught fishing or foraging at lunchtime, they were given planting to do before being allowed home again. And if they came back for work late, the . . . chief would complain, and they would disappear.[17]

Eng saw one boy caught planting potatoes "killed on the spot."[18]

This seems insane, and so it seemed to the peasants. People complained to each other. The Khmer Rouge understood that in muttering lies the possibility of revolt.

Seng was an "old" person, a Khmer Rouge supporter and a teacher in the southwest. In his village:

> [T]he problems began in 1975. . . . The work was demanding, and food inadequate. In some places it ran out, and people starved or swelled up. . . . From early 1976, if you said the food was not tasty, or if you stole corn, you would be killed.[19]

This was everywhere. And the more people died or were killed, the more hatred people felt. They would not look the Khmer Rouge cadres in the eye—that might get them killed. But the cadres could still imagine what the people with downcast faces were thinking.

Many of the new people from the cities had relatives among the "old" villagers. After all, the new people were 30 percent of Cambodia. Many of them had found their way to the villages their families originally came from. The regime understood quite quickly that the old villagers would grieve for their "new" kin. So these old villagers were reclassified into reliable old villagers and "candidates"—those old villagers with kin among the new people. And as the candidates were killed or starved, and as the old people who spoke back or looked wrong were killed, the regime knew its enemies were multiplying.

Sen Osman said that in Takeo village from early 1977, there was "a search for internal enemies and agents—enemies in words, enemies at work, inactive [people]. . . . So if you said something a little wrong like 'We are all tired,' they would take you away and kill you."[20]

As one of the Cham ethnic minority, Sen Osman was particularly vulnerable. Pol Pot's government began as extreme nationalists and therefore racists. Ethnic minorities were treated harshly from the beginning. Minority people who had supported the Khmer Rouge were still treated like Lon Nol's city people.

But as the regime found itself more and more unpopular, it began to look harder for ethnic enemies. There were several reasons for this. It knew it had enemies, but could not fully accept that its own people hated it, so it looked for foreign enemies and traitors. It was already nationalist, and an ethnic nationalism always carries with it a racism towards those not truly of the nation. And the regime thought that racism might unite the Khmers, who seemed to be dividing against it.

The regime was racist from the beginning. This made genocide possible. It is not clear whether it intended genocide from the beginning. What is clear is that mass ethnic killing escalated as the regime came under pressure from below.

The Chams, for instance, were Muslims, and therefore were suspect as religious believers. From the beginning, they were killed if they refused to eat pork. In some places, pork was served twice a month to test the Chams, even when there was little other food. In places where there was no pork, they were simply asked if they would eat pork and killed if they said no.

Tep Ibrahim, a Cham, was exiled to the north. In 1977 the Chams in his village were told that Malaysia was sending gasoline to ransom them because they were fellow Muslims. Tep Ibrahim, like the others, was happy to go. But he was late when they loaded the trucks with Chams. He ran after the truck but could not catch it. Of those who went in the trucks, he said, "there are none of us left. . . . Two days after they had left, their scarves and shirts were brought back and distributed to children. . . . They were taken and thrown [into pits], killed off." Later he cut bananas near where the trucks had been taken, and "the whole district was smelling" of bodies.[21]

The Vietnamese minority were particularly suspect. They were villagers along the Vietnamese border and immigrant workers in the cities. The Khmer Rouge leaders felt Hanoi had betrayed them many times, and that the Vietnamese were "ancient enemies" of the Khmer Empire. They began killing some, but not all, Vietnamese in 1975. Four hundred thousand ethnic Vietnamese then managed to flee to Vietnam. Many ethnic Cambodians (Khmers) fled with them across the border to escape the hunger and repression. At this point, Vietnam was still an ally of Cambodia. The Vietnamese government accepted the fleeing Vietnamese Cambodians. But the Vietnamese army forced the ethnic Khmers back across the border into Cambodia and almost certain death as enemies of the regime there.

The Khmer Rouge raided across the border, slaughtering whole Vietnamese villages. The Vietnamese authorities forbade Vietnamese journalists to publish the photographs of the dead and the tales of the survivors. They did not want to anger the Chinese government, the ally of the Khmer Rouge.

Tension still grew between Vietnam and Cambodia. As the hatred grew in the villages, the Khmer Rouge leadership looked for enemies. On 1 April 1977 the order went out from Phnom Penh to arrest "all ethnic Vietnamese, and all Khmers who spoke Vietnamese or had Vietnamese friends."[22] People who were arrested were not taken to prison. Genocide had begun.

Heng Chor was an ethnic Khmer in Pursat. There in March 1977, a "Khmer Rouge cadre killed his former wife, who was of Vietnamese descent, along with five of his sons, three daughters, three grandchildren, his mother-in-law, eight from his sister-in-law's family, [and] seven from his brother-in-law's family."[23] The cadre may have been trying to protect himself from the regime. He was, after all, a man with Vietnamese friends and relatives.

The Khmer Krom were suspect too. They were the ethnic Khmer minority in Vietnam. Some Khmer Krom had also migrated back into Cambodia. They spoke Cambodian with a Vietnamese accent. Pol Pot said they had Khmer bodies but Vietnamese minds, and they too were killed. Several times Khmer Rouge units raided across the border into Vietnam, rounded up Khmer Krom villagers, and took them back into Cambodia because that was their real home. Once there, though, they became the Vietnamese enemy and were killed.

But the more killing, the more hatred from below. Then the regime took the children. Those over three, or sometimes over five, were taken to special children's centers, where their parents could see them only rarely. Those of ten or so were taken to special children's work camps, and their parents could not see them at all. This policy was tried in a few places in 1975 but did not become general until 1977 and 1978. This one policy, more than all the hunger and all the killing, turned the reliable "old" villagers against the Khmer Rouge.

Even as they took the peasants' children away, Pol Pot and the other leaders appointed more and more of their own relatives to leading positions. Their kin were now the only people they could trust.

The people the government feared most, and killed most, were the cadres of the Khmer Rouge. These cadres were revolutionaries. They had joined the struggle out of a desire for equality and social justice. And they were the only people who commanded organizations with guns.

In place after place, the Khmer Rouge cadres saw what was happening and were sickened by what they were ordered to do. They were also terrified. But because they were almost all spread out in villages, they found it difficult to combine, difficult even to know if cadres in other areas felt the same. To plot a rebellion, a cadre had to talk to a lot of people. One of them, out of loyalty or fear, usually informed the central government. Moreover, it was difficult for the Communists to turn against their party, to fully admit to themselves what was happening.

So the cadre turned at different times, at different speeds. As they did so, one after another was taken away "for study." The Khmer Rouge leadership were justifiably terrified, because they knew they were hated. But the general fear meant that the rulers could not know precisely who hated them. It became a race between the regime trying to break rebellion and the cadres trying to nerve themselves to rebel.

The regime usually won the race. But they had to send specially picked cadres into the northwest to exterminate almost all the cadres there. In the east, the Vietnamese border provided a haven, and thousands of cadres and tens of thousands of villagers fought their way to safety. After that, the regime launched a pogrom of the eastern cadres who had remained loyal.

When people were arrested in Cambodia they were usually killed, not sent to prison. But the senior cadres of the Khmer Rouge were the exception. The government had to find out what they were doing. Like many other governments, what the Khmer Rouge leaders feared most were Communists. So when senior cadres were arrested, they were taken to Tuol Sleng prison, a former girls' school in Phnom Penh, where they were tortured and forced to write long confessions. Of the 20,000 people who went into Tuol Sleng, seven survived. The regime was afraid the relatives of these prisoners might take revenge, so it also executed their husbands, wives, and children, and sometimes their mothers.

By the end of 1978 Cambodia was full of bitterness. Many people were imagining rebellion. The regime was imploding. It reacted by escalating raids into Vietnam and pogroms against the Vietnamese in Cambodia. Pol Pot's hatred for the Vietnamese was sincere enough, but this policy was also calculated to bring a disintegrating country together under Khmer Rouge leadership.

It didn't work. In December 1978 the Vietnamese army invaded Cambodia. Both the Vietnamese leaders and the Khmer Rouge leaders expected stiff Cambodian resistance to the Vietnamese. It didn't happen. The highway to Phnom Penh lay open, and within a week the Vietnamese army was in the capital. The Khmer Rouge troops had not fought to defend the Khmer Rouge regime. The Vietnamese installed a new government headed by two former Khmer Rouge commanders who had rebelled and fled to Vietnam, Heng Samrin and Hun Sen. Pol Pot and the leadership fell back into the countryside, counting on a prolonged guerrilla war. In a matter of weeks, they were driven back into small enclaves in remote areas on the Thai border. The Vietnamese were about to smash them when the Americans stepped in.

The American government and media publicized the crimes of the Khmer Rouge. Pictures of the mass graves and the piles of skulls went around the world as proof of the evils of Communism. At the same time, the military dictatorship in Thailand, the Chinese Communists, and Jimmy Carter all worked together. The Khmer Rouge were allowed to rest in Thailand and then go back across the border. Under cover of humanitarian aid to refugees, the American and Chinese governments supplied food, money, and arms to the Khmer Rouge. Without this support, the Khmer Rouge would have gone under. At the same time the United States led successful fights at the UN, year after year, to keep Cambodia's UN seat for Pol Pot.[24]

The Americans were supporting Pol Pot to punish the Vietnamese for winning the Vietnam War.

WAR WITH CHINA

While the American and Chinese governments began to rebuild Pol Pot's tattered forces in 1979, the Chinese army invaded Vietnam along the northern border. The intention was to teach Hanoi a lesson and force it to retreat from Cambodia. Vietnamese resistance was fierce and the Chinese army had to withdraw.

The victims of this war were the Chinese minority in Vietnam. Already in 1978, the year before, the "boat people" had begun to flee Vietnam. At first they were the Vietnamese of Chinese ancestry in the south—the many businessmen and even more workers who had lost their jobs when the state took over the Chinese businesses in Saigon. After the Chinese invasion in the north, the Vietnamese government began a propaganda attack on Chinese people. More of the Chinese in the south fled, and the Chinese in the north, mostly peasants and fishermen, fled too.

The majority of the refugees crossed the northern border into

China. But in the south many left by small coastal boats. The local bureaucrats took their gold in bribes, and individual officials took over the houses of the rich as they left. Many boat people drowned in storms. Many who pushed ashore in Thailand or Malaysia were pushed out to sea again. Those who reached Hong Kong were put in detention camps by the British. At first the American government refused to take any boat people. Pirates, mostly local fishermen in Thailand and Indonesia, boarded many boats, robbed the people, killed some, and raped many women.

Then economic crisis hit in 1979 and 1980. Now most of the boat people were ethnic Vietnamese.

The economic crisis hit for four reasons. First, American and Chinese aid dried up. Second, the American boycott isolated the Vietnamese economy. Third was the cost of the Cambodian war and a standing army of 1.5 million. Fourth was the refusal of the peasants to grow more grain for the state.

As the crisis hit in cooperative after cooperative across the north, the local authorities instituted various local contract systems that allowed families to farm more of the land, and to keep and sell more of the rice they grew. In 1981 this was formalized at a national level. A new law allowed individual peasant families to, in effect, rent land on a long-term basis. The peasants then worked harder and grew more rice because they could keep more of what they grew. For the moment, famine was averted.

THE OCCUPATION OF CAMBODIA

Back in Cambodia the Khmer Rouge, with American and Chinese support, were gradually rebuilding their strength in the jungle. King Sihanouk was in alliance with them again, and they were helped by the way the Vietnamese government behaved after the invasion. The Vietnamese had received a wary welcome. Anybody was better than the Khmer Rouge, and if ever an invasion of another country was justified, the Vietnamese invasion of Cambodia was. But it was not simply a humanitarian operation. Had it been, the Vietnamese army would simply have turned power over to the Cambodian opponents of Pol Pot and left. Instead it kept 300,000 troops in Cambodia for ten years. Cambodians headed the government but Vietnamese made policy. According to the French anthropologist Marie Martin:

> All officials had a Vietnamese superior in the hierarchy who supervised a single person or an entire department. At the head of each ministry was a Cambodian minister and a "Vietnamese minister," as the Khmers called them. . . .
>
> Cambodians who held high positions . . . unanimously stated that each text written by a Khmer had to be approved by the Vietnamese authority in the department before circulation. All administrative, political and economic decisions had to have at least the endorsement of the adviser and were usually dictated by him.[25]

A Cambodian civil servant put it this way: "In the ministries [the Vietnamese] used to be called advisors. Now they are administrators, making all the decisions. People leave for that reason. Those who stay work with clenched teeth."[26] The advisors and the soldiers ate the Cambodian rice. Trucks of rice went north and east to Vietnam.

This occupation corrupted Cambodia. Everything was for sale—free care in public hospitals, for instance, and education. By 1991 the bribe for admission to medical school was $7,500 in gold.[27]

In this situation, Pol Pot's Khmer Rouge managed to survive in the forests and mountains of the west. They would not have done so without American and Chinese money and guns, and refuges in Thailand. But they also would not have lasted without the distaste many ordinary Cambodians felt for their new rulers. They could not take power, but they could harass the government and kill.

Roughly 50,000 Vietnamese soldiers were killed in Cambodia in the ten years after the invasion, and 200,000 were wounded.

Many of the wounded stepped on land mines supplied by America to the Khmer Rouge, and their limbs had to be amputated. Moreover, in the American War the children of top Communist cadres had gone south to fight. In the occupation of Cambodia, the Vietnamese troops were the conscript children of poor people, particularly peasants from the south. And with them went other poor Vietnamese, until the majority of prostitutes in Phnom Penh were Vietnamese.[28]

It was another colonial situation. Why? Vietnam took rice and got Russian aid. But this in no way made up for the cost of the war over ten years. Moreover, Vietnam had to maintain a standing army of 1.5 million with modern weapons, an enormous drain on a poor economy. The Vietnamese army were in Cambodia as proxies for the Russians, just as the Khmer Rouge had become proxies for the Chinese and Americans.

One thing showed this clearly. When the Russian dictatorship fell in 1989 and Russian aid was withdrawn from Vietnam, the Vietnamese government promptly pulled its troops out of Cambodia.

Suddenly Washington faced the possibility of an American-backed Khmer Rouge victory in Cambodia, which would be appallingly embarrassing. The United Nations intervened, with American sponsorship but no American troops. Its official mission was to hold Pol Pot back and restore democracy. It organized elections. The party led by King Sihanouk's son beat the ruling party led by Hun Sen. Hun Sen then annulled the elections, and the United Nations continued to support him. Sihanouk and his son, ever the opportunists, formed a coalition with Hun Sen. Hun Sen began learning English. The end result was that a corrupt client regime of the Vietnamese had become a corrupt client regime of the United Nations. The Chinese and Americans then cut off aid to the Khmer Rouge, and they gradually withered.

The UN spent $2 billion to do this. UN civilian workers in Cambodia had an extra daily hardship allowance of $130 a day, 195 times the 67 cents a day paid to Cambodian teachers and civil servants. Cambodians saw that legal UN corruption far out-stripped illegal Cambodian corruption. They began to steal what-ever they could, led by Hun Sen and his government. Martin writes: "Khmer summarize the life-style of their rulers in a short sentence: three wives, three villas, three cars."[29]

VIETNAM IN THE 1980s

The Vietnamese had troubles of their own. The rice supply in Vietnam had increased after 1981. But that increase was a one-off. By 1983 farmers were already working as hard as they could. The government then began raising rents on land and lowering the price they paid peasants for grain. The peasants began to react as they had in the 1970s, by growing only enough rice to feed themselves.[30]

What did the continuing economic crisis mean for people's lives? Some important things did get better for a while after 1954. By 1983 infant mortality was a third of what it had been in 1960, and life expectancy had increased from forty-two to fifty-nine years. But after 1978 the weight of newborn babies began to fall, and in 1987 the Ministry of Health estimated that half of children were suffering from malnutrition. The average height of adults was getting shorter, and the real wages of city workers were fall-ing. State employees had always counted on rations of rice and other staples at very low prices, but by 1979 a month's ration lasted only a few days. In 1976 city people spent 70 percent of their income on food. By 1980 it was 80 percent.[31]

Bui Tin was a senior Communist Party member, an editor, and a veteran of the French and American wars. In 1990 he went into exile in France at the age of 63. He wrote that on his street in Hanoi:

There is a worker over forty years old with four children, three boys and a girl. He had been laid off from a state-run factory, his wife is a street sweeper and he survives as best he can. He does a bit of building work, carpentry, repairing bicycles or tailoring. In winter he even makes Western "NATO" jackets according to a pattern which emanates from Thailand. In the evenings too, he takes a young son along to set up a stall selling tea and cigarettes outside the district finance office where they collect lottery tickets. . . .

Meanwhile an old lady of over eighty hawks titbits to the children. Also down the street, a retired colonel who specialized in anti-aircraft warfare now sells yoghurt [on the street]. A more junior officer who made a name for himself in 1954 at the time of the battle for Dien Bien Phu by sabotaging French aircraft before they took off from the airfield near Hanoi, now makes a living by pumping up bicycle tires. His problem is that even his pump is old and requires frequent repairs. . . .

Such people are intent on surviving all these hardships on their own. They are accustomed to electricity and water cuts as well as the stinking environment. They even cheer when the light comes back on. But what do they really feel inside about human fate?[32]

In 1988 Duong Thu Huong, a Communist Party member and veteran of the Chinese and American wars, wrote a novel attacking the rulers of her society. The heroine of *Paradise of the Blind* is a worker. Here she thinks about the smiling faces of Japanese tourists:

Hundreds of faces rose in my memory: those of my friend, people of my generation, faces gnawed with worry, shattered faces, twisted, ravaged, sooty, frantic faces. Our faces were always taut, lean with fear. The fear that we might not be able to pay for food, or send it in time, the fear of learning that an aged father or mother had passed away while waiting for our miserable subsidies, the fear that some embassy official just might not. . . .

We had daring, calculating faces: You had to think of everything, weigh everything. All the time.

You had to think to survive, to feed your loved ones, to hustle for a day's wages sharecropping or sweeping on a train. You had to think too of the life that stretched out ahead, the pain that still waited for you, of a future as unsure and unfathomable as sea fog. . . .

[I] have the eyes of a wild animal, darting about, razor sharp, ready to quarrel over goods at a shop counter or scuffle in a line for food. And there was the shame, the self-loathing, in the mirror of another's gaze. Life as one endless humiliation.[33]

The rice was not coming in from the countryside, and in 1988 the prospect of famine loomed in the north. The state capitalist model of development was not working in Vietnam. Russia under Gorbachev and China under Deng were adopting the market. In 1989 Russian aid stopped. The Communist ruling class in Vietnam knew they had to do something different.

What? The only ideas on offer in the world in 1988 were the ideas of the market. They had swept the West, Japan, Russia, and China. And in Vietnam, village after village and factory after factory had made unofficial free market deals that seemed to offer the only way to keep the enterprise going. There was a sort of creeping free market at the base of society—the Vietnamese called it "fence breaking."[34] And in 1988 the rulers at the top formally adopted Doi Moi, the "New Change." They hoped the market would solve their problems.

For the villagers, this meant that land was shared out. Each family got one share of the village land for each person in the family. In the cities the factories were not shared out. Instead foreign investment was welcomed. By one means or another, state managers turned their enterprises into private companies owned by themselves. The government looked to the International Monetary Fund and the World Bank to tell it how to run the economy.

The new strategy was to make Vietnam a low-wage economy exporting cheap goods. The model was the other southeast Asian economies, particularly Thailand, Indonesia, and Malaysia.[35] Vietnam had the poorest people in Southeast Asia. The government tried to attract foreign investment by promising its people would work harder, for less, for longer hours, and in less safe conditions than any workforce in Southeast Asia. But trying to undercut Indonesian workers, for instance, meant squeezing labor very hard indeed.

The government also gave up trying to control the peasants' rice. Now private traders, with government support, bought the rice cheaply and exported much of it to China. Vietnamese still ate an average of just over 2,000 calories a day—not enough—but Vietnam became the third-largest exporter of rice in the world.

In the countryside, peasants could now sell land.[36] By 1990 official figures estimated that half the peasants were already in debt. Those who got too far in debt had to sell land. By 1993 the Vietnamese economist Dang Phong wrote that "concentration of land is occurring quite strongly in the southern provinces and some central provinces."[37] The new rich in the villages were mostly the old administrators of the cooperatives. When the land was shared out, they took more than their share. As one villager said, "[T]he authorities could not stop this corruption. What could they do—"arrest themselves?"[38] And when the other villagers went too heavily into debt, these new rich were the people who could buy them out. In Vinh Hung district in the Plain of Reeds (the marshes south of Saigon) in 1993, while the district vice president "is kept busy with his work in the district, his wife runs the family business. In addition to their 100 hectares of land, they own a tractor and thresher, a pump, a petrol station which serves the entire area, and a truck."[39]

This one family had 100 hectares while the average family farmed one hectare. This is an extreme example, but the same thing was happening all over the country, particularly in the south. And of course the only way such a rich household could farm the land was to rent to the newly landless or hire them as laborers.

A similar process was happening in the cities. The ministries, the army, and the old factory managers now ran their own businesses. There was a complex mixture of state companies, private companies in partnership with state companies, and private companies paying state officials large bribes to get around the regulations those same state officials had constructed. The opportunities for profit, bribes, and stealing were enormous. The old Communist cadre split in two. The majority became poorly paid minor officials or unemployed ex-officials. Now they took small bribes or made out the best they could with bicycle pumps. Their old ideals had been betrayed from the top, and now they had to betray those ideals to feed their families. They became empty men and women, hollowed out by corruption, ashamed and angry.

A minority of the officials became a new rich class of combined state-private capitalists. (They were more private than state—by 1997 private capitalist Malaysia had more of the economy in public ownership than Vietnam.) The Communists had always said they were servants of the people. Now the people sang a little verse about their "servants":

The servant travels in a Volga [car],
The families of the masters wait at the station for a train.
The servant has a nice villa,
The families of the masters use oil paper to keep out the rain.
The servant attends banquets, noon and night,
The families of the masters eat greens and pickles every day.[40]

At the end of the American War, Vietnam had been a poor country but a relatively equal one. There were rich and poor, but the gap was nothing like that in Indonesia or the United States, and the village cooperatives and city workplaces provided free education and medical care. After 1988 people had to pay for medicine and schooling. They took sick children to the doctor less often and took more children out of school. Rationing had made sure that everybody got some food. Now that has largely gone.

An unequal society is unequal in every respect. One window on that inequality is what happens to women. The Danish anthropologist Tine Gammeltoft did a study of IUD (birth control coil) use by women in one village in the Red River Delta near Hanoi in 1993–94.[41]

The population of Vietnam doubled between 1975 and 1994, and the government promoted birth control. The women of this village supported the campaign. They had to bear the children. Since the village cooperative had been divided, men looked for work outside the village while women did most of the farming, bending over or squatting all day long. Family incomes had risen because women worked harder. But their backs ached from work and their heads ached from worry. There was never enough money, and women worried about food for the children. The worry and the pain kept them awake at night. As one woman said, "I often have headaches because of thinking a lot. When I don't think, there is no problem."[42]

Another woman said, "You go to work, come home tired in the evening, the children are a nuisance, the pig screams, you have to cook food for it. You go to sleep, already exhausted, so tired, the child has to be breastfed all night, the husband demands [sex]."[43]

If the woman doesn't give the husband sex, they may fight. If she does, she often resents it. One woman put it this way: "Women can't bear having a lot of sex. It makes you feel tired and worn out like a boiled vegetable."[44]

The women used birth control. Until the mid-1980s they had a choice of the pill, the condom, or the coil. Most Vietnamese used the condom. But then the government decided that the health system would only supply the coil. Foreign exchange was short and a coil was cheaper. Moreover, women controlled their use of the pill and men controlled condoms. The state, through the nurses who put in the coils, controlled the coil.

So women used the coil. In America and Europe, a large minority of women who use the coil have unbearable pain. Sometimes they put up with it, but usually they stop eventually. Three things are likely to increase with use of the coil—back pain, poor nutrition, and anemia. The women in this Vietnamese village had all three. But the coil was their only choice, so they used it.

Some were all right on the coil but the majority were not. It hurt their bellies. It made their periods longer, so they bled more and became weaker and more anemic. It gave them headaches, and they lay awake at night, their muscles in pain, their backs in pain, their wombs in pain, worrying about their children and their husband's anger.

They endured, because they had few choices.

The women in this village were part of a far larger system. During the wars against the Americans and the French, the government had encouraged women's rights because it wanted to mobilize women, wanted them to fight passionately for the cause. Now, as the whole society grew more unequal, the government cared less.

And many of the old ways linger. In the villages, childless women still fear their husbands taking a second wife. Prostitution has not gone away either. In Saigon the government effectively encourages it as part of the tourist trade. During the American War, the Rex Hotel in Saigon was famous among Vietnamese as a home of American debauchery. In 1998 I asked a rich American who had been to Vietnam several times in recent years what he recommended doing in Saigon. He said get a massage at the Rex Hotel.

But there is resistance among women too. In the Red River Valley in the north, there are many women without husbands because so many died during the war. The old moral code says they should not have sex or children. The government's new birth control policy says single women should not have children. But in all villages, many single women have children anyway. They often pay men to have sex with them enough times to conceive, and then they pay a fine to the authorities when they have the child. But they refuse to be ashamed because they have suffered enough from the war.[45] And because so many have done it, it is now accepted.

Resistance

The increasing inequalities in Vietnam have produced increasing resistance. The peasants had fought the French, the landlords, and the Americans. Then they fought the collectives to keep their rice. Now they fight the market.

The land was divided in 1988. In the first two years, 200,000 people filed official complaints about the way it was done.[46] In many cases, old landlords in the south were trying to take back by force the lands they had before 1975—there were 976 reported cases of this in Ben Tre province alone in just the first half of 1993. Throughout the country, local officials tried to take land by tricks or brute force. In other cases, a village claimed that local officials had given their land to a neighboring village. By 1990 this had happened in 6,000 villages nationwide, and in most cases people suspected bribery.

The peasants petitioned, demonstrated, and marched in thousands of villages. In the four years to 1992 in Thai Binh province, for instance, there were fifty "serious clashes" over land. Benedict Kerkvliet summarizes a report in the newspaper *Nong Dan* about a village in Thanh Hoa province in the north:

> [The villagers] had been disgusted for some time with corruption by commune officials. Efforts to change the situation had brought no result. In fact, things worsened, as district officials pressured people to stop making allegations of misbehavior. In early 1989 villagers chose, by an election, the leaders of two production groups within the village.[47]

The officials rejected their choices. The villagers "refused to change their minds":

> Eleven investigators and public security officials [came] to arrest several villagers, including the two elected leaders. . . . The officials

were suddenly surrounded by a huge crowd of angry, shouting villagers, who prevented them from arresting anyone. Instead, the officers found themselves trapped. The crowd would not let them leave. When district and commune authorities sent in security police to rescue the eleven officers, "thousands" of villagers fought back, using sticks, bricks, and anything else they could find. The security police found themselves overwhelmed; several were even disarmed by swarms of people. The security police retreated, leaving the villagers still with five "captives"—three security police and two investigators.[48]

In exchange for their hostages, the villagers demanded that the authorities drop all criminal charges, dismiss several local officials, "conduct a thorough investigation," and "organize democratic elections by which trusted people are chosen to be village leaders."[49] This is an extreme example and we do not know what happened next. But demonstrations were common—in 1988, farmers even marched on a provincial capital in the Mekong Delta.[50]

In the cities the workers went on strike. There is an official union, but it does not defend workers: only 12 percent of workers in private industry belong to it, and the government does not allow it to organize in foreign-owned companies. But, as Gabriel Kolko writes:

> Since the worst abuses—from beatings, forced overtimes, and unsafe conditions to withholding pay—have occurred in joint ventures and foreign owned plants (especially Korean) that expect to make the most of Vietnam's promised comparative advantages, they have experienced the most labor disputes. . . .
>
> Strikes have varied greatly in size and duration. An initial official estimate of at least 214 strikes nationally from 1989 to March 1996 is too conservative. The union paper reported thirty-two strikes in the first ten months of 1994 alone. There were "dozens"

of unauthorized strikes in 1995, the party admits publicly, nearly double the number in 1994—and even more in 1996. These strikes technically are all independent of the official union.[51]

This is a very high rate of strikes in a small working class. In the 1990s Vietnamese workers have been far more militant than British or American workers. And, as Kolko points out, these strikes are illegal, but they are reported sympathetically in the Vietnamese press and nobody is prosecuted. Leaders of peasant demonstrations have been arrested, and very occasionally sentenced to death. Strike leaders may lose their jobs, but the government does not dare to punish them.

This is because the rulers of Vietnam have some idea of what a mass strike in Hanoi or Saigon (Ho Chi Minh City) could do to them. Vietnamese independence started with the risings in Hanoi and Saigon in 1945. More recently, they have seen the example of Tiananmen Square in China in 1989. Mass urban movements, largely composed of workers, have overthrown dictatorships in Iran, the Philippines, Thailand, and Indonesia. Vietnam's ruling class is frightened of attacking workers' leaders lest other workers rally around. It can live with a large demonstration of peasants marching on a provincial capital. A mass demonstration in one of the two big cities might change everything. A general strike could overthrow it.

So, for the moment, it allows the strikes to happen, and sometimes to win. But in the long run that gives workers a confidence that makes a rising from below more likely.

Conclusion

The history of Vietnam after 1975 is a tragedy. The Vietnamese people fought for thirty years against French and American power and for a better world, with great courage and great losses. They ended up as the subjects of a new ruling class. That class was itself both the prisoner and agent of a world market and a world capitalist system. Vietnam today is a better place than it was under the Americans or the French. But it is not the kind of society all those people fought and died for.

The tragedy was that when those five men started meeting in the village of Beautiful Waters to talk about their village and how to change their country, they could only see a choice between the private capitalism they lived under and a state capitalist "communism." This book has been written in the conviction that another way is possible—not inevitable, but possible. In Chapter 1, I quoted Ngo Van, who fought with a few dozen Trotskyist comrades in the rising of the Saigon working class in 1945. They marched in the great demonstrations that August under banners that called for peasants to take the land and workers to take the factories. They wanted to carry through what the Russian workers and peasants had tried to do in 1917. Most of them were killed, and the few survivors like Ngo Van were driven into exile. But what they fought for still remains, I think, the hope for humanity—democratic workers' power from below.

8

AMERICA AND THE WORLD
AFTER THE WAR

This chapter is about the consequences of the war in America, and for American power in the world. The first part deals with the attempts by American governments from 1975 to 2000 to erase the memory of Vietnam and the movements of the 1960s. The second part deals with the resurgence of American power in the world after September 11. That resurgent power has confronted a worldwide anti-capitalist movement, which has also produced a global movement against war. The echoes of Vietnam and the 1960s are everywhere now. The book ends with a consideration of how this new movement is different from the old, how it is similar, and what can be learned from both the achievements and mistakes of the movement against the Vietnam War.

The U.S. government lost the war in Vietnam. Three things made the defeat worse. First, America was a great power and Vietnam was a small peasant nation. Second, the whole world had watched the defeat. Third, the American people had turned against the war and the American armed forces had refused to fight. The American ruling class had lost the war to the Vietnamese and the Americans.

This gave heart to anybody who opposed American power in the world. It also demoralized rulers in the Third World who looked to America for support.

Moreover, the anti-war movement in America had been closely related to the black movement, the women's movement, and the gay movement. The students had marched, the cities had burned, and the soldiers had mutinied at the same time.

So after the defeat in Vietnam, the American ruling class needed to reestablish their power. They tried to do this in several ways. As we have seen, they tried to isolate the Vietnamese economy and keep the Vietnamese poor as punishment for winning the war. They supported Pol Pot and Khmer Rouge in Cambodia because they were the enemies of Vietnamese Communism. They tried to blame the cruelty of the war on American veterans. They tried to rewrite history so that the anti-war movement became the enemies of the veterans. They tried to reverse the social gains made by the movements of the 1960s, particularly by weakening unions and imprisoning black men. Finally, they tried to persuade the American people to let their children fight ground wars for Washington again.

All these strategies can be summed up in one word—backlash. This chapter shows how that backlash worked, at home and abroad. It ends with Seattle, the anti-globalization movement, September 11, the war on terror, Afghanistan, and Iraq.

THE VIETNAM SYNDROME

After 1975 the American establishment faced what it called the "Vietnam syndrome." By this, they meant the difficulty in getting American workers to give their lives for American imperialism again. The liberals and the media spoke as if it were an illness, a "syndrome," a bad thing. They also said that the problem was that Americans were cowards—they were afraid of body bags coming home. In fact, the images that people remembered from the Vietnam War were not body bags. They were the photographs of the soldier with the empty thousand-yard stare, the naked little girl covered in burning napalm running down the road screaming, the Saigon chief of police shooting a prisoner through the head up close, a marine using his cigarette lighter on the thatch of a house. These were images of cruelty, and of American and Vietnamese suffering. Americans had fought bravely in other wars. It wasn't that they were cowards. It was that they had learned not to trust people asking them to die for a cause that wasn't theirs.

By 1998 almost all liberal academics and public commentators argued that the Vietnam War had been a mistake. That same year 63 percent of the American public still felt that the war had been "fundamentally wrong."[1] This was not acceptable to the media and government consensus, so they talked of syndromes and body bags. And from 1975 on, the government tried to get Americans to agree to fight in foreign wars.

This section looks at five situations where America's rulers wanted to use ground troops—Angola, Iran, Lebanon, the Gulf War, and Kosovo.

Angola

The first example is Angola. The nationalist movement there had won independence from Portuguese colonialism in 1975. Angola had a long border with South Africa. The blacks in South Africa could see the writing on the wall for their own white rulers, and there was a mass movement of schoolchildren's strikes in the townships and union strikes in workplaces. The South African white apartheid government fought back by invading Angola. The Russians then cleverly sent Cuban troops to fight the South Africans in Angola.

Henry Kissinger, the U.S. secretary of state, quite correctly saw this as a major blow against American power in the Cold War. Nelson Mandela's ANC in South Africa was at that time funded and supported by Russia, not the United States. South Africa was the most important concentration of private capitalism in the continent. And now the Russians, in the person of their Cuban clients, were able to use ground troops in Africa when the United States could not.

Kissinger said in 1975, "The United States will not accept further communist military intervention in South Africa." But Congress, haunted by Vietnam, "voted 323 to 99 to ban covert military aid to Angola."[2] Kissinger later asked the Pentagon to come up with a plan for fighting the Cubans in Angola. The Pentagon replied that it would take a very long time to come up with such a plan. Kissinger understood that the generals were preventing him from even thinking about fighting in Angola.[3] It is not hard to imagine what the generals might have thought about using an army with a lot of black soldiers to defend white racism in another Vietnam.

Iran

This inability to intervene weakened American power. Then came the 1979–80 revolution in Iran.[4] Iran was a major oil producer ruled by an American-backed dictator, the Shah. Months of mass demonstrations and strikes in the banks and oilfields finally drove the Shah from power. Two different political trends led this mass movement. One was the Left, and the other was the Islamists— often called "Muslim fundamentalists"—led by Ayatollah Khomeini. After the Shah was overthrown in Iran, they competed for leadership of the revolution for over a year. The Islamists won. Crucial to this victory was the occupation of the American embassy by Islamist students, who held the white men inside hostage for a year. (They let the women and African Americans go, on the grounds that they were oppressed in America.)

Before Vietnam, the U.S. government would have responded to the embassy occupation with an invasion of Iran. In 1980 they dared not. The result was a massive, and very public, humiliation for American power. This humiliation, the successful revolution, and the call for a more equal world all inspired strong Islamist opposition movements in Iraq, Turkey, Syria, Bahrain, Saudi Arabia, Lebanon, Israel and Palestine, Egypt, Sudan, Tunisia, Algeria, and Morocco.

These Islamist movements are often called "Muslim fundamentalists." The term is misleading, as it suggests a similarity with Christian fundamentalists in the United States. The Christian right in America is certainly political, but is also racist and supports the established order. The Islamists in the Middle East talked of decency in human relations, of an end to corruption, of more welfare provision by the government for the poor, and of opposition to American imperialism. A much better parallel than the Christian right is the religiously based politics of Martin Luther King, or the liberation theology of Catholic priests and nuns. Indeed, one good way to understand the appeal of Islamism is to read *The Autobiography of Malcolm X*, the leading American thinker of political Islam.[5]

These Islamist movements in the Middle East were something new.[6] For most of the twentieth century, mass opposition to the old order in the Middle East had been led by secular nationalists, socialists, and Communists—men like Ataturk in Turkey, Nasser in Egypt, and Arafat in Palestine. Most people who supported them were Muslim believers who saw no contradiction between socialism and Islam. But then many of the nationalist and socialist leaders came to power, usually with Communist support. These new leaders became dictators over grossly unequal capitalist societies, rather like the Communist leaders in Vietnam after 1975. By 1980 people in the Middle East, deeply disillusioned, were looking for an alternative that seriously meant to fight social inequality.

After the Iranian revolution, Islamism seemed to provide that alternative. It was not one uniform movement. Some Islamists were moderate parliamentary reformers, some were radicals, some were terrorists, and a few were revolutionaries like Malcolm X. There was also a constant tension within Islamist movements. The mass following, mostly workers and peasants, were attracted by the fiery rhetoric of opposition and the promise of a just society. Their leaders, however, were much more right-wing. They basically accepted the logic of business and the market. Where they came to power, as they did in Iran, Afghanistan, and Sudan, the leaders presided over an unjust society much as the nationalists had.

This contradiction between the leaders and the led could be seen in their sexual politics. Many educated young women in the Middle East, whose sisters and mothers had not worn the veil, now put on a headscarf to show their opposition to all established society. Iraq, for instance, was led by the determinedly secular dictator Saddam Hussein. A headscarf there was a very public way for a woman to express her opposition to both Saddam and the Americans.[7]

The women who did this did not intend to express support for masculine power. Indeed, their very rebellion was an assertion of their own power. It was not that simple, however. Wearing a headscarf is also an assertion that women are somehow different, just like the taboo on women, but not men, walking topless on American streets. For the leaders of the Islamist movement, the new dress codes fitted with a much more general conservatism in social matters. Again, perhaps the best way for an American reader to understand the contradictions here is to think of the Million Man March on Washington led by the Nation of Islam. There too you can see genuine anti-racism and a mass yearning for a more decent society—but also the separation of men and women, a conservative vision of the family, and a leadership wedded to business values.

The problem for the American government and the oil corporations after the Iranian revolution, however, was not the social conservatism of the Islamist leaders. It was that the new movements in the Middle East were a challenge by tens of millions of people to the dictatorships in each country. They were also a challenge to the American power that stood behind the dictators, who controlled the largest source of oil in the world. The Middle East and its oil were important for profits, strategically crucial, and essential to the industries of Japan and Europe.

Unable to intervene militarily themselves, the U.S. government attacked the Islamists by proxy. They encouraged Saddam Hussein, the military dictator in Iraq, to invade Iran. Saddam Hussein was only nominally a Muslim, and in no way an Islamist. His roots were in the secular Arab nationalist movement. He had come to power in a coup backed by the CIA. Then, during the 1970s, he had been allied with the Soviet Union. Now he swung back to the American alliance. The Iraqi invasion of Iran led to a war that lasted seven years and cost a million lives. That long, grinding war isolated and weakened the new Iranian regime. The dictatorships in Saudi Arabia and Kuwait, both American clients and both afraid of popular support for their own Islamists, gave Iraq billions to fight the Iranians.

America's other proxy was Israel. In 1982 the Israeli army invaded Lebanon, where an alliance of Islamists and secular Palestinian refugees were winning a civil war. But the Israelis were unable to hold the Lebanese capital, Beirut. So they were replaced by a multilateral force spearheaded by American marines, and American naval ships began long-range shelling of Lebanese villages. An Islamist suicide bomber then drove a truckload of explosives into an American base, killing 230 people, mostly marines. The marines were soon withdrawn.[8]

Back home, the U.S. government reacted to their humiliation in Iran with a campaign to whip up anti-Muslim prejudice that lasted for the next twenty years. All Muslims, not just political Islamists, were portrayed as sexist, terrorist, irrational, medieval fanatics—unlike Christians and Jews. Official prejudice continued for so long, and so strongly, that if you read almost any American newspaper article on Islamic fundamentalism and simply substitute the word "black" or the word "Jew" for "Muslim," the racism will leap off the page at you. The point of this long campaign was to persuade Americans that it would be necessary, and justifiable, to kill Muslims in the Middle East.

Then the dictatorships in Russia and Eastern Europe fell in 1989. The United States and the West had won the Cold War. U.S. President George Bush Sr. announced a "New World Order." Suddenly, it seemed possible to the American ruling class that they could dominate the world as the only military and economic superpower. Then came the Gulf War.

The Gulf War

In 1989 Saddam Hussein was still an ally of the United States. His war with Iran had now lasted seven years, but the Iranian army was finally winning. In response, Bush sent the U.S. fleet to the Persian Gulf. He made it clear the United States was backing Iraq. An American naval ship shot down an Iranian civilian airliner, killing all the passengers and crew. The United States did not apologize, and the captain was not disciplined. Iran, unwilling to risk war with the United States, made peace with Iraq.

But Saddam Hussein was still in trouble. He had just been defeated in war, a dangerous moment for any military dictator. And the war had exhausted the Iraqi economy. Saddam Hussein turned to the royal family dictatorship in neighboring, oil-rich Kuwait for help. The Kuwaiti royal family had promised Saddam billions to fight Iran, but had not yet delivered. Now, the war over, they refused to pay up. They were also increasing their own production of oil, which was driving down the price of Iraqi oil. Kuwait had been a part of Iraq until 1920, when the British had carved it out as a separate colony. Saddam Hussein decided to invade Kuwait. That way he could solve his economic problems and win a victory that would shore up his power at home. He checked with the American ambassador, and her ambiguous response gave him the impression that the United States would not try to stop an invasion of Kuwait.

Kuwait fell quickly—Kuwaitis were not prepared to die for their royal family. But the Iraqi victory threatened Saudi Arabia, the world's largest oil producer and the main U.S. ally in the Middle East. The people of Saudi Arabia hated the dictatorship of their royal family.[9] Saddam was not about to invade Saudi Arabia, but if the Kuwaiti royals went and the Americans did not defend them, it would encourage the Saudi people. Something had to be done to protect the oil and the dictatorships.

Kuwait was a key test for American power, and U.S. President Bush had to go to war. He organized a military coalition, based in Saudi Arabia, of most European powers and almost every dictatorship in the Middle East. When Saddam would not back down and was not allowed another way out, the coalition bombed massively and then sent in troops. The bulk of the allied fliers and soldiers were Americans.

The American government kept tight control of media coverage of the war, allowing only a few handpicked correspondents into Saudi Arabia and Kuwait. These correspondents had military minders at all times. The job of these minders was not to stop the journalists from talking to Saudis, Kuwaitis, or Iraqis. It was to stop them from talking to American soldiers and pilots.[10] That was what the American military had learned from Vietnam.

The coalition bombing killed between 100,000 and 200,000 Iraqi troops. U.S. bulldozers buried more alive in their trenches. The draftee Iraqi army were terrified by the bombing, and like most Iraqis they hated Saddam. They fled or surrendered.

The American troops rode into Kuwait with very few losses, many of them from friendly fire. Bush announced on American radio that he had finally buried the Vietnam syndrome. It was not that simple. Bush had said over and over again that the war was intended to overthrow Saddam, who was as evil as Hitler. Saddam's army was disintegrating, driving and running away as fast as they could. The Kurdish minority in the north and the people in the cities of southern Iraq rose in revolt against Saddam, expecting American help.

Yet the American army stopped at the Iraqi border and allowed Saddam Hussein to smash the revolts, when they could have overthrown him. There were two reasons. One was that the southern revolt was led by Islamists, and a Kurdish victory in the north would have encouraged the Kurdish rebellion in Turkey, an American ally. But the other reason was that the American generals were not prepared to invade. General Colin Powell, chairman of the Joint Chiefs of Staff, had done two tours of duty in Vietnam. He was determined that such a thing would never happen to his army again.[11] When push came to shove, the generals were still terrified of fighting on the ground.

An American–organized economic boycott over the next ten years cut off medical supplies, cut back the food supply, and pulverized the economy. Infant mortality soared, and according to studies by the School of Public Health at Harvard and by the United Nations, a million Iraqi children died as a result of the boycott.[12] But Saddam remained, exposing Iraq to all the limits of American power.

Kosovo

Our last example is the Kosovo war in 1999. There is not space here to fill in the complex background to that war.[13] The important point here is that the Vietnam syndrome was still working. In the spring of 1999, the American government and its NATO allies began bombing Serbia and Kosovo, in support of Kosovan rebels against the Serbian leader, Slobodan Milosevic. NATO expected the Serbians to crumble in the face of the bombing. They did not. The bombing went on for weeks and weeks. The British general in charge of the NATO operation thought ground troops would be needed, and many in the American government agreed with him. It began to look as if Serbia might hold out and American power would suffer a very obvious defeat.

The Pentagon said it would take many months to get American troops in a position to fight in Kosovo. This was a transparent lie. The United States had bases all over neighboring Albania. For forty years, the NATO forces had been prepared to fight Russian troops in Europe at a few hours' notice. But the Pentagon was still looking over its shoulder at Vietnam.

The NATO command did insist that the American army send Apache helicopters. These were the most modern and expensive helicopters the Americans had. They could fly low over Kosovo and engage the Serbian army up close and personal. The American generals saw this as a bridge to using ground troops. They allowed Apache helicopters to go to bases in Albania, but then announced they could not be used because the weather was bad, there were clouds, the pilots were not properly trained, and it would take months to get everything right. The generals were prepared to trash-talk one of their most treasured and expensive weapons to prevent any possibility of another Vietnam.[14]

In the end, opposition to the war grew in Serbia, there were protest demonstrations in several cities, and the Serbian government gave up. The lesson the Pentagon drew was that bombing worked.

But from 1975 to 2000 the United States was a strange sort of superpower. It was the world's leading economic power. Military spending in the United States was greater than in the next eight countries combined. U.S. military technology led the world. But the United States was effectively a great power without an army. And there would be times when they would absolutely have to have an army.

That was a problem the American ruling class was trying hard to solve.

Veterans

The backlash against the Vietnam War was not simply a matter of trying to use ground troops abroad. It involved rewriting history as well. Central to this were the American veterans of that war. What happened to them was taken from them and made into something else. Hollywood generally portrayed veterans as dangerous and violent men.[15] The most famous examples are *Taxi Driver*, *Rambo: First Blood*, and *Coming Home*, but dozens of B movies portrayed the same dangerous veterans. These men were suffering from psychosis produced by flashbacks on screen well before psychiatrists discovered "post-traumatic stress syndrome" and decided to call men's memories "flashbacks." And the point

Hollywood was making was the same point as the psychiatrists—the violent wishes of GIs were the cause of the violence in the Vietnam War.

The blaming of veterans for the cruelty of the war went in the face of the facts that they had been ordered to do it, that they had been rewarded for doing it, that attrition had been the strategy, and that they had finally refused to fight. It also went in the face of the fact that far more Vietnamese were killed by planes than guns.

But Hollywood had to blame somebody for the cruelty of the war, because Americans had not forgotten that it was a cruel war. The majority of them were still saying so in public opinion surveys twenty years later.[16] The truth was that liberals were responsible for Vietnam—John Kennedy, Robert Kennedy, Lyndon Johnson, and Robert McNamara. Now that most people knew the war was a mistake and wrong, the blame was being dumped on the GIs.

At the same time, the history was rewritten to divide GIs and the anti-war movement. First, the soldiers' refusal to fight was forgotten. But then, ten years after the war ended, there began to be many stories of anti-war protesters or hippies spitting on returning veterans. Jerry Lembcke began researching these spitting stories at the time of the Gulf War. Lembcke was a Vietnam veteran and a former activist in Vietnam Veterans Against the War, and he didn't remember any spitting. He remembered that most veterans had been against the war and that people had behaved decently to them when they came home—especially the anti-war protesters. So Lembcke went back and looked for reports of spitting on veterans by anti-war types or hippies in the 1960s and 1970s.[17] He found none at all anywhere in the papers or the magazines. He found no accounts of it at the time in right-wing magazines. He found no accounts for many years afterwards, and he found opinion surveys of veterans at the time who said they had been well received by people their own age. The only accounts of spitting on veterans Lembcke found were pictures and news stories of anti-war veterans protesting against the war and being spat on by supporters of the war.

Lembcke also found that returning veterans were spat on in the movies first, before there were any other accounts of spitting. And he pointed out that the movie *Coming Home* showed an anti-war crowd protesting against returning soldiers at an airport, something that never happened. Instead the peace movement protested at induction centers, ports, and airports against soldiers having to go and fight.

So the media and the politicians tried to blame the soldiers for the war and separate them in retrospect from the anti-war movement. In the 1980s politicians, particularly Reagan and Bush Sr., began insisting that they were the true friends of the veterans. The trouble, they said, was that America had not honored its veterans properly (the liberals spat on them). The symbols of this were the "prisoners of war/missing in action," Americans captured during the war and still held by Hanoi. There could be no proper diplomatic relations with Vietnam until these men were returned.

These prisoners did not exist. There were men whom the Pentagon had listed as missing in action and never accounted for. As the Vietnamese government kept insisting, they were dead. But their nonexistence made them the one group of veterans that the right wing could really support. They could not support the men who were actually still dying from the war, the victims of Agent Orange.[18] The men who had worked on Operation Ranch Hand, dumping pesticides from planes, were particularly badly hit. But many other GIs had been exposed. More and more of them became sick and listless, depressed and unable to work or do anything much. They got rashes, they began to come down with cancers, and more and more of their children were born with terrible birth defects.

The federal Veterans Administration (VA) hospitals told them over and over that it was in their heads—they were suffering from "post-traumatic stress." And indeed they were stressed, for they felt themselves dying, they were unable to work, and they had no explanation for what was happening to them.

Gradually they realized. What made their medical condition obvious was that very much larger numbers of people in Vietnam were suffering from the same thing, and that hundreds of thousands of children had been born there terribly deformed; now a third generation are being born with the same defects. But the U.S. government and the politicians fought as hard as they could to resist any compensation or treatment for the Agent Orange victims in America. To do so would be to admit what had been done in the war. It would open the question of whether the Vietnamese children, unborn when the war ended, should be compensated. And it would allow pictures of those children on American TV screens. That would make another war far harder to wage.

So the politicians supported veterans who did not exist, blamed the living veterans, and ignored the dying. They did so because they wanted to be able to go to war again.

STRESS

Most Vietnam veterans coped, as people do, and got on with building their lives. Although the great majority were not psychopaths, some did suffer greatly afterwards. Vietnam Veterans Against the War had left a legacy of political organization, and the veterans were able to insist something had to be done. The Veterans Administration was already responsible for the medical care of all veterans. In the 1980s it began to offer help to people suffering from what psychiatrists now called "post-traumatic stress disorder." Allan Young, an anthropologist, spent a year watching and listening to staff and resident patients in one such VA psychiatric center in 1986–87.[19]

What happened in that hospital is interesting for two reasons. First, it shows how the veterans were blamed for the cruelty of the war. But it also shows the class struggle in miniature, in one hospital, between psychiatrists and working-class patients. The backlash in America was not simply a campaign in the media. It was something that was pushed and fought through in the details of people's daily lives.

One man was both manager of the center staff and director of the treatment offered. He had a model of post-traumatic stress the staff had to use. It went as follows:

Men with post-traumatic stress disorder are split between their aggressive and sexual sides. At one moment in the past, they did one wrong thing, and they did it because they enjoyed it. After they enjoyed that thing, they were overwhelmed with guilt. So they split their desire from their aggression. The cure for them is to recall that moment in group therapy. When they have returned to that moment and accepted that they wanted to do evil, they can leave the guilt behind and become whole people.

Note carefully—they did one wrong thing. Terrible things that were done to them and terrible things that they saw did not count. It had to be an atrocity they wanted to commit, and only one atrocity. A lot of time in therapy was spent trying to find that one event.

It was all nonsense, as Allan Young shows clearly in his book on the VA clinic, *The Harmony of Illusions*. But the nonsense served a function. This center treated men wounded by the war, but it was a government center. It could not say, "The officers and the government are to blame." It could not say, "What was done to you in Vietnam is of a piece with what has been done to you since." And it could not allow the patients to say these things. So the psychiatric theory blamed the men—they wanted to kill.

The men kept trying to talk about what had been done to them. Young quotes from a group therapy session where "Henry" explains some of why he is upset:

HENRY: Maybe I am crazy. I was raised a Baptist. I went to church every Wednesday and Sunday, and I went to Bible camp. By the time I was eighteen I was in Vietnam. After I was in-country for only three days, I killed a sixteen-year-old boy. I began questioning my religion. I was asking myself what kind of god would put me in a position like this and let me do this. At first, I felt sad. But then people started telling me, "Way to go," and the captain and the sergeant congratulated me for having a kill after such a short time. After a while, I fell into the program. I'd see guys lose legs and other shit happen, and it didn't bother me anymore. I began to enjoy it and went back for a second tour. I wanted to get revenge, and I wanted to do as much destruction as possible.[20]

Here is part of group therapy a week earlier. Lewis, a junior psychologist, explains the theory:

LEWIS: Forgetting traumatic events originates in a conflict. You don't want to remember. Your conflict is always driving you back to the original event, but you don't want to go back to it. Stress responses do two things for you. First, you don't have to face your conflict, and second, you punish yourself. . . . One of the jobs of combat training is to remove some of the conflict over aggression, so that you can be aggressive. . . .

MARTIN [another patient]: Well, I can tell you we had no problem being aggressive in Vietnam.

LEWIS: OK, Martin. Give us an example, but use the word "I" instead of "we."

Two weeks later Carol, a counselor, shuts Henry up in group therapy:

CAROL: Yesterday you were wearing all black, Henry, a black shirt, black jeans. And what was Paul's response? He said the clients are like troops being shot at by [Vietnamese] people in black pajamas.

HENRY: Listen, the people who were shooting at me in Vietnam weren't wearing black uniforms. Black clothes don't mean anything to me. There was no aggressive intent. After the session, when I realized my clothes produced a stress response, I went to my room and changed, and I came to lunch in different clothes.

CAROL: Even if it were not your conscious experience right now, its meaning will come to realization. Same thing about the meaning of your remark yesterday, about the Vietcong not being your enemy.

HENRY: Well, that's right. The Vietcong were acting the same way we would have acted in their place. I had no anger against them. My anger's against the people who sponsored the war.

CAROL: Which is equivalent to saying, "My anger is against all Americans."[21]

Which shut him up and forced him to blame himself.

The class struggle in therapy went on all day, every day, in this clinic. The therapists, controlled by the managing psychiatrist, tried to make the veterans responsible for the war. The veterans fought back:

CAROL: Say to yourself, I've been punishing myself and people around me for twenty years. Say, Jack, you can choose to stop!

JACK: Listen, Carol. On some nights, I feel anxiety going through my body like electricity. It started in Vietnam. It wasn't just a feeling. It was an anxiety together with terrible chest pains and difficulty breathing. Just like having a heart attack. They sent me over to the field hospital to get an EKG. The doctors told them there was nothing wrong. They said I was just hyperventilating. They told me to breathe into a paper bag when I got those feelings, and they gave me a supply of Valium to take back. But I got those attacks anyway. And I'm still getting them. . . .

CAROL: The model says that we're dominated by two drives, aggression and sex, and that—

JACK: Listen, Carol. When I got those attacks, I sure didn't want to get fucked, and I can't believe it was my aggression.[22]

The staff had a way of explaining away the patients' anger towards them. They said anger is a defense: "The patient gets angry so he doesn't have to get in touch with his feelings of guilt about what he did. He seems to be angry with me. Actually, he's angry with me because I'm pushing him to reveal his guilt."

Sometimes patients tested the "limits" set by the staff. They threatened violence or left the room during group therapy to have a piss. They wore dark glasses in the group or disagreed with the therapists too effectively. If they broke these limits, they faced a "panel."

This panel was made up of all the staff the patient had told his intimate secrets to. They discussed everything about him behind his back. Sometimes they threw him out of the hospital. The other patients regarded this as a punishment—just like the army. The staff disagreed. They felt they were only setting limits.

And the center Allan Young studied was one of the best in the Veterans Administration. It was Freudian and progressive, and the patients were encouraged to talk. Many of these men had been to other hospitals before, where they were drugged to the eyeballs, shot full of thorazine, strapped to tables for weeks, and given electric shocks over and over, given electric shocks even while they were awake.

These were men without jobs whose median income—except for Veterans Administration disability benefits—was less than $1,000 a year. If they did not get a good report from the staff, they could lose those benefits. If the staff decided that they had "post-traumatic stress disorder," they could get $40,000 to $60,000 in back benefits. So there was a lot of pressure on them to be good. But not too good—if they were cured, they might lose benefits and still not have a job.

In that situation it's hard to be honest and open in therapy. Yet these men often were. They tried desperately. They had suffered for years and it was the only help available.

And so they waited days or weeks for each man to gather the courage to say what he did and what was done to him. As each man told the group his worst "event," they sat silent, leaning forward, willing him on to tell the truth. They wanted to tell and hear the truth. They had seen enough lies. But they also hoped the therapists were right and this would cleanse them.

The men told the truth. It did not cure them. The therapists said that once a man had returned to that moment and owned his responsibility, he would be whole. But he was not. He was ashamed. And in the eyes of the men who were there too, he was right to be ashamed.

The therapists said he could put his guilt behind him. But he could not. Somebody had to bear that guilt. It should be the guilty—not the working-class boys sent to hell, but the rich and powerful men who sent them there.

It would have helped those veterans in pain to be angry with the men who sent them there—titanically angry, encouraged in their anger, supported in their anger, honored for their rage. Instead they were silenced, so those who ruled America then could still rule it now, and hope to send other men to other Vietnams.

THE BACKLASH IN AMERICA

America's rulers were also trying to break the power and memory of the movements of the 1960s in America. Weakening movements against the ruling class at home would make it easier to allow American intervention abroad. And the class struggle at home was still what mattered most to the American ruling class.

In the 1960s and 1970s it had been shaken by the anti-war movement, the black movement, and the women's and gay movements. At every level, in every cranny of American society, opposition from below had grown stronger. From 1975 on, all American governments and employers tried to reverse this. They were helped in their efforts by the political confusion of American radicals.

The movements of the 1960s and 1970s were massive. Most of the millions of people involved were blue-collar workers or lower-level white-collar workers. These were the majority of the marchers in the civil rights movement, the rioters in the northern cities, and the soldiers in revolt in Vietnam. Many of the students in the anti-war movement came from these backgrounds, and opposition to the war was strongest in the working class.

But these movements were led by middle-class professionals. More important, they saw themselves as sectional movements, fighting for blacks or women or peace. Most of the people involved did not see the possibility of a united movement of all the oppressed, trying to unite all workers and concentrate their struggle against the corporations at work. The few organized revolutionaries they met looked to the example of Russia or China or Cuba, places where workers were ruled by dictatorships and oppressed in their daily working lives much as American workers were. Because these organized revolutionaries looked to the example of dictatorships, their own organizations also had unpleasant internal regimes that repelled people who were looking for more democracy.

As a result, the most radical elements in all the movements looked not to the whole working class but to some more radical version of their own sectional struggle. Some of the peace activists became terrorist bombers. Many of the most radical women became separatists, and many of the radical blacks became separatist nationalists. All of these movements stalled because the great majority of women, black people, gays, lesbians, and people who wanted peace had to continue living and working in a system run by the corporations. By the end of the 1970s, almost all these radical separatists realized they had trapped themselves in dead ends. They felt defeated but did not know why.

As these movements ran into the sand, the American establishment was making a space for the professional class that had led the movements. Job and educational opportunities opened up for women and blacks. By 1990, a sixth of black households made over $50,000 a year. This was not riches, but it did create a black middle class with some feeling of a stake in the system. Many of them got jobs as congressional representatives, junior diplomats, army officers, police chiefs, judges, and other administrators and defenders of the system.

Women too saw a rise in their wages. But most of this rise was concentrated in the top 20 percent of women earners, and really large gains only happened for the top 10 percent. These women still faced all sorts of "glass ceilings," but they too could, and often did, feel they had a stake in the system.

So when America's rulers started to push a domestic backlash after 1975, the radicals felt defeated, and many of the liberal leaders who workers had looked to, and still looked to, were now reluctant to really fight the ruling class.

The backlash reached into every corner of American life. Susan Faludi, in her excellent book *Backlash*, has detailed the attack on women's rights.[23] A central fight there was over abortion. But gays too suffered as the Reagan and Bush governments refused to do anything about AIDS and blamed gay men for their own suffering.[24] In the universities, there was a sustained attack on the ideas of the 1960s. But the two main weapons in the backlash were an attack on the unions and the imprisonment of blacks.[25]

Two important things mark America between 1975 and 1999 as very different from the rest of the industrialized world. In America and Eastern Europe, the real take-home hourly wages of workers fell. In the rest of the industrialized world, they rose. And in 1971 there were 200,000 prisoners in America. By 2000 there were over 2 million—a tenfold increase. No other country except Rwanda imprisons anything like that proportion of its population, and such a thing had never happened in America before. Both the fall in wages and the rise in prisoners were treated in the American media as if they were normal events. Both weakened the American working class.

The fall in wages was made possible by a sustained attack on the unions.[26] The key battle here was a national strike by air traffic controllers in 1981. The air traffic controllers were federal employees, and President Reagan fired all of them, hired scab labor, and refused to let the strikers have their jobs back. The leaders of the other unions in the airline industry, frightened of massive government fines, told their members to cross the air traffic controllers' picket lines.

Because there was no radical network in the unions and workplaces to organize people not to scab, the airline workers felt helpless without the backing of their leaders and went into work. That broke the strike. After that, workers in other industries realized that if the government and employers could do that to the air traffic controllers, they could do it to anybody.

At the same time there were large-scale layoffs and plant closures in heavy industry, the traditional heart of the union movement. Here again the union leaders told their members they could not fight the logic of the capitalist market, and if they did not agree to work for lower wages in worse conditions, then the jobs would simply go to workers in Third World countries. Again, there was no socialist network in the unions to argue that the enemy was the corporations, not workers in other parts of the world.

That led to a rash of give-back contracts accepting cuts in wages and job conditions. Because the unions were not fighting, people in the new service industries did not join unions and the unions did not lead the fights necessary to recruit them. Labor unionism was not abolished, but union membership shrank and the unions were weaker.

Most people still had full-time jobs. But the men who lost jobs in industry had to take jobs at lower wages in the service sector, and an increasing minority had to work one or more part-time jobs with lower wages and often no health benefits. Real hourly wages for blue-collar and routine white-collar workers fell, and work got harder and more dangerous. Family incomes stayed more or less steady, because many more women went out to work and both men and women worked longer hours. But families were running harder and harder to keep up. Without unions, or with weaker unions, and with the threat of losing the job they had, people got more scared of standing up for themselves at work.

From 1997 on, with almost full employment, real hourly wages did begin to rise again a bit. But during the 1990s the main corporate attack was on workers' health care. Most of the big strikes in the 1990s were in defense of what little health care insurance workers had, and many had none at all. The corporations increasingly forced their employees into health plans run by HMOs, health care organizations that were cheaper for corporations because they rationed the treatment workers could get.

The attack on workers as workers was one big weapon in the backlash. The other was prison. Any major social policy has to be understood in terms of its consequences. What is important is not what the people at the top say is their motivation. It's what their policies do that matters. What mass imprisonment did was pulverize the lives of black workers and subdue them as a political force.

By 1999, 45 percent of prisoners were black, mostly men, and another 20 percent were Latinos. The number of women prisoners was rising more rapidly than ever, but they were still a small minority of prisoners. At any one time, over a third of black men between the ages of 18 and 30 were in prison, on probation, or awaiting trial. In the black working class and in the inner cities, the proportion was even higher. Behind the almost 2 million people in prison were the many millions more who had been to prison in the previous twenty years. And behind those men were their parents and wives and children, tens of millions of them. Almost every black worker had some relative who had been to prison.

Prison destroys relationships. It brutalizes people, weakens and frightens them so they come out harder on the surface and more terrified inside. Prison management often relied on the more criminal and brutal prisoners to control the rest, and so prisons became factories for rape. A society that babbled about post-traumatic stress built mass factories for trauma. And because even rape could not control so many men, there were more and more special units with men locked down for twenty-three or twenty-four hours a day for years.

With the mass imprisonment went increases in police numbers, in "zero tolerance" daily harassment on the streets, in torture in police stations, and in paramilitary police SWAT teams with body armor, automatic weapons, grenade launchers, and helicopters. Under the pressure of the movements of the 1960s, the U.S. Supreme Court had suspended the death penalty in 1972. As the backlash gained force, the Supreme Court reversed itself in 1976. The number of executions increased steadily over the next twenty years. By the end of 1999, 598 Americans had been executed. That same year, all the countries of Western and Central Europe insisted that Turkey could not join the European Union until it abolished the death penalty, because no country could be considered civilized if it executed even one prisoner. And the American media still talked as if there were nothing odd about America.

What was happening was both breaking and demonizing the black working class. This did white workers no favors. The proportion of black prisoners was rising, but the number of white prisoners was rising too. Millions of Latino and white families went through the same suffering. This made everybody more frightened.

It also divided black and white workers. There is little evidence that white workers became more racist. However, black workers had been at the heart of the movement of the 1960s and 1970s. Anybody who wanted to fight back in those years looked to the black movement as an example. When white workers thought of black workers, they saw in their minds a grandmother in a southern city leading her church choir out of church, down the road to the courthouse, singing their defiance at the police dogs. Or they saw a black man in a northern city riot with a Molotov

cocktail in his hand. By 1999, when many white and black workers thought of the inner cities, the images that came to mind were
likely to be junkies and street gangs.

This was the result of the policy of mass imprisonment. A
beacon of hope had been turned into an object lesson of what
could happen to you. The American ruling class had reacted to
the mass union movement between 1938 and 1946 with a persecution of Communists that jailed a few hundred and lost less
than 20,000 people their jobs. In the 1980s and 1990s, they reacted
to the civil rights movement and Vietnam with a persecution of
blacks that sent millions to prison.

This was only possible because the leadership of the black middle class did not organize against it. The centerpiece of the prison
drive was the war on drugs. This was not actually a war on drugs
but a war on drug takers. And Jesse Jackson, the leader of the
black middle class, was part of that war on drugs. The black may-
ors, police chiefs, and spokesmen and women joined in too. Some
of them said we have to clean up our cities by imprisoning our
children. Others, to their credit, did not say that, but were still
far enough into the system that they did not organize mass resistance to the war on drugs and imprisonment.

But by 1999 this was changing. Some middle-class black leaders
were campaigning hard against police brutality. The union leaders,
too, were looking for ways to fight back. In both cases, this was
happening because there was widespread bitterness among both
black and white American workers about their lives, and an increasing hatred of class injustice. That feeling of bitterness was
beginning to break through into action.

The bitterness had been building a long time. Mostly you noticed it if you talked to people, and the mood during demonstrations was both angry and hopeful. It was not much reported in
the newspapers, but it kept breaking through.

In 1992, Los Angeles saw a riot against police brutality when
police were caught on video beating a black man, Rodney King,
and were then acquitted. The riot was on the scale of the black

riots in the 1960s, but this time it spread to Latino and white neighborhoods. There were supporting demonstrations in many cities, made up of mixed black and white crowds chanting, "No justice, no peace!" This was new.

Through the 1990s, Latinos were becoming increasingly important in American politics. In the 1960s African Americans had been the militant minority. Latinos had been there, in every movement, but not deeply politicized. Since that time there had been considerable immigration. Earlier waves of immigrants, with the exception of African slaves, had come to a country that was by and large freer than the one they left. Latino immigrants came to a country that they knew was partly responsible for the oppression where they came from. As they became more political, they changed the shape of radical feeling in America. By 2000 an eighth of the country was black, and just over an eighth was Latino. A new phrase was created—"people of color"—that also included Asians and Native Americans. They were now almost 30 percent of the population.[27]

In 1997 the Teamsters Union members at United Parcel Service (UPS) went on a national strike. UPS was well-known as a corporate pioneer in part-time and casual work. The central demand of the strikers was more full-time jobs. There was support for them right around the country. This time, unlike other strikes in the 1990s, UPS could not use scabs. The one place it tried, in Massachusetts, UPS and other workers fought the police on the picket line and stopped them. The UPS workers won.

Then in 1999 there were weeks of demonstrations in New York City after the police shot down an unarmed and innocent African immigrant, Amadou Diallo, on the street. There were thousands of protestors in each demonstration. At one point they blocked the Brooklyn Bridge, and the crowds were both black and white. Over 2,000 people were arrested for civil disobedience.

These demonstrations were in effect against Mayor Rudolph Giuliani of New York, the apostle of "zero tolerance" policing. They gave the unions of the people who worked for New York

City the confidence to call a rally for a decent wage for all work-ing families. 50,000 people came. This too was new.

And then came the demonstration in Seattle against the World Trade Organization (WTO) in December 1999.

GLOBALIZATION AND SEATTLE

Seattle was the beginning of a worldwide revolt against "global-ization."[28] The word is misleading. There had been an integrated global economy for over a hundred years. Globalization was actually an attempt to restructure this world economy. Basically, from the early 1980s on, the American government and corpo-rations were trying to do to the world what they were doing to American workers. First, the power of corporations over workers was increased throughout the world. Second, the power of Amer-ican corporations over other corporations increased.

Globalization was a response to both an opportunity and a problem. The opportunity was created by the fall of the Soviet Union. Suddenly the United States was the only superpower on the planet, and the Left all over the world was demoralized. Most of the Left had believed that the Soviet Union was in some sense socialist—with flaws, yes, and mistakes, and not very democratic, yes, but in some way the only alternative to world capitalism. This feeling, it turned out, extended far beyond Marxists and Communists. Many in the British Labour Party, the European so-cialist parties, and the academic Left in the United States felt the same way. Now it seemed to most people that there was no al-ternative to the rule of the market. Socialist, Communist, and Labor parties all over the world swung right. The ideas of the market now dominated people's heads.

The strategy of globalization was also a response to a problem.[29] Since the 1960s, there had been a long-run decline in the rate of profit in the industrialized world. Economists have debated the extent of this decline. The figures vary from country to country, and they vary depending on what system of accounting is used.

But whatever set of figures is used, there has clearly been a problem with profit rates in the United States, Canada, Western Europe, Eastern Europe, and Japan. This meant that the corporations, governments, and ruling classes in all these countries were looking for ways to drive profits back up. Globalization was a strategy to do this.

Globalization tried to drive profits up by reducing the wages and government expenditure going to working people. So across the globe, in every country, social programs and benefits were cut—pensions, health, education, unemployment pay, welfare, public housing, public transport, and subsidies to the price of food. Corporations and banks were deregulated, and health and safety rules at work repealed or not enforced. Taxes on the rich, and on corporations, were reduced in most countries. Publicly owned utilities and services were privatized, so corporations could make further profits. The jargon phrase for all of this was "neo-liberal economics."

Globalization was also an attempt by American corporations to dominate other corporations and governments. This was called "free trade." In practice free trade meant that foreign markets were opened to U.S. companies. American companies refused to let Third World countries make their own cheap medicines without patent fees. They got rid of laws that prevented foreign investment, and they eliminated customs duties on U.S. goods and health and safety regulations that American products did not conform to. Whenever public services were privatized, they made sure American companies were able to get in there.

One little fact shows how unfree "free" trade was. The North American Free Trade Agreement (NAFTA) is over 300 pages long. A genuine free trade agreement would be one page long. The other 300-odd pages mostly protected American industries. Poor countries all over the world were opened to Western industrial products without being able to sell agricultural products back.

The U.S. government led and organized this global process. Their tools were the U.S. Federal Reserve Bank under Alan

Greenspan, the International Monetary Fund (IMF), the World Bank, the World Trade Organization (WTO), and the North Atlantic Free Trade Agreement. Their leading spokesman was Bill Clinton.

The other governments and ruling classes in the world had an ambivalent reaction to globalization. They liked the rule of the market and their increased power over their own workers. They didn't like the increasing American power over them. So there were constant tensions. But globalization and neoliberal economics were presented as a package. If they wanted to cut and privatize and glorify the market, they had to follow the Americans.

The World Trade Organization meeting in Seattle in December 1999 was supposed to be one more milestone in American and capitalist dominance of the world economy. Demonstrators came from all over the United States and Canada, with many agendas. Some were brought by labor leaders to protest the loss of American jobs. Some were protesting the effects of the world market in the Third World. Some were against sweatshops. Some were defending sea turtles. Some of them wanted to reform the WTO, and some wanted to abolish it. The union leaders talked of America while young radicals talked of capitalism.

The union leaders told their members to march separately from the environmental and political campaigners. Rank and file Teamsters refused, and forced their way through police lines to join the "turtle kids." Together the union members and the Left stopped the opening day of the WTO conference. The police waded into them with gas and rubber bullets. Some of the demonstrators replied by breaking windows of corporate chain stores, starting with Starbucks, home of the $5 cup of coffee, that symbol of yuppie arrogance. When the first Starbucks window broke on television, a shout went up in living rooms across America.

A riot followed. President Clinton had to react to this riot by saying the demonstrators had a point, because he knew ordinary people all over the country supported them. The delegates of the other big and little capitalist powers gathered for the WTO said to themselves, "Clinton can't even control his own people—why should we do what he tells us?" The conference ended with nothing decided and no agenda for the next one.

It was a very public victory for the demonstrators. They had arrived supporting many causes. But it turned out that what united them was a hatred of capitalism. They kept saying so to the reporters, and the word "anti-capitalism" was suddenly part of the mainstream media vocabulary. The American Federation of Labor had never been part of a national demonstration against capitalism. Now suddenly it was.

The wind changed in American politics. For the first time in sixty years, there is a mass movement in America against capitalism as such. That movement had a resonance around the world. In 1989 students in Saigon protested against their course content and conditions by holding meetings and seminars at their university. They called this form of protest a "teach-in"—Ann Arbor, Michigan, had come to Saigon. In 1999 Vietnam was in Seattle. The memory was there as the police attacked the crowd and they chanted, "The whole world is watching," as they had chanted in Chicago in 1968. And the present was there, as many demonstrators came as part of the movement against sweatshop conditions in the Third World, the same thing the workers in Saigon were striking against through the 1990s. The American workers in Seattle were also fighting corporations that wanted a low-wage, non-union economy. In Seattle and Saigon the enemy was the world market. As one anonymous demonstrator said to a reporter, "Our parents had Vietnam. This is our Vietnam." *Newsweek* reported:

> Two young men stood chest to chest, screaming in each other's faces, both tear-stained from the pepper gas wafting along Sixth Avenue in downtown Seattle. One wanted to smash the Nike window, the other to stop him. "How do you think they stopped Vietnam?" demanded the one with the rock.[30]

It wasn't that simple in the 1960s and it won't be that simple this time around. You could say that tens of thousands of union members marching make far more difference than a few people with rocks. And you would be right. But if you worked in one of the Nike sweatshops in Vietnam, you would know that the man with the rock was your brother.

The anti-globalization movement had not begun in Seattle. The Zapatista farmers in southern Mexico had launched their fight against NAFTA in 1994, and the French public sector workers had held a general strike against neoliberal policies in 1995. There had been similar struggles in many places, particularly in the poorer countries. But when 30 million workers in India held a one-day general strike against neoliberalism, no one outside India noticed. Seattle happened in front of Clinton, in the center of the world system, and everyone noticed.

That launched a series of demonstrations at meetings of world leaders in Sweden, South Korea, Canada, the United States, Papua New Guinea, Thailand, Australia, Italy, France, Switzerland, Austria, Czechoslovakia, Germany, Belgium, and other places. The largest of these was at the summit of George Bush Jr. and the other G8 leaders in Genoa, Italy, in June 2001.[31] Three hundred thousand people demonstrated, and the police attacked them. Many hundreds of thousands more demonstrated across Italy in protest at police brutality, and the government, humiliated, had to back down.

Opinion polls in one country after another showed the protesters had majority support on almost all the issues they were demonstrating about. Globalization, and American corporate power, it seemed, finally faced a real challenge. The market was losing its dominance of ordinary people's heads. A movement that at first called itself "anti-globalization" was now referred to in most countries as "anti-capitalist." And the main slogan of that movement was "Another World Is Possible."

Then came the War on Terror.

THE ROOTS OF TERROR

On September 11, 2001, nineteen Islamist suicide bombers hijacked four American passenger planes and flew two of them into the twin towers of the World Trade Center in New York City, and one into the Pentagon; a fourth plane crashed in a field in Pennsylvania. Nearly 3,000 people died. There was an outpouring of sympathy in the United States, and across much of the world. Many people were seeing for the first time, live on television, just what the sort of bombing that had engulfed Vietnam and Iraq looked like. In America they were seeing interviews with survivors, ordinary people like themselves speaking a language they could understand. This bombing was wrong, for the same reasons the bombing in Vietnam and Iraq had been wrong. It followed the same logic—if you don't like the policy of a government, you punish the people who live in that government's country.

Sixteen of the nineteen hijackers were from Saudi Arabia. They were not poor people, envious of American wealth. Many, in fact, were graduate students in Germany. What had driven them to such desperate measures was the political situation in their own countries. Saudi Arabia has been an ally of the United States, backed by American power, for fifty years. It is one of the most brutal and reactionary dictatorships on earth.

They also saw American power as the enemy in Iraq and Palestine. Roughly a million Iraqi children had died in the last ten years because of U.S.-organized sanctions on imports. This was known across the Middle East. So was the fact that when Madeleine Albright, Clinton's secretary of state, was asked about the deaths of these children by a journalist, she had replied that sometimes there was a price that had to be paid.[32]

Palestine was important too. To understand why, it is important to know that most of the Arab population had been driven out of the new state of Israel in 1948. The Zionist militias had killed thousands of Arabs. In one village of Deir Yassein, they killed all the men, women, and children. This was done in order to scare most of the rest of the Palestinian Arabs into fleeing to neighboring countries.[33] Fifty years later, many of them still lived in refugee camps in neighboring states. Many, however, lived in Jerusalem, the West Bank, and Gaza, in territory that was conquered by Israel in wars in 1967 and 1973.

The terror that drove the Palestinian refugees out in 1948 is well known in the Arab world. In the West, it was rarely mentioned until recently. In 1948 there was no word for what happened. It was not genocide. The Zionist militias did not want to exterminate the Arabs, only to persuade them to leave. Since the troubles in the former Yugoslavia in the 1990s, however, we now have a name for what happened—ethnic cleansing. That more recent example allows Westerners to understand more easily the fear, sorrow, and long-lasting hurt the Palestinians carried after 1948.

In the 1980s the newly conquered Palestinian refugees in the West Bank and Gaza launched an "Intifada" (uprising) that lasted seven years. Most of the activists in the Intifada were schoolchildren, and their main weapon was stones thrown at Israeli soldiers, who fired live ammunition back. The result of this uprising was an agreement between Israel and the leadership of the Palestine Liberation Organization that seemed to promise an independent Palestinian state in the West Bank and Gaza.

It didn't happen. Despairing, the Palestinians began another uprising, the Second Intifada, in 2000. Again, the main activity was young men and boys throwing stones and Israeli soldiers shooting them. This time, however, the Palestinians became increasingly angry at watching their children die, and despairing that Americans or Europeans would respond to their pleas for help and mediation. Some turned to suicide bombing. Each such bombing produced Israeli attacks that killed more people than the bombing itself. By 2000 something like three times as many Palestinians as Israelis had died.

The United States was Israel's main backer. For many years, Israel had been the leading recipient of American foreign aid. In 2000 Israel, a country with a per capita income of $19,000, received 25 percent of all American foreign aid. Without this backing, the Israeli economy would collapse. The hijackers, like people across the Arab world, held the United States responsible for what was being done to the Palestinians.

The hijackers, however, were different from the Viet Cong. The Viet Cong had organized a mass movement from below, village by village and town by town. They had killed a few government officials so the peasants would have the space to organize freely. The hijackers, by contrast, were elitist. They relied on the terrorism of a small number of martyrs, not a mass army. And they were not, in practice, fighting for social justice. They were anti-imperialists, but not socialists, and all of them were part of the educated middle class. They did not encourage the peasants in Egypt to take the land, or the workers in Saudi Arabia to go on strike. Vietnam had been a war for land. The hijackers were unable, and unwilling, to organize the same energy. That was why they were desperate.

By contrast, the Vietnamese Communists had been very clear with American supporters throughout the war that they wanted no terrorism in the United States. It would only weaken them. Instead, they wanted and hoped for the support of ordinary Americans for peace, and in the end they got it.

What the hijackers did on September 11, however, strengthened both the position of the President George W. Bush in America, and U.S. power in the world. They made it far easier for Bush to go to war. Indeed, the bombing of the Twin Towers pushed him into war.

September 11 was a serious challenge to American power in the Middle East. In one way or another, the United States stood behind all the important dictatorships in that region, except for Iraq. But American power in these countries rested mostly on fear, not consent. The sight of the Pentagon in flames weakened that fear. If the American military could not even defend their own headquarters, why should people fear them?

There would have to be bombing and war somewhere to restore that fear. The Bush administration began to talk about a war in Afghanistan. This was not just a reaction to the challenge to their power, however. An Afghan war also provided the Bush team with a set of opportunities. First, it was a chance to finally reverse the Vietnam syndrome. Most Americans had been horrified by September 11. Now they might well consent to American ground troops fighting in large numbers, and accept that some of them would die.

Second, a successful war on Afghanistan might tip the balance of power in the surrounding countries of Central Asia. These countries—Kazakhstan, Kyrgyzstan, Tajikistan, Uzbekistan, Turkmenistan, and Azerbaijan—were rich in oil and gas. Until 1989 they had been part of the Soviet Union. Now they were independent, and their oil fields and gas reserves were up for grabs.

Third, a war on Afghanistan, followed by a wider war on terror, might shore up Bush's power, and American corporate power more generally. The U.S. government was facing economic recession. When faced with economic troubles at home, many leaders have been tempted to change the subject to war. In the process, the growing anti-capitalist movement might well be weakened across the world, and decisively so inside the United States.

Finally, the American ruling class had emerged from the Gulf War in 1991 as the dominant power in the world. Their military predominance there had set the stage for a decade of economic domination. Now the United States was still the dominant military power, but the European Union had as big an economy. The United States and Western Europe were drifting apart. A new war in Afghanistan, and a continuing "war on terror," could reestablish U.S. dominance.

As Washington looked around the Middle East, however, they knew they had to be careful. Many of the key people in the Bush administration came from the oil industry—Bush himself, his father, Vice President Dick Cheney, and Secretary of Defense Donald Rumsfeld. Condoleeza Rice, the national security advisor and a former oil executive, even had an oil tanker named after her. These people knew the Middle East. Their constant fear was what they called "the Arab street." The tight control by the dictatorships in the Middle East meant they were also fragile regimes. If a large demonstration turned on their own government, it could fall in hours. If 300,000 people were to march on the American embassy in Cairo, for instance, the Egyptian army would face a choice. If they opened fire on that crowd, the Egyptian government would fall. If they did not open fire, the crowd would reach the embassy and the government would still fall. If any major regime in the region fell, others might follow quickly, and the United States would lose control of the oil.

The tight control of the dictatorships also meant that it was difficult for both the American government and the radicals in those countries to gauge the strength of popular feeling. No one could know that things were about to change drastically until the moment they did. So the risk was there, and the American government had to worry about it constantly.

But the American government also had to restore their power after September 11. They had to bomb somewhere. In the months that followed, their policy would be a constant seesaw as they tried to stamp their authority on the region without provoking popular revolt.

As the Bush administration looked around the Middle East in September 2001, Iraq was a tempting target. But it would involve a serious war, with considerable resistance, and might lead to large demonstrations in other countries. So was Saudi Arabia, home to sixteen of the nineteen hijackers. But intervention there, even in cooperation with the Saudi government, might provoke an uprising. The Taliban in Afghanistan, however, had few friends. Their brand of hard-core, right-wing Islamism was widely despised across the Middle East. Afghanistan had seen twenty-two years of invasion and civil war. It was a shattered country, unable to resist. Afghanistan became the first target in the "War on Terror."

AFGHANISTAN

It is necessary now to explain what had been happening in Afghanistan. My account here is based on published sources, two years of field research in the 1970s, and many conversations with Afghans since.[34]

In 1978 the Communists in Afghanistan took power in a coup led by military officers. Rural risings, led by mullahs and Islamists, spread across the country. The Russian government, fearful that revolt would spread across the border into their largely Muslim southern provinces, sent tanks into Kabul in 1989. Many of the urban Afghans who had supported the Communists now switched sides. The rebellion lasted seven years. It was, everyone noted, Russia's Vietnam. Again, helicopter gunships, bombers, and napalm faced a guerrilla war. Out of a population of about 20 million, between half a million and a million died, roughly another million were maimed, and 7 million refugees fled from the countryside to Afghan cities and refugee camps in Pakistan and Iran.

The guerrillas were the Afghan farmers in arms, fighting under the banner of Islam. This made sense, for the Afghans had fought three wars against the British colonialists—in 1838, 1878, and 1919—under the banner of Islam, and won all of them.

The leadership of this rebellion was across the border in Pakistan. These leaders were right-wing Islamists, divided into seven parties, supported with money and arms by the Pakistani, Saudi, and American governments. The CIA turned to the Saudi intelligence service to organize foreign volunteers to fight with the Afghan resistance. Saudi intelligence found a young man for the job, Osama bin Laden. His volunteers were called al Qaida.

Within three years, most Afghans were deeply fed up with the American-backed parties in Peshawar, Pakistan. They talked Islam, but stole much of the money intended for arms and for food for refugees in the camps.

In 1988 the Russian army left, defeated. The next year the Communist dictatorship in Russia itself collapsed, and the CIA withdrew support for the Afghan Islamists. They had served their purpose of weakening Soviet power, and the United States did not want to be identified with an Islamist government in power.

From 1988 onwards, and particularly after 1992, there was civil war between the different Islamist parties in Afghanistan. Most Afghans were shocked and angry. They had fought for peace and justice, but they had endless war and corruption. For forty years, politics in Afghanistan had been polarized between Communists and Islamists. Now most Afghans had lost faith in both, and politics was polarized along ethnic lines, between the Pushtun people of the south and the Turkic and Persian-speaking peoples of the center and the north.

In 1989 Osama bin Laden, deprived of American financial support and appalled by the infighting among the Islamists, left Afghanistan and went home to Saudi Arabia. There he initially supported the American war on Iraq—he was a Saudi patriot. But the bombing of Iraq seemed all too similar to the Russian bombing of Afghanistan. And the Saudi government now allowed permanent American bases on their soil. The whole legitimacy of the Saudi government relied on being the guardians of the most holy cities in Islam, Mecca and Medina. Bin Laden saw the American—Christian—soldiers as an affront to this guardianship. He became part of the underground opposition movement in Saudi Arabia, and soon had to go into exile in Sudan.

In 1995 the U.S. government intervened in Afghanistan again. The reason was the newly independent countries of Central Asia. The key to controlling their oil and gas fields was a pipeline. The existing oil pipelines ran through Russia, and the Russian government and oil companies were able to pay much less than the market rate for this oil. The easiest and shortest route for a pipeline to the sea, though, ran through Iran, still an enemy of the

United States. The U.S. government, and the American oil company Unocal, wanted an alternative short pipeline down through Afghanistan to the coast of Pakistan.

Pakistani army intelligence organized a new force, the Taliban, backed by U.S. and Saudi money. Many of the Taliban soldiers were young students of religion from the refugee camps in Pakistan, and they were overwhelmingly Pushtun. They invaded from Pakistan, promising peace and an end to corruption. Most Afghans had reservations about the Taliban, but after seventeen years of fighting they felt a bad peace was better than a good war. And the American support, they said, meant the Taliban might actually be able to bring peace.

Within a year the Taliban controlled most of Afghanistan, but not all. In the north, resistance was led by a coalition called the Northern Alliance. The U.S. government and Unocal decided the Taliban could not make the country safe for pipelines. The United States withdrew support.

Then bin Laden returned to Afghanistan. He and al Qaida had exploded bombs outside American embassies in Kenya and Tanzania, killing almost 300 people. Sudan was no longer safe for him. The Taliban, who remembered his support for them during the Russian War, felt obliged to provide him with asylum. This too turned the U.S. government against the Taliban.

Then came September 11. The U.S. government immediately claimed that bin Laden had been the mastermind behind the attacks. The evidence, such as it is, points to Mohammed Atta as the leader and organizer of the hijackers. But bin Laden did give them public backing.

The Taliban were now terrified of an American invasion. The Pakistani government tried to negotiate a hand over of bin Laden, but before they could conclude one the United States began bombing Afghanistan to remove the Taliban government. They also sent some American special forces and paratroops, but not ground troops in force. They were still worried about the Vietnam syndrome. And inside Afghanistan, memories of the Russian invasion were still fresh. American tanks and troops would revive that, and might well lose local support for the United States inside the country.

Invading troops in any numbers would also have to go through neighboring Pakistan, ruled by a military dictatorship allied to the United States. As the bombing began, there were angry, sizeable demonstrations in Pakistan. A full-scale invasion might lead to the overthrow of the Pakistani government. After all, a popular uprising had thrown out an earlier military dictatorship in Pakistan in 1971.

So the American government combined bombing with support for the Northern Alliance, the army of the opposition in the north of Afghanistan. The Alliance had only a few thousand troops, who were reluctant to fight. Like other Afghans, they had had enough of war. The Alliance were also supported financially and with arms by Iran, Uzbekistan, and Russia. A victory for the Northern Alliance might not be a victory for the United States.

Perhaps 3,000 civilians died in the bombing, more in the devastation, flight, and hunger caused by the invasion, and perhaps several thousand Taliban troops also died. Yet the war inside Afghanistan was a stalemate. Bush came under pressure. There were demonstrations in Pakistan, Britain, and parts of the Middle East. Bush was also losing support inside America for a war that seemed to be going nowhere. So a compromise was reached. This compromise was not public, but my Afghan sources are clear as to what the outlines were.[35]

First, the Taliban were allowed to retreat from Kabul in safety. Most of them, and their leaders, went home to their villages in southern Afghanistan, where they remain in control of the most of the Pushtun countryside. Some of the top leadership took refuge in the Pushtun areas of Pakistan, along the border, and bin Laden escaped.

As the Taliban left, Kabul fell to the Northern Alliance, and American troops began arriving in strength. Behind them came British, Turkish, and other UN troops. The Americans installed a new president, Hamid Karzai, who shared power in Kabul with the Northern Alliance. Karzai was a Pushtun Afghan who lived in the United States. Everyone in Afghanistan, of all political complexions, believed Karzai to be a long-standing career CIA agent.

The rural areas remained largely under the control of local leaders—senior Taliban, former rebels against the Russians, or former Communists. In the summer of 2002 the deputy president was shot dead leaving his office in Kabul, possibly by Islamists, or possibly by competitors in the heroin trade. American troops replaced Karzai's Afghan bodyguards—there were no Afghans left he could trust. By the fall, there were almost daily attacks on American troops, and riot police opened fire on student demonstrators. There was widespread despair about Karzai's government, even among the Afghan exiles who had returned from Europe and America to take senior positions in his government.

When the war began, the American government had said that they did not intend to remain in Afghanistan. By November 2002 it was clear that if they left, Karzai would soon be dead. That month they changed policy, decided to station troops in Afghanistan for some time to come, and began to try to break the local leaderships.

Within the country, the occupation had had a quite limited success. But that was not how it looked internationally. Abroad, it seemed the United States had broken the Taliban government. Suddenly there were American military bases in every Central Asian country but Turkmenistan, which gave them control of Central Asian oil. More than that, the United States had come out of the war a more dominant power in a more militarized world.

There were problems. Osama bin Laden and the Taliban leader, Mullah Omar, had escaped, which meant that some Americans asked what the war had been for. If the United States withdrew from Afghanistan, or was driven out, there would be more questions. So, for the moment, they had to stay. Also, not that many

people had died—20,000 or less. American power looked for-
midable in the Middle East, but it did not look terrifying.

These problems pushed the Bush administration to look for
further ways to establish their power. In his state of the union
address to Congress in January 2002, Bush had already named the
next enemy in the "War on Terror"—Iraq.

IRAQ AND PALESTINE

In targeting Iraq, Bush raised doubts among many who had supported the Afghan War. The Iraqi regime was widely despised,
but it was not a sponsor of terrorism. The attack on Afghanistan
had been partly justified by the Taliban's reactionary policies towards women and by their "fundamentalist" brand of Islam.[36] Iraq
was a secular country where the status of women was relatively
high. Many of those in the United States and abroad who felt
something had to be done after September 11 now began to suspect that Bush was using the War on Terror to pursue his father's
old enemy, Saddam Hussein.

The American corporations and the Bush administration, however, saw glittering prizes. Iraq was the world's second-largest producer of oil. If the United States won in Iraq, American oil
companies planned to take control of that oil. And the United
States had come out of the Afghan War with considerably en-
hanced power. If they humiliated Iraq, they could dream of un-
precedented global power. The American government was on a
roll, and the temptation was enormous.

So were the risks. The first problem was Palestine. The uprising
there was still in full swing. Children were throwing stones, suicide bombers were killing Israelis, and the Israeli army was killing
far more Palestinians. Feeling for the Palestinians had long been
strong in the Arab world. In the spring of 2002, Israeli tanks
occupied the cities of the West Bank in force, enforcing twenty-
four-hour curfews and forbidding ambulances to rescue the
wounded. This led to pictures of the dead rotting in the streets

shown on television across the Arab world. Very large demonstrations took place in most Arab countries.[37]

In Egypt, students marched out of the University in Cairo. They rapidly gathered many workers on the streets. The crowds began by chanting slogans against Israel. Within an hour, they were fighting the police and chanting against the Egyptian regime. The main chant was, "We have reached rock bottom." Within days, there were hundreds of thousands demonstrating, and President Mubarak had sent his wife to lead the marchers and show his government's solidarity with Palestine. Mubarak called Bush several times that week. He had long been an American client. Now he was screaming down the phone at Bush that something had to be done.

In Morocco a million took to the streets, and there were other marches across the Arab world. In Lebanon all the sides in the twenty-year civil war, from the right-wing Christian Phalange party to the Islamists and the Palestinians, united to demonstrate against the Israeli onslaught. The Lebanese police sent a delegation to say they would not police the march—they too sided with Palestinians. In Saudi Arabia, a very tightly controlled dictatorship that allowed no demonstrations whatsoever, 20,000 people demonstrated outside the main American base at twelve hours' notice.

The invasion of Iraq had to be delayed. The demonstrations created a debate in Washington about tactics in Iraq. The Pentagon were leery of any war in Iraq. Colin Powell, now secretary of state but an army man through and through, personified this hesitation. If there was going to be a war, the generals wanted saturation bombing of Baghdad for weeks beforehand, followed by 500,000 American troops. The right wing in the administration, personified by Secretary of Defense Rumsfeld, wanted a quick attack by a smaller number of troops, without saturation bombing. They were worried that the sustained bombing of a city of 4 million would produce mass demonstrations throughout the Arab world and beyond, and allow weeks for those demonstrations to build. A quick attack by soldiers might kill Saddam and take the city before this could happen. The downside, the generals saw, was that many more American soldiers would die. They were still haunted by Vietnam. And they felt that support in America for an Iraqi war was wide but shallow. Significant casualties, and the cruelty of house-to-house urban fighting, might well turn Americans against a war.

Anti-capitalism

The American government and the corporations were also facing a resurgence of the anti-capitalist movement, particularly in Latin America and Europe. During 2002, left-wing populist candidates won elections in Brazil and Ecuador. In Venezuela a popular rising beat back a U.S.-backed coup against the left-wing president, Hugo Chavez. In December 2001, 2 million Argentineans took to the streets of Buenos Aries all night to protest economic crisis and IMF-backed government policies. The protestors removed three governments in quick succession.

In Europe the anti-capitalist movement had hesitated right after September 11, and most activists had put their efforts into protesting the war in Afghanistan. But in December there were 130,000 marchers, mostly Belgian trade unionists, outside the European Union summit in Brussels. In March 2002, 500,000 people demonstrated in Barcelona, Spain, under the slogan "Against a Europe of Capital and War." Most were local people, and Barcelona is a city of only 3 million.

The anti-capitalist movement was spreading to involve the major unions in several parts of Europe. In the spring and summer, there were separate one-day general strikes against privatization, pension cuts, and neoliberal government economic policies in Spain, Italy, and Greece. Three million people demonstrated for the general strike in Rome. Seven hundred thousand marched in Barcelona this time, a million marched in Madrid, and 85 percent of all employed people in Spain joined the strike. Two days later, 120,000 anti-capitalists marched outside the European Union summit in Seville, in southern Spain, led by the Spanish trade unions. I was there, and I had been on the local union demonstration for the general strike in Seville two days before. Both demonstrations were of the same size, with the same banners, and they looked, sounded, and felt the same. The anti-capitalist movement and the unions were becoming one.

The European anti-capitalist movement was also becoming an anti-war movement. In September 400,000 people joined an anti-war march in London, the largest demonstration ever in Britain. In Germany the center-left government was losing an election campaign until Chancellor Gerhard Schröder decided to come out strongly against a war in Iraq, and thus won a convincing victory. In Turkey a moderate Islamist party won by a landslide. In November the European anti-capitalist movement held a conference, the European Social Forum, in Florence, Italy, attended by 60,000. The forum was supported by the major Italian unions, and by the official federation of unions from across Europe. On the third day of the forum, a million people came to Florence to demonstrate against war. The march was led by international demonstrators under a big anti-war banner. Behind them came the auto workers' union. The forum was confident enough to call for coordinated demonstrations in every capital in Europe against war in Iraq on February 15, 2003.

Public opinion in every country in Europe was against war. The governments of Europe, caught between that feeling and the American alliance, went backwards and forwards, agreeing to an American-sponsored UN resolution on Iraq, but saying they wanted no war without another UN authorization.

In America things were harder for the peace movement, not surprisingly after September 11. Three days after the Twin Towers, anti-globalization activists in New York had been able to organize a peace vigil of about 1,500 as close to Ground Zero as they could get. There were soon small peace demonstrations on almost 200 college campuses and in over 200 towns. In January 2002, 20,000 people demonstrated against the World Economic Forum meeting in Manhattan. All these protestors, however, were very conscious of being a small minority.

By April there were two demonstrations of about 50,000 each in Washington on the same day, one against the IMF meetings, largely white, and one in solidarity with Palestine, largely Arab American. The coalitions involved brought the two demonstrations together, and they became 100,000 marchers. They were still very much a minority, but a larger one.

In October about 150,000 demonstrated for peace in Washington, and 80,000 in San Francisco, on the same day. That had been the strength of the peace demonstrations in early 1967.

THE PEACE MOVEMENT NOW

I write this in December 2002. It looks likely that the Bush administration will go to war in Iraq. The risks are large, but so are the prizes if they win. Moreover, they have staked enough on removing Saddam that if they back down now, their standing and power in the world will be significantly reduced.

The American government will win any war in Iraq militarily. It is not clear how quickly the Iraqi army will crumble this time. There will be very large demonstrations and civil disobedience in Europe. No one knows if these will be large enough to break the European governments from supporting American intervention. And no one knows if demonstrations or uprisings in the Middle East will bring down any of the governments there.

But even if Bush wins a quick victory and loses no important allied governments, the War on Terror will continue, and so will the peace movement. Washington has made it clear that regime change in Iran is next on the list. And if not in Iran, there will be more wars. The U.S. government's ambition for global dominance means that any popular movement or uprising, anywhere, becomes another challenge to their power. If they learn from Iraq that war works, they will do it again.

And conquering Iraq will be one thing, but ruling it will be another. Washington has made it clear that they do not plan on elections in Iraq. They want, instead, a colonial governor, probably General Tommy Franks. A prolonged occupation will produce either terrorism, or mass urban demonstrations, or both, as it has begun to do in Afghanistan.

The War on Terror is becoming a war for the world. I said at the beginning of this book that my reason for writing it is that I have ambivalent feelings about the movement against the Vietnam War. I am proud of what we were and did. But we also made major mistakes. I have written this so a new generation of activists can learn from what we did, and do better. So what lessons does the past hold?

First, we have to realize that history does not simply repeat itself. On a world scale, the anti-capitalist and peace movements are stronger in several ways than they were at a similar stage in the 1960s. It took eight years from the lunch counter sit-ins of 1960 to 1968. The new movement is only three years old. The movement of the 1960s began at the edges of the world system, in the American South. This one began in Seattle, outside the World Trade Organization summit, at the center of the world system. The movement of the 1960s began with resistance to segregation, and then to the Vietnam War. This one began with opposition to the capitalist system as such.

One great weakness of the U.S. movements of the 1960s is that they saw themselves as divided, into blacks and women and gays and lesbians and Native Americans—the list is endless. One strength of the new movement is that the different social movements and trade unions combine in demonstrations and campaigns, most strongly in Europe and Latin America. The new movements see that all their problems stem from the same system, and that in one way or another they have to combine against a common enemy.

Second, there is also more at stake now for the American government and the corporations. Intervention in Vietnam was important to prevent the contagion of revolt from spreading to the parts of the world Washington really cared about. Vietnam itself produced rice, not oil. This time the oil reserves of the Arab world and Central Asia are keys to the center of the world economic system. A decisive defeat for American hegemony in the Middle East and Central Asia would be far worse than the fall of Saigon in 1975. So the American government may well fight harder, with fewer allies, and certainly will take greater risks than they did then. At the same time, the risks for their power are greater. American defeat in the Middle East would also strengthen an already resurgent anti-capitalist movement in the rest of the world.

It is because the risks are greater, because most people somehow know that Iraq is more important, that the movement against the war is now so much larger across the world than it was at a similar stage in the 1960s.

A third difference, however, is that Saddam Hussein and the Taliban are not Ho Chi Minh and the Viet Cong. The Vietnamese peasantry were a massive social movement, with deep roots, fighting for equality and land. The regimes in Iraq and Afghanistan have no such popular support, no cause that millions will die for. So far, only in Palestine have American power and its clients confronted a genuine national movement. This may change, as mass movements build in other countries, and American power may be forced to confront one of them.

A final difference is that the movements of the 1960s grew in a world where people in most countries had lived through twenty-five years of economic boom—even in most of the Third World. These were movements of hope, of people who wanted more and better. This time the movements are growing after a generation of economic crisis and cuts. The bitterness this has produced across the world among many ordinary people is at the root of the global anti-capitalist movement. Recessions and unemployment do not necessarily produce revolt. Most workers have two reactions to economic crisis. One is anger, the other is fear for their jobs. These two reactions pull in different directions. What is critical are the ideas in workers' heads. In the 1970s, recession produced fear and acquiescence in most places in the world. This time around, the ideas of the anti-capitalist movement are available.

In short, circumstances are very different now. But there are similarities, too. I was part of the movement of the 1960s in the United States and am part of the European movement now. The hope, the illusions, the smiles, the chaos, the energy, and the delight in unexpected uprisings remind me joyfully of my youth.

The American movement, then and now, is of central importance in the world, because America is at the heart of the world system. What happens in the United States affects the rulers of this world particularly strongly. Any movement there also gives heart to people across the world, as Seattle showed. The Vietnam War was ended by protests coming from American college campuses and revolt in the U.S. armed forces. This history will not necessarily be repeated. A revolt across the Middle East, or in Europe, could be decisive this time. But the movements in each country affect each other even more than they did thirty-five years ago. The demonstration of 400,000 in London against war was seen on television and was front-page news in every country in the Middle East. Demonstrations in Washington are even more important in giving Europeans and Arabs hope. So the lessons of the movement in the United States are important now not only there, but across the world.

The first lesson is that people change. Movements against war begin with minorities. If those minorities demonstrate and argue, if they are big enough for people to hear an alternative, that alternative gains ground. People are not stupid, and they learn from the experience of war.

The second lesson is that when enough people change, they can stop a war. The hope, above all, is in the example of the American GIs.

The third lesson is that political ideas matter. The ideas of the new anti-capitalist and peace movements began with Seattle. These ideas are mostly the same as the ideas of the American movement of the 1960s. This is particularly true in the movement in the United States, but to some extent across Europe as well. This is not surprising. Many of the protestors in Seattle were the children of parents who protested in the 1960s. It was only natural to pick up where their parents left off. The idea that all these ideas were new had also been a dominant idea in the American movement in the 1960s.

The crucial weakness here lies in a cluster of ideas that hold ordinary working Americans in contempt. In Chapter 5, I quoted a firefighter's wife, the mother of a young man who died in Vietnam. She said she was against the war, but she could not hear the voices of people like her in the anti-war movement. People like her, and like everybody she knew, were not respected by that movement. That attitude is still strong in the new movement in the United States. It goes along with a feeling that protestors are naturally a minority, and that educated people are more radical than working-class people. It also goes with a movement that believes two-thirds of America is comfortable. So when you reach out to the oppressed, you go to the third, the desperate, the under class, the "community," rather than to the unions. White American workers, it is still widely believed, are reactionary. People of color may resist, it is believed, and so will people in Mexico or Brazil. But America is a special case, a particularly reactionary place. The phrase radicals often use for this is that they are working "in the belly of the beast."

It is of course true that African Americans and Latinos are by and large, but with many exceptions, more radical than many white people. But it was white, black, and Latino soldiers together who stopped the Vietnam War. Any movement in the United States that wants to change anything central will have to involve white, black, and Latino working people. And that's perfectly possible, because the United States is not a two-thirds comfortable society. It is ten percent very comfortable, and ninety percent anxious and driven.

We can be concrete about what that means in practice. It means taking the anti-globalization movement into the unions, as is being done in Europe, to create a movement that protests war and goes on strike at home. It means that for a demonstration in Washington, you put flyers through every African American door in the city before the demonstration and then start the march from the ghetto. This makes sense. When you protest the World Bank and the IMF, you are protesting policies that hit Africa and black America particularly hard. It is the children of working America, too, who will die in any new American war.

But a movement without the confidence to go out to working America will not have the confidence to knock on the doors of black working America.

Again, many in the new American movement feel anti-globalization is something separate from the unions. This is despite the fact that when the North American unions are involved, as in the demonstrations in Seattle and Quebec, they are more than half the demonstrators. The view of ourselves as an enlightened minority is a recipe for isolation and powerlessness.

There are organizational consequences of such a view, too. If you think of the movement as an elite left-wing minority, then you look for ways and styles of organizing that reflect that minority. If, instead, you keep in mind all the time that it takes a majority to change the world democratically, then you look all the time to your right, and ask how you can win over and include more and more people.

Finally, there is one more important difference from the 1960s. In those years, millions of Americans who went through the mass movements ended up feeling a revolution was the only solution. The radical ideas on offer, though, were the ideas of Stalinism, of regimes that brutally repressed their own working people. Most radicals rejected those ideas. They remained prisoners of lifestyle and separatist politics, or felt they would like to be more radical but couldn't be. The tens of thousands who embraced Stalinist parties found themselves in organizations with unpleasant internal regimes who could not relate to ordinary workers. The combination of separatism, abstention, and apathy meant that no long-term radical trend could be built inside working America.

This time the Stalinist tradition is exhausted. The dictatorships of Eastern Europe have fallen. This time the radical ideas on offer are the ideas of anti-capitalism. There is intense debate now, throughout the movement across the world, about what another world would look like. Almost everybody in the movements, however, agrees that democracy is central to the world we want. And the slogan most often heard on marches, and chanted with most fervor, is "Another World Is Possible."

FURTHER READING

There is a very large number of good books on the Vietnam War. The books listed below are just some of the places to begin reading on each topic. Full citations are given in the bibliography.

General: A moving and funny collection of contemporary documents from all points of view: John Pratt, *Vietnam Voices: Perspectives on the War Years 1941–1982*; and Marilyn Young, *The Vietnam Wars: 1945–1990*.

Vietnamese Communism: Gabriel Kolko, *Anatomy of a War: Vietnam, the United States and the Modern Historical Experience*, which is also a very good history of the whole war; David Marr, *Vietnam 1945: The Quest for Power*; and James Trullinger, *Village at War: An Account of Revolution in Vietnam*, about the village of Beautiful Waters.

The air war: James Gibson, *The Perfect War: Technowar in Vietnam*.

GIs: Christian Appy, *Working Class War: American Combat Soldiers and Vietnam*; and then, among many good memoirs, Michael Clodfelter, *Mad Minutes and Vietnam Months: A Soldier's Memoir*.

North Vietnamese soldiers: Duong Thu Huong, *Novel Without a Name*.

Viet Cong guerrillas: Tom Mangold and John Pennycate, *The Tunnels of Cu Chi*.

Washington policymakers: David Halberstam, *The Best and the Brightest*.

The anti-war movement in America: Tom Wells, *The War Within: America's Battle over Vietnam*, which is also good on the policymakers; and Fred Halstead, *Out Now! A Participant's Account of the American Movement Against the Vietnam War*.

Vietnam Veterans Against the War: Ron Kovic, *Born on the Fourth* *of July*; and Richard Stacewicz, *Winter Soldiers: An Oral History of the Vietnam Veterans Against the War*.

The soldiers' revolt: Joel Geier, "Vietnam: The Soldiers' Rebellion," *International Socialist Review* 9, 1999; Richard Cortright, *Soldiers in Revolt: The American Military Today*; and Richard Moser, *The New Winter Soldiers: GI and Veteran Dissent During the Vietnam War*.

My Lai: Michael Bilton and Kevin Sim, *Four Hours in My Lai: A War Crime and Its Aftermath*.

American veterans: Jerry Lembcke, *The Spitting Image: Myth, Memory and the Legacy of Vietnam*; and the second half of Allan Young, *The Harmony of Illusions: Inventing Post-Traumatic Stress Disorder*.

Vietnamese veterans: Bao Ninh, *The Sorrow of War*, a great novel.

Cambodia: William Shawcross, *Sideshow: Nixon, Kissinger and the Destruction of Cambodia*; and Ben Kiernan, *How Pol Pot Came to Power: A History of Communism in Kampuchea, 1930–1975*.

Thailand: Daniel Fineman, *A Special Relationship: The United States and the Military Government in Thailand, 1947–1958*; and Ji Ungpakorn, *The Struggle for Democracy and Social Justice in Thailand*.

China and Vietnam: Quiang Zhai, *China and the Vietnam Wars, 1950–1975*; and Nayan Chanda, *Brother Enemy: The War After the War*.

Vietnam after 1975: Start with Gabriel Kolko, *Vietnam: Anatomy of a Peace*; then a novel by Duong Thu Huong, *Paradise of the Blind*; and two anthropology books, Tine Gammeltoft, *Women's Bodies, Women's Worries: Health and Family Planning in a Vietnamese Rural Community*; and John Kleinen, *Facing the Future, Reviving the Past: A Study of Social Change in a Northern Vietnamese Village*.

State capitalism: Tony Cliff, *State Capitalism in Russia*; and *Revolution Besieged: Lenin, 1917–1923*; Chris Harman, *Class Struggles in Eastern Europe, 1945–1983*; and Charlie Hore, *The Road to Tiananmen Square*.

The Russian Revolution of 1917: Leon Trotsky, *History of the Russian Revolution*.

The Chinese Revolution: Harold Isaacs, *The Tragedy of the Chinese Revolution*, on the 1920s; and Jack Belden, *China Shakes the World*, on the 1940s.

The anti–globalization movement: Jonathan Neale, *"You Are G8, We Are 6 Billion": The True Story Behind the Genoa Protests*; Andrew Hsiao and Rachel Newman, *Anti-Capitalism: A Field Guide to the Global Justice Movement*.

Afghanistan: Ahmed Rashid, *Taliban: Militant Islam, Oil, and Fundamentalism in Central Asia*; and Jonathan Neale, "The Long Torment of Afghanistan," *International Socialism*, 2001.

Iraq and Saudi Arabia: Anthony Arnove, *Iraq Under Siege: The Deadly Impact of Sanctions and War*; and Said Aburish, *The Rise, Corruption and Coming Fall of the House of Saud*.

NOTES

INTRODUCTION

1. I take the phrase from Appy, 1993.

CHAPTER 1

1. Trullinger, 1980.
2. Trullinger, 1980, p. 11.
3. Trullinger, 1980, p. 36.
4. Trullinger, 1980, p. 36.
5. Kolko, 1985, p. 15.
6. Trullinger, 1980, pp. 24–5.
7. Trullinger, 1980, pp. 24–5.
8. Trullinger, 1980, pp. 24–5.
9. Lacoutre, 1968. For Ho Chi Minh's life see also Chapter 3 of Marr, 1995; and Duiker, 2000.
10. For the background to the view taken here, see Cliff, 1974; and Cliff, 1987. Also very useful in understanding the period are Lewin, 1968; Rees, 1997; Deutscher, 1959; and Ciliga, 1979.
11. See two very good books: Harman, 1982; and Isaacs, 1961.
12. I am simplifying a complex story. For the full details see Isaacs, 1961.
13. Trullinger, 1980, p. 29.
14. Young, 1991.
15. Trullinger, 1980, p. 42.
16. Trullinger, 1980, p. 43.
17. Marr, 1995, pp. 208–209. For the famine as a whole, see Marr, 1995, pp. 96–107 and 207–210.
18. Marr, 1995, pp. 392–401.

19. Young, 1991, p. 11.
20. Halberstam, 1983, p. 104.
21. Ngo Van, 1990, p. 23.
22. Ngo Van, 1995; and articles by various people in *Revolutionary History* 3:2 (1990): pp. 8–43.
23. Trullinger, 1980, pp. 45–6.
24. Young, 1991, p. 29.
25. Luong and Nguyen, 1988, p. 157.
26. Luong and Nguyen, 1988, pp. 63–4.
27. See, for instance, Bui Tin, 1995; and many passages in Duong Thy Huong, 1993. For an intermediate position see Luong and Nguyen, 1988, pp. 186–200; and for a more sympathetic account, Moise, 1983.
28. Eisenhower, 1963, p. 372.
29. Thayer, 1989, pp. 2–3; and Young, 1991, pp. 38–9.
30. Trullinger, 1980, p. 75.
31. Race, 1972, p. 35.
32. Race, 1972, p. 34.
33. For capitalism in the South, see Kolko, 1985, pp. 208–230.
34. Young, 1991, p. 56.
35. The most detailed source for the passionate arguments in the party is Thayer, 1989. Kahin, 1986, is also very good.
36. Race, 1972, pp. 99–100.
37. Race, 1972, p. 110.
38. Race, 1972, pp. 112–6.
39. Kolko, 1985, p. 104.
40. Chanoff, 1986, quoted in Bergerud, 1991, p. 18.
41. Race, 1972, pp. 129–130.

CHAPTER 2

1. The answer to this question is complex, but again relates to the broader picture of U.S. foreign policy interests. See German, 1999.
2. Halberstam, 1983, pp. 10–13. For more on the American ruling class, see Domhoff, 1967; Aldrich, 1988; and Munkirs, 1985.
3. For American foreign policy after 1945 the best places to start are Kolko and Kolko, 1972; and Ambrose, 1993.

4. The account of anti-Communism that follows leans particularly heavily on Schreker, 1988; Caute, 1978; and Navasky, 1980. Three books are very useful for the causes of anti-Communism: Lipsitz, 1981; Fones-Wolf, 1994; and Harris, 1993.

5. Fine, 1969; Preis, 1964, pp. 3–85; and Dubofsky and Van Tine, 1977, pp. 181–279.

6. Preis, 1964, pp. 257–86.

7. Lipsitz, 1981, p. 129.

8. Lipsitz, 1981, p. 126.

9. Powers, 1987.

10. Schrecker, 1988, p. 285.

11. Navasky, 1980, describes the process in detail.

12. For Hollywood, see Ceplair, 1980; and Schwarz, 1982.

13. Schrecker, 1988, pp. 267–268.

14. Schrecker, 1988, p. 276.

15. Schrecker, 1988, 144.

16. Schrecker, 1988, p. 363, estimates that 10,000 to 12,000 who lost their jobs can be counted, but more would have gone quietly and disappeared from the statistics.

17. Zhai, 2000, pp. 133–9.

18. Kahin, 1986, p. 131. Knute Rockne was a famous football coach at Notre Dame.

19. For the full argument on Kennedy's complicity, see Chomsky, 1993.

20. Kahin, 1986, p. 296. This discussion on the coup relies on Kahin, 1986, pp. 121–235, although I disagree on the possibility of a neutralist solution working.

21. McCoy, 1991, pp. 193–261.

22. Kahin, 1986, p. 226, his emphasis.

23. For Johnson's role, see Kahin, 1986, pp. 347–402.

24. McNamara, 1995, p. 31.

25. McNamara, 1995, p. 32.

26. Pratt, 1984, p. 194.

27. Robinson, 1995, pp. 235–72.

28. Kolko, 1988, p. 181.

29. Kolko, 1988, p. 181.

30. Kolko, 1988, p. 181; and Robinson, 1995, pp. 273–303.

31. Brackman, 1969, p. 192.
32. Brackman, 1969, p. 197.

CHAPTER 3

1. Gibson, 1986, p. 319.
2. Pratt, 1984, p. 243.
3. Appy, 1993, pp. 164–7.
4. Caldwell, 1971, pp. 123–4.
5. Young, 1991, pp. 129–30.
6. Young, 1991, p. 191.
7. Gibson, 1986, pp. 374–5.
8. Pratt, 1984, p. 227.
9. Burchett, 1966, p. 19, quoted in Gibson, 1986, p. 376.
10. Broughton, 1969, p. 113, quoted in Gibson, 1986, p. 377.
11. Clodfelter, 1995, p. 228.
12. Young, 1991, p. 130.
13. Gellhorn, "Suffer the Little Children," *Ladies' Home Journal*, January 1967, p. 109, quoted in Wells, 1994, p. 84.
14. Tuso, 1990, pp. 186–7.
15. Tuso, 1990, p. 182.
16. Appy, 1993, pp. 17–38. This section and the next lean heavily on Appy's magnificent book.
17. Coles, 1971, p. 131.
18. Appy, 1993, pp. 25–6.
19. Bergerud, 1991, p. 128.
20. Appy, 1993, p. 124.
21. Appy, 1993, pp. 16–7.
22. Baker, 1981, pp. 77–8.
23. Baker, 1981, pp. 77–8.
24. Bergerud, 1991, p. 133.
25. Bergerud, 1991, p. 133.
26. Halberstam, 1983, p. 268.
27. Halberstam, 1983, pp. 305–306.
28. Appy, 1993, p. 156.
29. This, and the quotes that follow, are all from a manuscript by Michael Clodfelter reprinted in Pratt, 1984, pp. 651–6. For a more detailed version, see the excellent Clodfelter, 1988.

30. Clodfelter, in Pratt, 1984, pp. 651–6.
31. Clodfelter, in Pratt, 1984, pp. 651–6.
32. Clodfelter, in Pratt, 1984, pp. 651–6.
33. Clodfelter, in Pratt, 1984, pp. 651–6.
34. Caputo, 1977, pp. xvii–xviii.
35. Appy, 1993, p. 156.
36. Bergerud, 1991, pp. 200–201.
37. Bergerud, 1991, p. 229.
38. P. Marin, "Coming to Terms with Vietnam," *Harpers*, 1980, quoted in Appy, 1993, p. 296.
39. Vietnam Veterans Against the War, *The Winter Soldier Investigation: An Inquiry into American War Crimes* (Boston, 1972), quoted in Appy, 1993, p. 294.
40. *Winter Soldier Investigation*, quoted in Appy, 1993, pp. 294–5.
41. Trullinger, 1980, p. 117.
42. Appy, 1993, p. 295.

CHAPTER 4

1. This account of life in the tunnels is based on Mangold and Pennycate, 1985. See also Bergerud, 1991; Bergerud, 1993; Schell, 1967; and Chong, 1999.
2. Mangold and Pennycate, 1985, p. 74.
3. Mangold and Pennycate, 1985, pp. 81–2.
4. Mangold and Pennycate, 1985, p. 83.
5. Mangold and Pennycate, 1985, p. 83.
6. Mangold and Pennycate, 1985, p. 89.
7. Mangold and Pennycate, 1985, p. 90.
8. Mangold and Pennycate, 1985, pp. 96–7.
9. Mangold and Pennycate, 1985, pp. 96–7.
10. Mangold and Pennycate, 1985, p. 153.
11. Mangold and Pennycate, 1985, p. 169. See also Schell, 1967; and Bergerud, 1991.
12. Halberstam, 1983, p. 786.
13. Shea, *Vietnam Simply*, quoted in Pratt, 1984, pp. 273–4.
14. Truong Nhu Tang, 1985, p. 236.
15. And there certainly were unions and strikes in South Vietnam, many

not led by Communists. For an account of one industrial dispute, see Wesseling, 2000, pp. 56–61.

16. Young, 1991, p. 223.
17. Bergerud, 1991, p. 218.
18. Truong Nhu Tang, 1985, pp. 168–70.
19. Truong Nhu Tang, 1985, pp. 168–70.
20. Chapelier, "Plain of Jars: Social Changes Under Five Years of Pathet Lao Administration," *Asia Quarterly*, 1971, pp. 18–19, 36, quoted in Branfman, 1972, p. 19.
21. Branfman, 1972, p. 97.
22. Branfman, 1972, p. 116.
23. Bao Ninh, 1993. Here and elsewhere in the book, I quote novels as evidence. I do this when they seem based on the author's own experience. Many of the people who fought in Vietnam chose to write of their experiences in novels partly because it was the way they could best tell the truth. Novels are particularly good sources for North Vietnamese society and for North Vietnamese soldiers. For the class prejudices involved in not using novels as sources, see the excellent discussion in Gibson, 1986, pp. 476–81.
24. Bao Ninh, 1998, pp. 2–4.
25. For Phoenix, see Valentine, 1982.
26. Snepp, 1977, pp. 42–43.
27. Snepp, 1977, p. 316.
28. Turner with Phan Thanh Hao, 1998, pp. 98–9.
29. Duong Thu Huong, 1995, pp. 2–3.
30. Bilton and Sim, 1992, p. 82.
31. Bilton and Sim, 1992, pp. 130–1.
32. Bilton and Sim, 1992, pp. 131–2.
33. Young, 1991, p. 189.

CHAPTER 5

1. Wells, 1994, p. 23. This chapter relies heavily on Wells, 1994; and Halstead, 1978.
2. Wells, 1994, p. 24.
3. Wells, 1994, pp. 36–7.
4. DeBeneditti and Chatfield, 1990, p. 158.

5. For the whole story, see Marqusee, 1999.
6. Moser, 1996, p. 41.
7. Halstead, 1978, p. 265; and Wells, p. 129.
8. Westheider, 1997, pp. 12–3.
9. Wells, 1994, pp. 107–111, 411.
10. Young, 1991, p. 203.
11. Wells, 1994, p. 112.
12. Marqusee, 1994, pp. 164–5.
13. Loewen, 1996, p. 133.
14. Wells, 1994, p. 133.
15. Wells, 1994, p. 191.
16. Wells, 1994, pp. 107, 197.
17. Wells, 1994, pp. 107, 373.
18. Halberstam, 1983, p. 779.
19. Wells, 1994, p. 112.
20. Young, 1991, p. 229.
21. Kolko, 1985, p. 319.
22. Wells, 1994, p. 319.
23. Wells, 1994, pp. 250–1.
24. Farber, 1988, p. 201.
25. For 1968 see Harman, 1998; and Ali and Watkins, 1998. For Chicago see Farber, 1988.
26. Young, 1991, p. 237.
27. Wells, 1994, p. 395.
28. Karnow, 1984, p. 609.
29. Wells, 1994, p. 422.
30. Heinemann, 1993, pp. 248–9.
31. Heinemann, 1993, pp. 248–9.
32. Halstead, 1978, p. 539.
33. The figure is from Heineman, 1993, p. 249.
34. Henry Kissinger, *The White House Years*, quoted in Wells, 1994, p. 430.
35. Wells, 1994, p. 180.
36. See Spofford, 1988.
37. Coles, 1971, pp. 133–4.

CHAPTER 6

1. Kovic, 1976, p. 20.
2. Kovic, 1976, p. 111.
3. Kovic, 1976, pp. 191–4.
4. For the Vietnam Veterans Against the War, see Stacewicz, 1997; Kovic, 1976; Moser, 1996; and Nicosia, 2001.
5. All of the above quotes are from Moser, 1996, pp. 113–4.
6. Moser, 1996, p. 117.
7. Cortright, 1975, p. 55.
8. Cortright, 1975, p. 60.
9. Cortright, 1975, p. 26.
10. Cortright, 1975, p. 26.
11. Cortright, 1975, p. 65.
12. Cortright, 1975, p. 66.
13. Cortright, 1975, p. 5.
14. Quoted in Moser, 1996, p. 79.
15. Cortright, 1975, pp. 10–15.
16. Cortright, 1975, pp. 10–15, 24–5.
17. Cortright, 1975, p. 34.
18. Terry, "Bringing the War Back Home," *Black Scholar*, November 1970, quoted in Westheider, 1997, p. 76.
19. Westheider, 1997, p. 98.
20. Westheider, 1997, p. 88.
21. Westheider, 1997, p. 78.
22. Cortright, 1975, p. 95.
23. Cortright, 1975, p. 97.
24. Cortright, 1975, pp. 56–7.
25. O'Brien, 1973.
26. O'Brien, 1973, pp. 120–2.
27. O'Brien, 1973, pp. 79–80.
28. O'Brien, 1973, p. 173.
29. Moser, 1996, p. 49.
30. O'Brien, 1973, pp. 113–4.
31. Trujillo, 1990, p. 35.
32. Cortright, 1975, p. 44.
33. Cortright, 1975, p. 45.

34. Moser, 1996, pp. 50–1.
35. Moser, 1996, p. 51.
36. Jury, 1986, p. 40.
37. Moser, 1996, p. 49.
38. Moser, 1996, p. 50.
39. Moser, 1996, p. 49.
40. Moser, 1996, p. 50.
41. Cortright, 1975, pp. 108–110, 295.
42. Cortright, 1975, p. 39.
43. Cortright, 1975, pp. 36–7.
44. Moser, 1996, p. 64.
45. Geier, 1999, p. 38.
46. Cortright, 1975, p. 48.
47. Cortright, 1975, pp. 11–12.
48. Halstead, 1978, p. 641.
49. Cortright, 1975, pp. 111–12.
50. Cortright, 1975, p. 115.
51. Cortright, 1975, p. 118.
52. Cortright, 1975, p. 122.
53. Cortright, 1975, p. 136.
54. Cortright, 1975, p. 137.
55. Young, 1991, pp. 178–9.
56. Young, 1991, p. 280.
57. Snepp, 1977, p. 271.
58. Snepp, 1977, p. 257.
59. Snepp, 1977, p. 249.
60. Trullinger, 1980, pp. 200–201.

CHAPTER 7

1. Chanda, 1986, p. 24.
2. Chanda, 1986, p. 133.
3. Porter, 1993, p. 137.
4. Ngo Vinh Long, 1988. The following account of cooperatives in the Mekong leans heavily on Ngo, 1988.
5. Porter, 1993, pp. 170–71.
6. Porter, 1993, p. 161.

7. Ngo Vinh Long, 1988, p. 165.

8. Fforde and de Vylder, 1996, p. 183, put it more diplomatically: the cooperatives were "weak and informal" and the figures should be treated "with caution."

9. Official statistics for the whole country in the 1980s said that the state's share of the trade in staples fluctuated between 14 and 21 percent; see Fforde and de Vylder, 1996, p. 94. These figures suggest that the state controlled less than 10 percent of the trade in rice in the Mekong Delta. Of course, one has to be careful with official figures in Vietnam for several reasons. Sometimes the authorities massage the figures. In recent years, corruption and local deals mean that official bodies cannot count accurately anyway, and the accounting conventions for national statistics assume a state-controlled economy that has never fully existed. For some of the problems with statistics, see Kimura, 1989, especially Chapters 1 and 2.

10. For the bombing, see Shawcross, 1979.

11. For the history of Cambodian Communism the best book is Kiernan, 1985.

12. Kiernan, 1996, pp. 172–3. This section on Cambodia leans heavily on Kiernan's book, the only one I have found that makes sense of what happened. I have pushed his argument further than he would in some places, and I disagree with Kiernan about the motives of the Vietnamese government, but that is not central to his argument.

13. Kiernan, 1996, pp. 172–3.

14. Kiernan, 1996, p. 175.

15. See Kiernan, 1996, pp. 235–6.

16. Kiernan, 1996, pp. 235 and 239.

17. Kiernan, 1996, pp. 183–4.

18. Kiernan, 1996, pp. 183–4.

19. Kiernan, 1996, p. 203.

20. Kiernan, 1996, p. 274.

21. Kiernan, 1996, p. 274.

22. Chanda, 1986, pp. 86–7.

23. Kiernan, 1996, p. 297.

24. The whole sorry story is best told in Shawcross, 1984.

25. Martin, 1994, p. 297.

26. Shawcross, 1984, p. 418.
27. Martin, 1994; and Kamm, 1998.
28. Bui Tin, 1995, p. 124; and Martin, 1994, p. 271.
29. Martin, 1994, p. 273.
30. Le Cao Dan, 1995, pp. 114–19.
31. Fforde and de Vylder, 1996, pp. 55, 80, 233–4; Porter, 1993, pp. 55–7.
32. Bui Tin, 1995, p. xvi.
33. Duong Thu Huong, 1993, p. 239.
34. This is a theme throughout Fforde and de Vylder, 1996.
35. For the positive view of this strategy, see Hiebert, 1996. For a negative view and the best explanation of what is happening, see Kolko, 1997.
36. In theory, the state still owned all the land, but in practice everybody was sure the state would never take it back and they could effectively sell it, so they did.
37. Dang Phong, 1995, p. 167.
38. Kerkvliet, 1995.
39. Dang Phong, 1995, p. 167.
40. Bui Tin, 1995, p. 109.
41. Gammeltoft, 1999. Her picture of women's lives is confirmed by the Vietnamese sociologist Pham Van Bich, 1999.
42. Gammeltoft, 1999, p. 146.
43. Gammeltoft, 1999, p. 163.
44. Gammeltoft, 1999, p. 165.
45. Pham Van Bich, 1999, p. 190.
46. Kerkvliet, 1995, p. 74.
47. Kerkvliet, 1995, pp. 78–9.
48. Kerkvliet, 1995, pp. 78–9.
49. Kerkvliet, 1995, pp. 78–9.
50. Porter, 1993, p. 162.
51. Kolko, 1997, p. 117.

CHAPTER 8

1. Chomsky, 1999, pp. 119–20 and footnote 3, p. 180.
2. Ambrose, 1993, pp. 276–7.

3. Kissinger, 1999, pp. 803–808 and 829–32.

4. The best short introduction to the Iranian revolution is Marshall, 1988. Bayat, 1987, is also very useful.

5. Malcolm X, with Haley, 1992.

6. For the politics of Islamism see Ali, 2002; Lindisfarne, 2001; Neale, 2001; Harman, 2001; and Alexander, 2001.

7. The best discussion of the Islamism and gender is Lindisfarne, 2002.

8. For the Lebanese civil war and American and Israeli intervention, see Fisk, 1990. For how the marines felt, see Petit, 1986.

9. For Saudi politics and the long-standing links between the royal family and the Americans, see the excellent Aburish, 1995. The same author's 1997 book is good on the whole region.

10. See MacArthur, 1991.

11. This is a recurring theme in Powell's memoirs: See Powell, 1995. See also Woodward, 1991; and Halberstam, 2002.

12. Simons, 1998; and Arnove, 2000.

13. For the details see Chomsky, 1999; Glenny, 1996; German, 1999; and the articles in *International Socialist Review* 7 and 8, 1999.

14. For the Apache saga see Priest, 1999.

15. The following discussion of films and spitting is based on Lembcke, 1998. There is also a very good discussion of films in Appy, 1993, pp. 310–14.

16. Chomsky, 1999, p. 180.

17. Lembcke, 1998.

18. On Agent Orange and U.S. government policy, see Wilcox, 1983; and Nicosia, 2001.

19. Young, 1995.

20. Young, 1995, p. 247.

21. Young, 1995, p. 251.

22. Young, 1995, p. 245.

23. Faludi, 1991.

24. See the magnificent Shilts, 1988.

25. The following discussion of imprisonment relies on Taylor, 1999; Tonry, 1995; and Parenti, 1999. The discussion of wages, incomes, and unions relies on Smith, 1992; and Mishel, Bernstein, and Schmitt, 1999. For what it is like to work for and live on low wages in the United States, see Ehrenreich, 2001.

26. Moody, 1988.
27. Davis, 2001.
28. The account of the anti-globalization movement in the rest of this chapter is based mainly on my experience in the movement. See also Neale, 2002; Neale, 2003; Charlton, 2000; Bircham and Charlton, 2001; and the videos *This Is What Democracy Looks Like* on Seattle and *Genova Libera* on Genoa.
29. For the economics of globalization, see Harman, 2001; Brenner, 2002; Neale, 2002; Bello, 1974; and Bond, 2002.
30. *Newsweek*, 13 December 1999, p. 32.
31. See Neale, 2002.
32. For Iraq see Simons, 1998; Arnove, 2000; and Aburish, 2002.
33. See Rose, 2002.
34. For Afghanistan see particularly Rashid, 2000; Maley, 1998; Griffin, 2001; Mousavi, 1995; Ali, 2002; Lindisfarne 2002; Neale, 1981; Neale, 1988; Neale, 2001; and Neale, 2003.
35. The discussion that follows is based partly on conversations with Afghans in the last few months, and partly on the press coverage.
36. See Lindisfarne, 2002, for how the Bush administration used feminism to justify invasion.
37. The following account comes from Alexander, 2002, and conversations with radicals in the Middle East.

BIBLIOGRAPHY

Aburish, Said. *The Rise, Corruption and Coming Fall of the House of Saud.* New York, 1995.

———. *A Brutal Friendship: The West and the Arab Elite.* New York, 1997.

———. *Arafat: From Defender to Dictator.* London, 1999.

———. *Saddam Hussein.* London, 2002.

Aldrich, Nelson Jr. *Old Money: The Mythology of America's Upper Class.* New York, 1988.

Alexander, Anne. "Powerless in Gaza: The Palestinian Authority and the Myth of the 'Peace Process'." *International Socialism,* 89, 2000.

———. "The Crisis in the Middle East." *International Socialism,* 93, 2001.

Ali, Tariq. *The Clash of Fundamentalisms: Crusades, Jihads and Modernity.* New York, 2002.

Ali, Tariq, and Susan Watkins. *1968: Marching in the Streets.* New York, 1998.

Ambrose, Stephen. *Rise to Globalism: American Foreign Policy Since 1938.* New York, 1993.

Appy, Christian. *Working Class War: American Combat Soldiers and Vietnam.* Chapel Hill, N.C., 1993.

Arnove, Anthony, editor. *Iraq Under Siege: The Deadly Impact of Sanctions and War.* London, 2000.

Baker, Mark. *Nam: The Vietnam War in the Words of the Men and Women Who Fought There.* New York, 1982.

Bao Ninh. *The Sorrow of War.* London, 1993; first published in Vietnamese 1991.

Bayat, Assef. *Workers and Revolution in Iran: A Third World Experience of Workers' Control.* London, 1987.

Belden, Jack. *China Shakes the World.* London, 1973.

Bello, Walden. *Dark Victory: The United States and Global Poverty*. London, 1994.

Bergerud, Eric. *The Dynamics of Defeat: The Vietnam War in Hau Nghia Province*. Boulder, Colo., 1991.

———. *Red Thunder, Tropic Lightning: The World of a Combat Division in Vietnam*. Boulder, Colo., 1993.

Bilton, Michael and Kevin Sim. *Four Hours in My Lai: A War Crime and Its Aftermath*. London, 1992.

Bircham, Emma, and John Charlton. *Anti-capitalism*. London, 2001.

Bond, Patrick. *Against Global Apartheid: South Africa Meets the World Bank, IMF and International Finance*. Lansdowne, South Africa, 2000.

Brackman, Arnold. *The Communist Collapse in Indonesia*. New York, 1969.

Branfman, Fred. *Voices from the Plain of Jars: Life Under an Air War*. New York, 1972.

Brenner, Robert. *Turbulence in the World Economy*. London, 2002.

Bui Tin. *Following Ho Chi Minh: The Memoirs of a North Vietnamese Colonel*. Translated and adapted by Judy Stowe and Do Van. London, 1995; first published in Vietnamese 1991.

Caldwell, Malcolm. "Report from North Vietnam." In Ken Coates, Peter Limqueco, and Peter Weiss, editors, *Prevent the Crime of Silence: Reports from the International War Crimes Tribunal Founded by Bertrand Russell*. London, 1971.

Caputo, Philip. *A Rumor of War*. New York, 1997.

Caute, David. *The Great Fear: The Anti-Communist Purge Under Truman and Eisenhower*. New York, 1978.

Ceplair, Larry, and Steven Englund. *The Inquisition in Hollywood: Politics in the Film Community, 1930–1960*. Garden City, N.Y., 1980.

Chanda, Nayan. *Brother Enemy: The War After the War*. New York, 1986.

Charlton, John. "Talking Seattle." *International Socialism* 86, 2000.

Chomsky, Noam. *Rethinking Camelot: JFK, the Vietnam War and US Political Culture*. Boston, 1993.

———. *The New Military Humanism: Lessons from Kosovo*. London, 1999.

Chong, Denise. *The Girl in the Picture: The Remarkable Story of Vietnam's Most Famous Casualty*. London, 2000.

Ciliga, Ante. *The Russian Enigma*. London, 1979; first published in French 1938.

Cliff, Tony. *State Capitalism in Russia*. London, 1974; first published 1948.

————. *Revolution Besieged: Lenin, 1917–1923*. London, 1987.

Clodfelter, Michael. *Mad Minutes and Vietnam Months: A Soldier's Memoir*. Jefferson, N.C., 1988.

————. *Vietnam in Military Statistics: A History of the Indochina Wars, 1772–1991*. Jefferson, N.C., 1995.

Coles, Robert. *The Middle Americans: Proud and Uncertain*. Boston, 1971.

Cortright, David. *Soldiers in Revolt: The American Military Today*. Garden City, N.Y., 1975.

————. "GI Resistance During the Vietnam War." In Melvin Small and William Hoover, *Give Peace a Chance: Exploring the Vietnam Antiwar Movement*. Syracuse, N.Y., 1992.

Dang Phong. "Aspects of Agricultural Economy and Rural Life in 1993." In Benedict Kerkvliet and Doug Porter, editors, *Vietnam's Rural Transformation*. Boulder, Colo., 1995.

Davis, Mike. *Magical Urbanism: Latinos Reinvent the US Big City*. New York, 2001.

DeBeneditti, Charles, and Charles Chatfield. *An American Ordeal: The Antiwar Movement of the Vietnam Era*. Syracuse, N.Y., 1990.

Deutscher, Isaac. *The Prophet Unarmed: Trotsky, 1921–1929*. New York, 1959.

Domhoff, G. William. *Who Rules America?* Englewood Cliffs, N.J., 1967.

Dubofsky, Melvyn, and Warren Van Tine. *John L Lewis: A Biography*. New York, 1977.

Duiker, William. *Ho Chi Minh: A Life*. New York, 2000.

Duong Thu Huong. *Paradise of the Blind*. London, 1993; first published in Vietnamese 1988.

————. *Novel Without a Name*. New York, 1995; first published in Vietnamese 1990.

Ehrenreich, Barbara. *Nickel and Dimed*. New York, 2000.

Eisenhower, Dwight. *The White House Years: Mandate for Change, 1953–1956*. New York, 1963.

Faludi, Susan. *Backlash: The Undeclared War Against American Women*. London, 1992.

Farber, David. *Chicago '68*. Chicago, 1988.

Fforde, Adam. *The Agrarian Question in North Vietnam, 1974–1979: A Study of Cooperator Resistance to State Policy*. Armonk, N.Y., 1989.

Fforde, Adam, and Stefan de Vylder. *From Plan to Market: The Economic Transition in Vietnam*. Boulder, Colo., 1996.

Fine, Sidney. *Sit-Down: The General Motors Strike of 1936–1937*. Ann Arbor, Mich., 1969.

Fineman, Daniel. *A Special Relationship: The United States and Military Government in Thailand, 1947–1958*. Honolulu, Hawaii, 1997.

Fisk, Robert. *Pity the Nation: Lebanon at War*. London, 1990.

Fones-Wolf, Elizabeth. *Selling Free Enterprise: The Business Assault on Labor and Liberalism, 1945–60*. Urbana, Ill., 1994.

Gammeltoft, Tine. *Women's Bodies, Women's Worries: Health and Family Planning in a Vietnamese Rural Community*. Richmond, UK, 1999.

Geier, Joel. "Vietnam: the Soldiers' Rebellion," *International Socialist Review* 9, 1999.

———. "Nader 2000: Challenging the Parties of Corporate America." *International Socialist Review* 13, 2000.

German, Lindsey, editor. *The Balkans: Nationalism and Imperialism*. London, 1999.

Gibson, James. *The Perfect War: Technowar in Vietnam*. Boston, 1986.

Glenny, Misha. *The Fall of Yugoslavia: The Third Balkan War*. London, 1996.

Griffin, Michael. *Reaping the Whirlwind: The Taliban Movement in Afghanistan*. London, 2001.

Griffiths, Philip Jones. *Vietnam Inc*. London, 1972.

Halberstam, David. *The Best and the Brightest*. London, 1983; first published 1972.

———. *Ho Chi Minh*. New York, 1983.

———. *War in a Time of Peace: Bush, Clinton and the Generals*. London, 2002.

Halstead, Fred. *Out Now! A Participant's Account of the American Movement Against the Vietnam War*. New York, 1978.

Harman, Chris. *The Lost Revolution: Germany 1918 to 1923*. London, 1982.

———. *Class Struggles in Eastern Europe, 1945–1983*. London, 1988.

———. *Explaining the Crisis: A Marxist Reappraisal*. London, 1999.

———. *The Prophet and the Proletariat*. London, 2001.

Harris, Howell. *The Right to Manage: Industrial Relations Policies of American Business in the 1940s.* Madison, Wisc., 1993.

Harris, Nigel. *The Mandate of Heaven: Marx and Mao in Modern China.* London, 1978.

Havens, Thomas. *Fire Across the Sea: The Vietnam War and Japan, 1965–1975.* Princeton, N.J., 1987.

Heineman, Kenneth. *Campus Wars: The Peace Movement at American State Universities in the Vietnam Era.* New York, 1993.

Hersh, Seymour. *The Price of Power: Kissinger in the Nixon White House.* New York, 1983.

Hiebert, Murray. *Chasing the Tigers: A Portrait of the New Vietnam.* New York, 1996.

Hore, Charlie. *The Road to Tiananmen Square.* London, 1991.

Hsiao, Andrew, and Rachel Newman, editors. *Anti-Capitalism: A Field Guide to the Global Justice Movement.* New York, 2003.

Isaacs, Harold. *The Tragedy of the Chinese Revolution.* Stanford, Calif., 1961; first published 1938.

Jury, Mark. *The Vietnam Photo Book.* New York, 1986; first published 1971.

Kahin, George. *Intervention: How America Became Involved in Vietnam.* New York, 1986.

Kamm, Henry. *Cambodia: Report from a Stricken Land.* New York, 1998.

Karnow, Stanley. *Vietnam: A History.* New York, 1984.

Kerkvliet, Benedict. "Rural Society and State Relations." In Benedict Kerkvliet and Doug Porter, editors, *Vietnam's Rural Transformation.* Boulder, Colo., 1995.

Kiernan, Ben. *How Pol Pot Came to Power: A History of Communism in Kampuchea, 1930–1975.* London, 1985.

———. *The Pol Pot Regime: Race, Power and Genocide in Cambodia under the Khmer Rouge, 1975–79.* New Haven, Conn., 1996.

Kimura, Tetsusaburo. *The Vietnamese Economy 1975–86: Reforms and International Relations.* Tokyo, 1989.

Kissinger, Henry. *Years of Renewal.* New York, 1999.

Kleinen, John. *Facing the Future, Reviving the Past: A Study of Social Change in a Northern Vietnamese Village.* Singapore, 1999.

Kolko, Gabriel. *Anatomy of a War: Vietnam, the United States and the Modern Historical Experience.* New York, 1985.

———. *Confronting the Third World: United States Foreign Policy 1945–1980*. New York, 1988.

———. *Vietnam: Anatomy of a Peace*. New York, 1997.

Kolko, Joyce, and Gabriel Kolko. *The Limits of Power: The World and United States Foreign Policy*. New York, 1972.

Kovic, Ron. *Born on the Fourth of July*. New York, 1976.

Lacoutre, Jean. *Ho Chi Minh: A Political Biography*. New York, 1968.

Lawrence, John. *The Cat from Hue: A Vietnam War Story*. New York, 2002.

Le Cao Dan. "Agricultural Reforms in Vietnam in the 1980s." In Irene Norlund, Carolyn Gates, and Vu Cao Dam, editors, *Vietnam in a Changing World*. Richmond, UK, 1995.

Lembcke, Jerry. *The Spitting Image: Myth, Memory and the Legacy of Vietnam*. New York, 1998.

Lewin, Moshe. *Lenin's Last Struggle*. New York, 1968.

———. *Russian Peasants and Soviet Power: A Study of Collectivization*. Evanston, Ill., 1968.

Lindisfarne, Nancy. "Starting from Below: Fieldwork, Gender and Imperialism Now." *Critique of Anthropology*, December 2002.

Lipsitz, George. *Class and Culture in Cold War America: "A Rainbow at Midnight."* South Hadley, Mass., 1981.

Loewen, James. *Lies My Teacher Told Me: Everything Your American History Textbook Got Wrong*. New York, 1996.

Luong, Hy Van, and Nguyen Dac Bang. *Revolution in the Village: Tradition and Transformation in North Vietnam, 1925–1988*. Honolulu, Hawaii, 1988.

MacArthur, John. *Second Front: Censorship and Propaganda in the Gulf War*. New York, 1991.

Malcolm X, with Alex Haley. *The Autobiography of Malcolm X*. New York, 1992.

Maley, William, editor. *Fundamentalism Reborn? Afghanistan and the Taliban*. London, 1998.

Mangold, Tom, and John Pennycate. *The Tunnels of Cu Chi*. New York, 1985.

Marqusee, Mike. *Redemption Song: Muhammad Ali and the Spirit of the Sixties*. New York, 1999.

Marr, David. *Vietnam 1945: The Quest for Power*. Berkeley, Calif., 1995.

Marshall, Phil. *Revolution and Counter-Revolution in Iran*. London, 1988.

———. *Intifada: Zionism, Imperialism and the Palestinian Resistance*. London, 1989.

Martin, Marie. *Cambodia: A Shattered Society*. Berkeley, Calif., 1994.

McCoy, Alfred. *The Politics of Heroin: CIA Complicity in the Global Drug Trade*. New York, 1991.

McNamara, Robert, with VanDeMark, Brian. *In Retrospect: The Tragedy and Lessons of Vietnam*. New York, 1995.

Mishel, Lawrence, Jared Bernstein, and John Schmitt. *The State of Working America 1998–99*. (Ithaca, N.Y., 1999).

Moise, Edwin. *Land Reform in China and North Vietnam: Consolidating the Revolution at Village Level*. Chapel Hill, N.C., 1983.

Moody, Kim. *An Injury to All: The Decline of American Unionism*. London, 1988.

Moser, Richard. *The New Winter Soldiers: GI and Veteran Dissent During the Vietnam War*. New Brunswick, N.J., 1996.

Munkirs, John. *The Transformation of American Capitalism: From Competitive Market Structures to Centralized Private Sector Planning*. Armonk, N.Y., 1985.

Murphy, John. *Harvest of Fear: A History of Australia's Vietnam War*. St. Leonards, Australia, 1993.

Navasky, Victor. *Naming Names*. New York, 1980.

Nazpary, Joma. *Post-Soviet Chaos: Violence and Dispossession in Kazakhstan*. London, 2002.

Neale, Jonathan. "The Afghan Tragedy." *International Socialism*, 12, 1981.

———. "Afghanistan: The Horse Changes Riders." *Capital & Class*, 35, 1988.

———. "The Long Torment of Afghanistan." *International Socialism*, 93, 2001.

———. *"You Are G8, We Are 6 Billion": The True Story Behind the Genoa Protests*. London, 2002.

———. "Afghanistan." In John Rees and Farah Reza, editors, *The Anti-War Movement*. London, 2003.

———. "The Anti-capitalist Movement in Europe." In Peter Dwyer and David Seddon, editors, *The Anti-capitalist Movement*. London, 2003.

Ngo Van Xuyet. "On Vietnam." *Revolutionary History*, 3:2, 1990.

————. *Revolutionaries They Could Not Break: The Fight for the Fourth International in Indochina 1930–1945*. London, 1995.

Ngo Vinh Long. "Some Aspects of Cooperativization in the Mekong Delta." In David Marr and Christine White, editors, *Postwar Vietnam: Dilemmas in Socialist Development*. Ithaca, N.Y., 1988.

Nicosia, Gerald. *Home to War: A History of the Vietnam Veterans' Movement*. New York, 2001.

O'Brien, Tim. *If I Die in a Combat Zone, Box Me Up and Take Me Home*. New York, 1973.

Parenti, Christian. *Lockdown America: Police and Prisons in the Age of Crisis*. New York, 1999.

Petit, Michael. *Peacekeepers at War: A Marine's Account of the Beirut Catastrophe*. Boston, 1986.

Pham Van Bich. *The Vietnamese Family in Change: The Case of the Red River Delta*. Richmond, UK, 1999.

Porter, Gareth. *Vietnam: The Politics of Bureaucratic Socialism*. Ithaca, N.Y., 1993.

Powell, Colin, with Joseph Persico. *My American Journey*. New York, 1995.

Powers, Richard. *Secrecy and Power: The Life of J. Edgar Hoover*. London, 1987.

Pratt, John. *Vietnam Voices: Perspectives on the War Years 1941–1982*. New York, 1984.

Preis, Art. *Labor's Giant Step: Twenty Years of the CIO*. New York, 1964.

Priest, D. "How Fear of Losses Kept Super-Copters from Kosovo Action," *International Herald Tribune*, 30 December 1999.

Race, Jeffrey. *War Comes to Long An: Revolutionary Conflict in a Vietnamese Province*. Berkeley, Calif., 1972.

Rashid, Ahmed. *Taliban: Militant Islam, Oil and Fundamentalism in Central Asia*. New Haven, Conn., 2000.

Rees, John. "The New Imperialism." In Alex Callinicos et al., *Marxism and the New Imperialism*. London, 1994.

————. "In Defence of October." In John Rees et al., *In Defence of October: A Debate on the Russian Revolution*. London, 1997.

————. "Imperialism, Globalisation, the State and War." *International Socialism*, 93, 2001.

Robinson, Geoffrey. *The Dark Side of Politics: Political Violence in Bali.* Ithaca, N.Y., 1995.

Rose, John. *Israel: The Hijack State.* London, 2001.

Schell, Jonathan. *The Village of Ben Suc.* New York, 1967. Reprinted in Jonathan Schell, *The Real War: The Classic Reporting on the Vietnam War.* New York, 1987.

———. *The Military Half: An Account of the Destruction of Quang Nga and Quang Tin.* New York, 1968. Reprinted in Jonathan Schell, *The Real War: The Classic Reporting on the Vietnam War.* New York, 1987.

Schrecker, Ellen. *Many Are the Crimes: McCarthyism in America.* Boston, 1988.

Schwartz, Nancy. *The Hollywood Writers Wars.* New York, 1982.

Shawcross, William. *Sideshow: Kissinger, Nixon and the Destruction of Cambodia.* New York, 1979.

———. *The Quality of Mercy: Cambodia, Holocaust and the Modern Conscience.* New York, 1984.

Shilts, Randy. *And the Band Played On: Politics, Plagues and the AIDS Epidemic.* New York, 1988.

Simons, Geoffrey. *The Scourging of Iraq: Sanctions, Law and Natural Justice.* New York, 1998.

Smith, Sharon. "Twilight of the American Dream." *International Socialism* 54, 1992.

Snepp, Frank. *Decent Interval: An Insider's Account of Saigon's Indecent End Told by the CIA's Chief Strategy Analyst in Vietnam.* New York, 1977.

Spofford, Tim. *Lynch Street: The May 1970 Slayings at Jackson State College.* Kent, Ohio, 1988.

Stacewicz, Richard. *Winter Soldiers: An Oral History of the Vietnam Veterans Against the War.* New York, 1997.

Taylor, K. "Racism and the Criminal Injustice System." *International Socialist Review* 8, 1999.

Thayer, Carlyle. *War by Other Means: National Liberation and Revolution in Vietnam.* Sydney, 1989.

Tonry, Michael. *Malign Neglect: Race, Crime and Punishment in America.* New York, 1995.

Trotsky, Leon. Translated by Max Eastman. *History of the Russian Revolution.* London, 1977.

Trullinger, James. *Village at War: An Account of Revolution in Vietnam.* New York, 1980.

Truong Nhu Tang, with D. Chanoff and Can Toai Doan. *A Vietcong Memoir.* San Diego, 1985. British edition, *Journal of a Vietcong.* London, 1986.

Tuso, Joseph. *Singing the Vietnam Blues: Songs of the Air Force in Southeast Asia.* College Station, Texas, 1990.

Ungpakorn, Ji. *The Struggle for Democracy and Social Justice in Thailand.* Bangkok, 1997.

Valentine, Douglas. *The Phoenix Program.* New York, 1982.

Wells, Tom. *The War Within: America's Battle over Vietnam.* Berkeley, Calif., 1994.

Wesseling, Louis. *Fuelling the War: Revealing an Oil Company's Role in Vietnam.* New York, 2000.

Westheider, James. *Fighting on Two Fronts: African Americans and the Vietnam War.* New York, 1997.

Wilcox, Fred. *Waiting for an Army to Die: The Tragedy of Agent Orange.* New York, 1983.

Woodward, Bob. *The Commanders.* New York, 1991.

Young, Allan. *The Harmony of Illusions: Inventing Post-Traumatic Stress Disorder.* Princeton, N.J., 1995.

Young, Marilyn. *The Vietnam Wars: 1945–1990.* New York, 1991.

Zhai, Quiang. *China and the Vietnam Wars, 1950–1975.* Chapel Hill, N.C. 2000.

INDEX